COLOPHON

BIS Publishers
Het Sieraad Building
Postjesweg 1
1057 DT Amsterdam
The Netherlands
T +31 [0]20 515 02 30
bis@bispublishers.com
www.bispublishers.com

ISBN 978 90 6369 470 8

AUTHOR
Galit Ariel, Amsterdam
info@wondarlands.com

EDITOR
Simone McKenzie, Toronto

COPY EDITOR
Jill Sheen, Amsterdam

CREATIVE DIRECTION & BOOK DESIGN
Galit Ariel, Amsterdam

CREATIVE DIRECTION & COVER DESIGN
Delux Design, Amsterdam

AUGMENTATION ART DIRECTION & APPLICATION
Nimi Ariel, Amsterdam

augmentingalice.com

AUGMENTING
ALICE

The Future of Identity, Experience and Reality

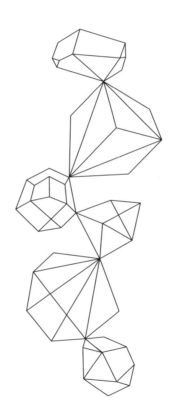

by GALIT ARIEL

How to Use
the Augmentation Layer
in the Book

This book contains an augmented layer, which provides an interactive experience and additional information. However, the book is designed in a way that ensures a full [physical] experience without the need for anything extra.

The information in the augmented layer will be updated periodically. If you would like to contribute or send remarks please contact us on: dev@wondarlands.com

Disclaimer:
While we have done everything in our power to enable a smooth augmentation experience, our use of a third-party platform removes our ability to have full control over system failures or changes to the application.

#1
DOWNLOAD OUR APP

Download the *Augmenting Alice* app, available for Android and iOS devices. Make sure you have the latest version of the app and that your smartphone [or tablet] has the latest operating system installed. Our app is available on the App Store or through augmentingalice.com

#2
CHOOSE OPTIMAL CONDITIONS

Make sure you have the optimal conditions to trigger the augmentation:

1. Sufficient and consistent light.

2. Source image/artwork is not distorted or damaged.

#3
LOCATE THE AR SYMBOL

Artwork with an augmented layer are marked with the AR eye symbol at the top of the page.

#4
USE FLAT SPREADS

Make sure that the book spread is as flat as possible, activate the *Augmenting Alice* app and enjoy an extra layer of information or animation.

Table of Contents

Preface

Hello, Augmented Explorers!

This book is written with the intent to contextualise and 'futurescape' Augmented Reality applications, considering the technology's implementation potential, challenges and risks. Whether you are an Augmented Reality or Virtual Reality developer, content creator or consumer, Augmented Reality will play a major role in our [near and far] future experiences and interactions. Augmented Reality has the potential to become a universal experience platform, that could be either beneficial or detrimental to societal, economic, political, identity, cultural and experiential systems.

I chose to reference *Alice's Adventures in Wonderland* as a framework, as this masterpiece of popular literature describes the adventures of Alice as she explores new aspects of reality and confronts her own limitations in a virtual world. Lewis Carroll – the pen name of Charles Lutwidge Dodgson – was a mathematician who explored the way we adhere to culture, politics and identity in a manner that was ground-breaking for its time, and still relevant today. If technology and new media could offer us a window into wonderland, Augmented Reality would enable wonderland to travel through the rabbit's hole and become a layer within our physical space, altering our sense of reality and culture.

We may have normalised the presence of a constant digital influence, believing that we can filter and disconnect from technology at will. If this is even partially true, Augmented Reality will be a transformative technology, one that will forge such an immersive experience, embedded within our spatial and bodily spheres, creating a seamless physical-virtual flow – a reality with a digital layer implemented within it – everywhere, and all the time. This is not a prophecy for a distant future. We are on the verge of this new era, and we must be prepared for it – the augmented era.

I Am a Nerd.

Being a self-proclaimed nerd has finally become a badge of honour.
A hypothetical passport that grants you passage to the land of the new tech
elites. Nerds have moved away from the social fringe, and now represent
mainstream future builders, members of the start-up crowd, the innovators,
the social disrupters, the unicorn breeders, and potential leaders of a new
social and economic order.

Growing up, I had no doubt that the alternate sociotechnical futures as
described by my personal holy sci-fi trinity – Isaac Asimov, William Gibson
and Phillip K. Dick – could materialise. What drew me to their writing was
that they did not focus on the science behind future technologies, but how
vividly they could envision and describe the complexities, challenges and
consequences of applying future technologies within the context of complex
human mechanics – on the mental, social and moral level. They created a vivid
sense of the near- and far-future zeitgeist, social conflicts and systems put in
place to regulate human-machine-digital interaction.

You should never underestimate nerds and their science fiction, as they play
a pivotal role in stimulating technology and creativity. Science fiction is the
ultimate playground for true innovators to seed ideas without being restricted
by mechanical, operational and financial issues. I consider myself lucky to be
one of the nerds who lives to see how the 'fiction' layer is peeled off science
fiction novels. We are seeing Moore's first and second laws [accelerated
computing capabilities and decreased cost/accessibility] unfold, and witnessing
how emerging technologies that were previously considered sci-fi concepts
have materialised, and been integrated into our everyday lives – including the
World Wide Web, mobile devices, Real-Time streaming, Artificial Intelligence,
and, of course, Virtual Reality and Augmented Reality.

My personal interest, or should I say obsession with other realities began as
a child – on board the USS Enterprise's *Holodeck*. It was such an incredible
notion for me that technology could enable exploring alternative, infinite
environments and experiences. But alas, all of this was happening light years
away, on a spaceship, and I had no clue how to get drafted into the Federation's

Intergalactic Fleet. I did try to research the subject, but it was quite challenging with only a dial-up Internet connection.

During my design studies in the 1990s, ideas about invisible computing technologies, Augmented and Virtual Reality were being explored, and were even being prototyped. My childhood dreams were suddenly being transformed into a tangible technology tool, but still out of reach - 'living' only in research labs, with early prototypes that were not available or ready for mass implementation. My 'technology calling' was yet to be realised, and I entered the working world as an industrial designer. After sharpening my skills on a varied portfolio of brand and product design strategies, I decided to focus on my Master's degree on technology innovation focusing on a social and user-engagement lens.

Along the way, I married a 3D game designer – of course! And halfway through my degree, he walked into our home carrying the best thing a man can bring his wife – an *Oculus Rift* Development Kit. He cleared his throat and said, "Honey, this is it. Virtual Reality is here. And it's ready to change our lives." I adjusted the Oculus goggles, and was ready to be immersed in my lifelong fantasy of a parallel universe.

And then... all of my childhood fantasies came crashing down around me. Where were these alternative, immersive and inspiring worlds? Instead, I had a mildly engaging experience that felt more like a party trick than transcending to another dimension. The visual feedback was disorientating and in fact – I became quite bored. I took off the clunky headset and was left feeling disillusioned, disappointed, and with a mild headache. I did not expect the technology to offer a high-fidelity experience, but I questioned the Virtual Reality itself. My husband shrugged, and told me that I am simply "experiencing it wrong". And so began our family feud.

Like every nerd challenged by a feud or a sense of disappointment, I sat down to write a paper that would explore Virtual Reality as an innovation platform. I was hoping to find out what should happen within this Virtual existence, but mostly I wanted to have an academic argument proving that I was not 'experiencing it wrong'. My conclusions drove me to shift my academic and professional focus towards augmented implementation strategies.

I Am a Digital Hippie.

How lucky am I to be living in the era that every nerd ever dreamed of – an era in which science fiction transforms into, well, just science. Still, my dream 'what if I was born then' epoch has always been the 1960s. Perhaps I have a false idea about the actual events and atmosphere of the '60s, but I perceive it as an era of self-exploration flavoured with the simple aspiration for a utopian civilisation, and spiced with an amazing soundtrack. A simpler era where reality was reality, and mortality was mortality. But I accept that within our limited lifespan as an evolving species, we have an urge and perhaps an obligation to look at the bigger picture. It is after all, what makes religions, social structures, and yes, even technology evolve. The belief that there is 'more', and that there is a better way of living, a more efficient or progressive way. How this should be achieved [for individuals and societies] is the root of ancient and modern conflict.

As a digital hippie, I believe that there is still room for progress in the innovation process. I am convinced that tech leaders and developers can do better to sustain the balance between technology and its end beneficiaries – humanity and society. I am optimistic about the way technology is and will be integrated into our society, yet urge the industry and the reader to apply critical thinking to its development and application.

Midway through my thesis, I took a short break to beautiful Lisbon, Portugal. Just as my vacation commenced, a pop-up window grabbed my attention, introducing the launch of a new Augmented Reality application, *Pokémon* Go, based on the yellow pop-culture anime character, *Pokémon*.

"Oh no!" I thought. "And so it begins..." I was already deep into researching the failed diffusion of past Augmented Reality devices and applications, looking into new and existing platform builders [notably Microsoft, Apple and Magic Leap]. The viral popularity of this [*Pokémon*] game shuffled some of my core theories. As the weeks went by, it became a global phenomenon [despite its inevitable and quick decline]. You could see how marketers and investors were moving their interest [and funds] from the development and implementation of Virtual Reality towards Augmented Reality. It became evident that Augmented Reality was finally here. And here to stay.

At that point, I wondered what the implications of the new tech in town would be. How would Augmented Reality change our relationship with technology, and with reality itself? I wasn't quite sure what I needed to do to tap into this universe of human, meaning and technology. Social sciences always fascinated me more than the exact sciences. Throughout my career, I constantly rebounded between my need to explore ideas about social and personal identity, and those about physical and virtual aesthetics and function. Following Steve Mann's extraordinary work on information streaming and data layering via head mounted devices, I become drawn to Augmented Reality as the field that I find the most impressive in terms of the hybridisation of technology into the physical realm. Seeing the first Magic Leap simulation videos made my heart skip a beat. And there you have it. The moment where fiction ceased to exist, and science bled into our reality. So I committed to converging the past, present and future aspects of emerging technologies and Augmented Reality, and delivering perspective and prospective thoughts regarding its development and implementation.

Augmenting Alice
— the future of identity, experience and reality —

"HOW DO YOU KNOW I'M MAD?"
SAID ALICE.
"YOU MUST BE," SAID THE CAT,
"OR YOU WOULDN'T HAVE
COME HERE."

— Lewis Carroll, Alice's Adventures in Wonderland

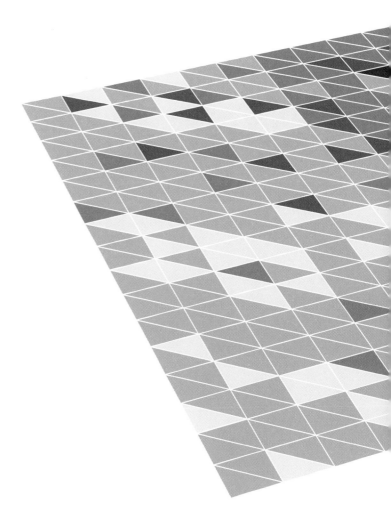

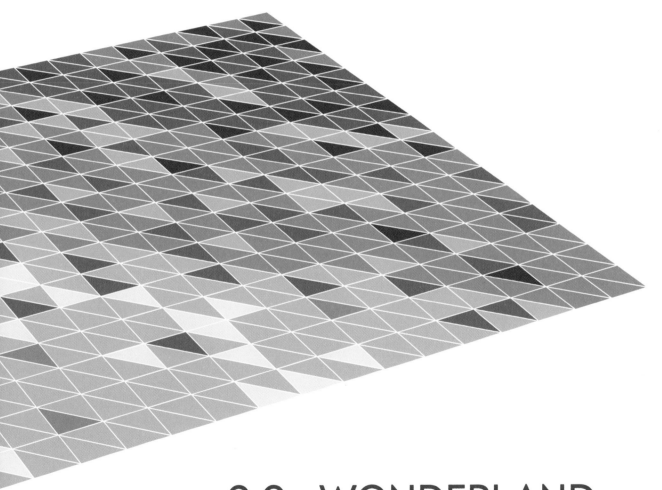

0.0   WONDERLAND
WITHIN REACH

Wonderland within reach

Subject Introduction

0.1 'Innovation Über Alles'

The wave of digital revolution Western society is surfing, marks significant social, demographic and economic changes. Over the past decade, Forbes' *World's Most Valuable Brands* list reveals a shift towards the domination of technology conglomerates in the top spots, easily surpassing former leading brands from the food and beverage, consumer goods, and automotive industries. We are witnessing an unprecedented consumer and market following, leading to investment growth in emerging technologies, notably related to the development of Augmented Reality and Virtual Reality. Both of these have already been applied to gaming, training, medical, retail and marketing tools, automotive interfaces, mobile applications and more.

Virtual Reality and Augmented Reality investments rose from US$ 692 million in 2015 to a whopping US$ 2.3 billion [!] by the end of 2016.[1] Along with the highly-anticipated launch of Magic Leap, a multi-million venture-capital-backed Augmented Reality start-up raising US$ 1.39 billion within 5 years of its foundation,[2] financial analysts predictions had extended predictions regarding the future value of the Augmented Reality market to be valued at anything between US$ 80 to US$ 182 billion by 2025.[3] This forecast in growth prediction is probably induced by the viral success that *Pokémon Go* gained. At the same time, we need to be cautious about such a rose glasses view, and consider forecasts that predict a slow consumer adoption rate. In fact, Q1 in 2017 already demonstrated a lower investment volume raising one fifth of the amount raised in the same quarter of 2016.[4] If we look at past experiences we would be wise to learn from examples

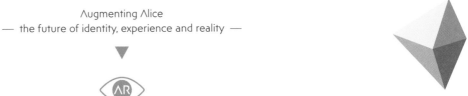

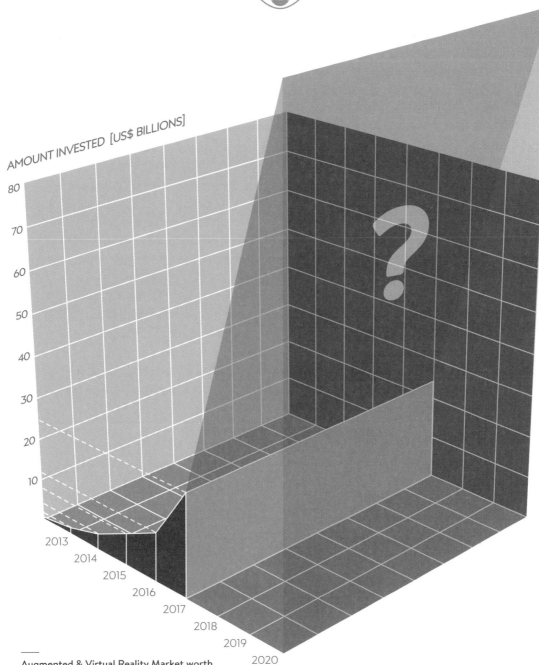

O.O
Wonderland within reach

AMOUNT INVESTED [US$ BILLIONS]

80
70
60
50
40
30
20
10

?

2013
2014
2015
2016
2017
2018
2019
2020

Augmented & Virtual Reality Market worth
An unprecedented investment growth inflates
the Augmented and Virtual market worth.
Author's Image, 2017.

0.0

Wonderland within reach

of Augmented Reality integrated hardware, software and applications – from *Google Glass* to *Pokémon Go* – which have shown initial promise and interest from users and investors alike, yet [arguably] failed to create a lasting impact or a more meaningful, long-term adoption. These cases show that when seeding and launching emerging technologies, simply following 'by the book' innovation implementation strategies does not guarantee their successful adoption and widespread diffusion. In order to understand the context and potential of Augmented Reality development and implementation, we need to review the context of current emerging technologies and the broader term of 'innovation'.

Globalisation has caused innovation to emerge as a key parameter and driver for competitiveness and growth. As manufacturing and consumption has moved into new territories [the BRIC and PIGS countries], economic competitiveness has relied more and more on process efficiency. This was followed by an increasing need to focus on unique design and service models, meaning that reviewing business models, creative and processes became critical to the survival of companies, brands and entities. Innovation as an independent practice gained popularity and led to widespread growth of innovation services, roles and educational degrees. New terms have come to the forefront of business as design thinking, service design and streamlined experience planning increasingly define product and service development processes.

For example, the term 'usability' is used more often and in a wider context when we speak about innovation development models. Beyond improved end-user productivity, usability engineering offers cost effectiveness in R&D, support, maintenance, training and marketing for both internal and external stakeholders. In turn, it improves development lead times and product marketability. Usability engineering and its insights provide a competitive edge, increasing brand and product value, user satisfaction, and driving sales and revenue.

Innovation has brought us global communication and manufacturing systems that act as a catalyst to creating innovation-driven processes and social structures. Capital value, entities, regions and nations are now measured by their present status and potential growth within the innovation field. Start-up hubs, nations, and individuals are becoming key influencers within economic, strategic and political systems, as they are all the gatekeepers to the new commodity and global driving force – information.

Despite all the hype and value brought by innovation, I, for one, cannot wait for the overuse of the word 'innovation' to fade out [and don't even get me started on 'disruptive innovation']. Buzzwords and industry trends are essential to triggering new approaches to value creation, yet when they become a 'one size fits all' or 'let's just repeat the word a lot of times in our business plan' solution, they may become not only counterproductive, but also destructive.

In Apple's heyday, I was often asked by clients to help them become 'like Apple'. I ended up creating a presentation deck that outlined the 'becoming Apple' process. I made sure that the entire executive board was present, created a slick layout, and used my best presentation voice. The first slide was titled 'How can you become Apple?' The room was silent, and the participants were sitting on the edge of their seats waiting for me to explain how to capture that Apple magic. As I clicked through to the next slides, I enjoyed watching their increasingly baffled looks and widened eyes as I amplified their need to purge out top management, perhaps lose relevance for a few years, re-hire the management, invest mostly in Research & Development, and release limited quantities of new products to the market.

"Oh," the CEO would say. "This is not what we had in mind. This wouldn't work for us at all…"

"In that case," I'd say, launching my second presentation deck, "let us discuss the meaning of innovation and its application according to YOUR company's needs." It was a neat trick that helped to embed a better internal perception of innovation, reiterate the need for innovation to become a relevant tool [rather than a slogan or a holistic outcome], and highlight the requirement – first and foremost – for streamlined processes. Unfortunately, the overused term and its meaning are still thrown around by midlife-crisis brands and start-ups alike.

Innovation was not always considered a positive attribute. Benoît Godin, a Canadian researcher, looked at the use of 'innovation' extensively. The term has existed for several hundred years, and was considered a derogatory term until the late nineteenth century. Conformity was an effective tool used by political rulers and the church to maintain religious dogmas, and social and political hierarchies. Disturbing the status quo was considered an action against church

and state, to the extent that England's King Edward VI ordered *A Proclamation against Those that Doeth Innovate* in 1548, threatening that innovators would: "suffer imprisonment, and other grievous punishementes". [5]

In 1636, Henry Burton published the pamphlet *For God and the King*, which acknowledged the ripple effect innovation could have as it spreads. The pamphlet also specifies the types of innovation:

» Innovation in Discipline

» Innovation in the Worship of God

» Innovation in the Civil Government

» Innovation in Altering of Books

» Innovation in the Means of Knowledge

» Innovation in the Rule of Manners

» Innovation in the Rule of Faith

Though Burton's condemnation of innovation was resisted by scholars of the time, his contribution to the definition and significance of innovation and innovators is indisputable.

0.2   Hate the Buzzword, Love the Game

Innovative strategies, products and processes are vital for companies to stay at the top of their game, and react to changing market and consumer needs. The challenge becomes greater for established companies to identify and cultivate disruptive technologies, and divert resources from a known customer need to a new product when the need for the new product is unknown or unproven.

But, what precisely is 'innovation'?

Burton's definition of innovation was related to 'alterations' in religious, public or state affairs, and this is indeed the source of the modern meaning. Innovation is commonly related to the act of change, yet the common trumpet-blowing of any product or process anomaly as 'innovation' is misleading. Perhaps this

is the reason why nine out of ten start-up companies fail. Innovation requires contextual or functional alterations – otherwise, it is 'merely' natural growth [which is also great]. However, there is a massive difference between the introduction of a new alteration or an 'invention' and the aspired deep and long-term impact created by true 'innovation'. It was economist Joseph Schumpeter who differentiated invention from innovation in 1939. He defined innovation as related to an advantageous shift within a business model. A single deviation from the norm cannot be considered innovation. The ability to embed or offer an alternative to typical paradigms and processes is what defines the outcome as innovation. For example, the Ford *Model T* on its own may have been a spectacular piece of machinery, but its innovative value lies in its broader context and significance as the source for establishing fast-paced assembly lines and mass-produced goods, the five-day work week, and product customisation.

Innovation and technology development are key factors in the realisation of globalisation. Both represent the human aspiration to rule the Earth – built on the desire to create a homogenous society, whether it is cultural, ecological or ideological.

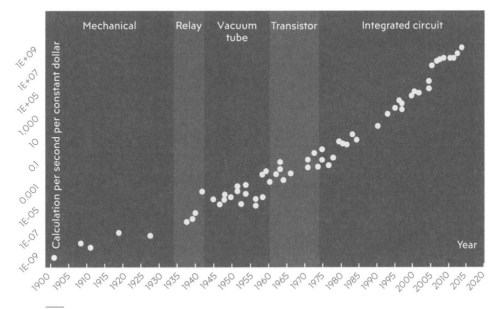

Moore's Law in Practice, 120 years overview
Author's Image, 2017.
[Adapted from Kurzweil, 2005]

0.0 Wonderland within reach

Comedian Louis CK has a great take on the reason we innovate. God approaches humanity, outraged by the destruction they have caused to a perfectly self-sustained ecosystem. "Why did you do it?" He [God] asks. "Food," answers the human. "I left you food all over the floor… What are you doing?" asks God, baffled. "It didn't have bacon around it," mumbles the human.[6]

The original sin described in the Bible is humans' dissatisfaction with an existing status quo, and our pursuit of an elevated state of mind. This was the root cause of Adam and Eve's Expulsion from Paradise. Our desire to gain the forbidden fruit of progress is what defines humanity. Going beyond the survival instincts of other species, humans look to increase effectiveness by elevating processes, quantities and quality.

But do we ever stop to ask ourselves to what end, and at the expense of whom and what? Many emerging technologies wave the flag of efficiency in the way they cater to existing and new needs, yet fail to evaluate whether these are essential to our survival and development, and – in other words – valid. The advertising industry has long trained us to cross-reference and swap our needs with desires, forming effective new consumption hooks and triggers. Not to underestimate the role of feelings and impulses within our decision-making process – after all, attraction, risk-taking and even acting on a whim are all part of our evolutionary survival mechanism.

Augmented Reality will have a tremendous effect on the way we form innovative interaction and content systems. As it matures, it will evolve beyond the visual aspect of the technology to encapsulate new interaction possibilities. This will require enhanced display and control design, based on more intuitive manipulation of and interaction with physical objects. The adoption of technology is influenced just as much [if not more] through an internal sense of reward rather than straightforward considerations of cost and benefit. The implications of launching a new technology within such a saturated market means that developers need to be more attuned to user needs – identifying hindrances, such as unnecessary layers of complexity, and balancing the paradox between ease of use and feature variation and optimisation.

0.3 My Precious

As the craze of 'innovation' as a hype word dies out, its value as a transformative tool will remain. Yet the focus of innovation will shift from a mere business tool to the creation of a more experiential value. We can see signs of this transformation in examples such as a recent LA Times article that declared that the word 'innovation' would finally clear the path for the word 'immersive'.[5] Let's take a closer look at the ripples Augmented Reality will create as it evolves, and it's further application in the public and private domain.

The rate of development has accelerated over the last few decades, and with it the dominance of technology in all areas of life. Regardless of the industry or platform, we are completing a cycle of digital transformation where disruption, access and immediacy become core values and factors for success. For those following the 'start-up soup' closely, relevant technologies, such as the Internet of Things, Real-Time, cloud storage, Global Positioning System [GPS] and wearables are all materialising into everyday tools.

> We are witnessing the era where science fiction becomes a tangible reality. Emerging technologies are being developed and merged, capable of achieving amazing thing, surpassing our wildest visions. The 'one ring to rule them all' is Augmented Reality.

Together with Virtual Reality, Augmented Reality shows unprecedented growth in both investment and interest within big technology platforms and accelerator industries. When we look at implementation case studies, products and processes, we can see that we have developed tunnel vision about Augmented Reality – by considering it as a technology product. Instead, the Augmented Reality horizon is to become the new standard platform for content creation and experience generation, becoming as essential as other common resources, with an impact that can only be compared with the global influence of the World Wide Web.

Spatially embedded interaction would give us greater freedom to use technology fluidly, creating new layers and relationships within our physical space. Sustainability entrepreneur Elon Musk's energy panels are revolutionary not only

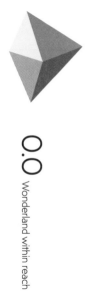

because they offer a sustainable energy source, but also because they offer the user the ability to be independent of the energy grid ecosystem. In the past, governments provided us with access to common infrastructure. Now, we see technology facilitators offering equivalent systems that both expand to a global reach and adhere to niche requirements. The reference to *Alice in Wonderland* is not coincidental – Augmented Reality will act as the rabbit hole that will enable the application of a world of endless possibilities within our everyday reality.

Our society is driven by technological interaction, yet one must remember that technological systems, interaction and perception are heavily based on pre-existing cognitive and social factors. Thus, successful digital interaction builds on, mirrors and enhances pre-existing behavioural cues. What has changed is the accelerated rate with which digital artifacts and systems integrate within a wide range of functions from communication to creation. This is partially due to the affordability of mobile devices, Internet connectivity and access to online knowledge systems, which have positively influenced the rate of diffusion of new digital technologies. The acceleration, miniaturisation and increased performance of technology also result in wider applicability, allowing smoother integration within everyday activities and objects.

All of this ensures even more widespread access to technology and data streaming devices across territories, societies and industries. As Moore's first and second law materialise, the majority of the human population either owns or has access to high-capacity computing devices. Mobile phone ownership, for example, has shown steady growth, increasing from 4.01 billion users in 2013 to 4.61 billion in 2016, and expected to reach 5.01 billion global users by 2019.[7] Now, consider the fact that your smart phone has a higher calculation capacity than all of NASA's 1969-era computers combined. In other words, the device we keep in our pocket, and use to capture and share selfies, is sufficiently powerful to achieve a successful moon landing.

With the diffusion and acceleration of technology, the Internet of Things [IoT] has started shifting from a prophecy to a reality. Internet of Things refers to the integration of communication systems within a variety of products – ranging from communication devices and small portable home appliances, to aircraft engines and furniture. IoT offers clear benefits to users when applied to consumer-centric design and interaction. We already have many

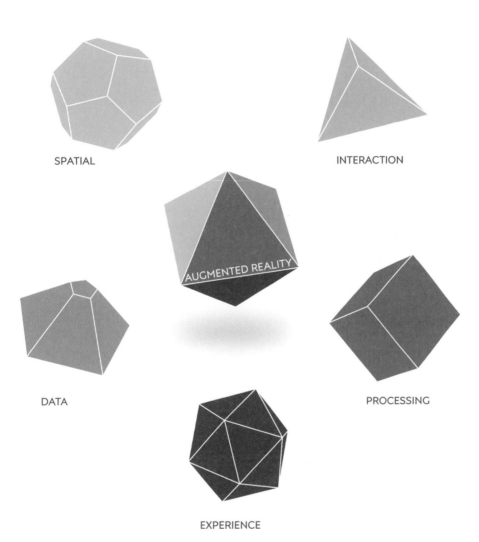

SPATIAL

INTERACTION

AUGMENTED REALITY

DATA

PROCESSING

EXPERIENCE

The One Ring to Rule Them All
Augmented Reality is the ultimate interface
platform that would integrate all emerging
technologies into a new interaction platform.
Author's Image, 2017.

0.0
Wonderland within reach

smart sensors – from smoke detectors to health trackers, which have been developed for remote activation and access, as they track and send output to the user via mobile applications. The next step is a range of interconnected devices. Concepts such as smart homes and smart kitchens include appliances that gear-up for your dinner, offering recipes containing the ingredients already in your cupboards and fridge, and preparing the food according to the recipes and users' dietary requirements.

The combination of big data and IoT will undoubtedly generate new physical/ digital hybrid models in product, interaction and service design. Outside the domestic realm, IoT implementation can be beneficial in a variety of fields and applications, such as monitoring premises, products, customers and supply chains. Its relevance and benefits extend to a wider scope of industries, environments and societal shifts.

Much like the question of the chicken and the egg, improved access and the accelerating rate of technological innovation keep us in a state where we constantly pursue newer and more efficient applications. At some point, we really need to ask ourselves how to ensure that the continuous acceleration of technology is a sustainable model. While it's true that technology and online communication have enabled global systems, for example, they have also enabled further ideological fragmentation. This is predominantly demonstrated in the development of localised, racial and nationalistic identifications and politics – from ISIS to Brexit and the 2016 US elections.

In light of this, we also need to consider Newton's third law, which states that every action has an equal and opposite reaction. This is applicable beyond the physical realm, and applies to social and technological phenomenon.
A recent example is the shared economy, which was hailed as the future of business models, and now seems to be losing steam. This is partially due to the increased caution from users who are demanding higher standards of quality and reliability from open-source service platforms and social media. Countries and regions are also applying restrictive legislation and regulations on these models. Established businesses, such as Airbnb and Uber, are being hit hard. To survive this assault they must expand their service offering – which Uber has done with the launch of UberEats food delivery service.

There are merits and consequences to such a technology-based society. It transforms relationships and social dynamics, and evolves notions such as time, intimacy, and human existence rather than seeing these as separate phenomena that cannot be separated from human structures and behaviours. Technology is already an enhancement, or augmentation of the human condition.

When we consider the context of Augmented Reality, we need to learn from past implementations of emerging technologies and platforms, moving towards a philosophy of 'design with intent' rather than design for the sake of 'innovation'.

"BEGIN AT THE BEGINNING," THE KING SAID, VERY GRAVELY, "AND GO ON TILL YOU COME TO THE END: THEN STOP."

— Lewis Carroll, Alice's Adventures in Wonderland

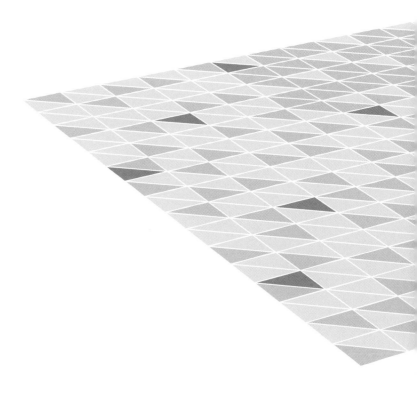

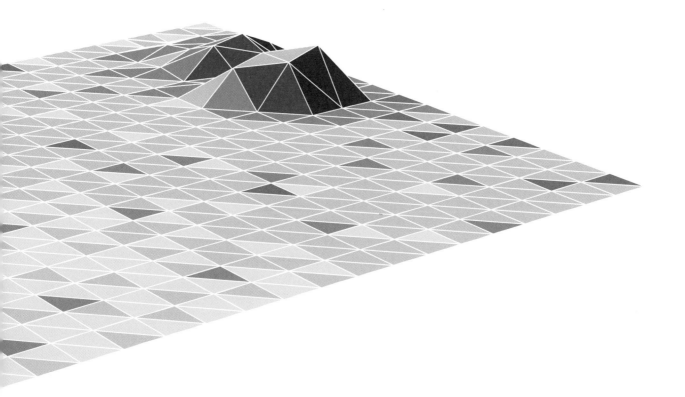

1.0 DOWN THE
RABBIT HOLE

Down the Rabbit Hole

The Road So Far

At this point in time, a variety of technologies are being developed that have the potential to change the nature of technology – from an applied system to an integrated system. Augmented Reality would be the 'one ring to rule them all' permitting us to form an interaction layer that would interlace the physical and the virtual. Before we move into the implications of such a change, let's take a step back and review what brought us to this point.

1.1 Understanding Augmentation

"The real world just doesn't offer up as easily the carefully designed pleasures, the thrilling challenges, and the powerful social bonding afforded by virtual environments. Reality doesn't motivate us as effectively. Reality isn't engineered to maximize our potential. Reality wasn't designed from the bottom up to make us happy."[1]

What an odd species we are, as Jane McGonigal stated [above] we seem to not accept reality as is. Always on a quest to decipher, explore and modify our experiences within it, always on a quest to augment it. Throughout history, we have created incredible technologies that do exactly that, allowing us to overcome the uncertain conditions of mother nature, enhancing our communication and social systems, inventing things and materials that we need, crafting ones that we simply enjoy, and exploring the very nature of the universe. These are truly amazing achievements. The creation of a hybrid space that exists between the digital and the physical has fascinated authors, researchers and scholars for decades. Augmented Reality stands out as one of the most interesting bridges between the two realms.

▼

As humans and technology embark on the journey to cross this bridge, let's look at the learnings and obstacles augmentation has faced so that we can better comprehend the path ahead. Don Norman, one of the most influential scholars focused on developing a human-centric approach to design and interactive systems, envisioned the future of computing as invisible information appliances, embedding computer processing features inside everyday objects. In his 1998 book, *The Invisible Computer*, he also concludes that this will heavily impact our interaction and relationship with our environment and the objects around us. Norman envisioned a future [that is currently unfolding before our eyes] where computing systems would be embedded within physical structures [interactive surfaces], where home devices would utilise the Internet as a data infrastructure [Internet of Things]. He envisioned the potential of wearables and body implants, and how everyday behaviour would change due to the access of portable information systems – or as he refers to them as 'pocket information displays'.

In their book, *Windows & Mirrors*, Jay David Bolter and Diane Gromala describe Norman's view of an invisible appliance as a window attribute. They argue that the additional role and potential of digital artifacts should be to reflect, enhance and evolve user actions. This means that while technology might become invisible, the interaction enabled through it acts as a mirror of our activities. So, in a sense, embedding even basic technologies generates new layers of interaction, which effect behaviours, rituals and cultures directly and indirectly. Smartphones are a great example. Within a relatively short period of time the frequency and quality of our mobile communication and related behaviour has shifted – sometimes with serious implications. There are new laws and awareness campaigns in place to deter people from texting while driving. Even our walking patterns have changed and to accommodate this new behaviour, some cities have created designated pedestrian lanes for texting pedestrians, and even placed pavement projected traffic lights to ensure that distracted 'texters' are aware of the traffic signals. Now, consider the context of Augmented Reality. We are trying to create a technology that applies a digital layer on top of [and within] our physical reality. As natural as it might feel to us, we ultimately aspire to manipulate our perception of physical reality. Even the term 'augment' means to achieve a higher or intensified state of reality itself, acting as a mirror and a window simultaneously.

1.0

Down the rabbit hole

Much like other forces intertwined with the path of humanity – be it nature, divinity or mortality – we have developed a dual approach towards those things made by man, with technology being a core focus for both dependency and concern. The popular television series *Black Mirror* narrates ominous predictions about the effects of emerging technologies and mass digital and social media. The show's title is a smart reference to our constant staring into our blackened mobile screens – it also derives from a divination method called 'scrying' – where future predictions are made by gazing into a reflective object, often a magic or darkened mirror. This method is attributed to Nostradamus, the French seer from the 1500s whose cryptic four-line prophecies are commonly quoted in relation to disastrous events.

Many developers tend to shrug their shoulders, and dismiss technology cautious individuals and policies as being overly conservative, or even regressive. The issue begins when valid concerns, considerations, and negative impacts are ignored, resulting in a technology-silo development bubble. Perhaps the myth of the genius visionary who disregards public opinion and social conventions has contributed to this.

The reality is that no technology is an island. Beyond its functional needs and features, every technology will eventually be used by humans. Technology at large is not a thing that is separate from a social context. Anyone developing and applying technology needs to consider the broader effect of its use. Embedding emerging technologies is likely to have some destabilising outcomes, controversy, and possibly alarming reactions. This is expected from any application of progressive processes and behaviours. And if this is a core expectation for the application of technology, why are we shrugging it off as a side effect?

The realisation of Augmented Reality is a natural progression – a merger of processes, and an evolution of the user interface. We have moved from vacuum tubes to transistors and on to integrated systems. This is the natural outcome of maximising computing power, miniaturisation and the commoditisation of mobile computing devices, as well as the ongoing development of multisensory input systems into human-sized machines. Today, we already need to consider a much broader aspect of system building – forming a seamless system that incorporates hardware, software, multi-platform, user interface, service design, brand, and content delivery. As big-data analytics evolves, we will see more micro-behavioural feedback integrated into applications and experience building. Yet the most interesting shift will be the strides toward biological machines and computational neuroscience – this is where cybernetics and Artificial Intelligence surpass science fiction hypotheses, and transform them into tangible futures. As these technologies become available and fully functional, they will enable the development of complex systems within user communication and feedback. We will see the creation of holistic and targeted experiences – Augmented Realities serving as the experience bridge between the digital and the physical.

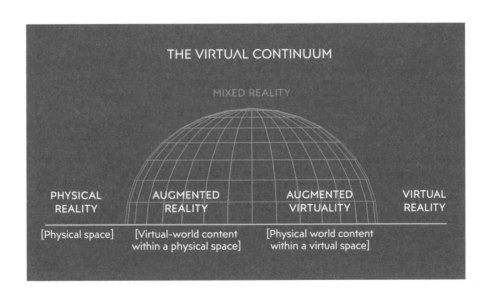

The Virtual Continuum
Author's Image, 2017.
[Adapted from Milgram and Kishino, 1994]

1.0

Down the rabbit hole

1.2   What Augmented Reality Is [and What It Is Not]

Many users and developers seem to loosely refer to Augmented Reality and Virtual Reality applications and devices as the same technology. Although they share many features and both sit within the virtual, there is a significant difference between the two. Virtual Reality's paradigm is to form a fully immersive simulation that replaces the user's environment, whereas Augmented Reality builds a digital layer onto or within the existing physical environment.

The term 'Augmented Reality' was coined in 1990 by Boeing researchers Tom Caudell and David Mizell, during the *Boeing Augmented Reality* Head Mounted Display [HMD] system project for the new *777 jet-liner*. Augmented Reality is often defined as "all cases in which the display of an otherwise real environment is augmented by means of virtual [computer graphic] objects."[2] In other words the enhancement of the user's existing environment via a digital layer.

An extended definition of Augmented Reality looks beyond the layered visual aspect, defining Augmented Reality as a view of a physical, real-world environment with elements that are augmented by computer-generated sensory input such as sound, video, graphics or GPS data.[3]

Regardless of the technique used to create the digital layer, these definitions imply that any digital layering within a physical space could fall within the definition of Augmented Reality. I prefer to stick to the registration definition[4] – where the augmented layer demonstrates a strong link and shares a spatial relation to the environment. A projection of digital imagery within a physical space does not qualify as Augmented Reality, unless it contains reactive features that transform according to variables within the environment – to form a truly digital/physical continuum by adapting and transforming to specific features, positions and interactions within the space.

Another misconception is that augmentation requires a complex application of high-fidelity technologies. However, the transcendence and the application of interactivity within an environment can be achieved in simple and effective ways, as demonstrated by Danish-Icelandic artist Olafur Eliasson. Known for his sensory transforming sculptures and installations, he focuses on manipulating and representing spaces and natural phenomena through the use of reflection, mist, water and light. Eliasson aims to create a sensual and surreal exploration of the physical environment and the sense of self. In 2003, he created The Weather Project installation in the Tate Modern Museum's Turbine Hall. It simulated what can best be described as an immersive sun-gazing experience. In his 2010 *Feelings Are Facts* installation, Eliasson used simple, yet highly-impactful methods to manipulate the senses and augment spaces. An empty space was filled with colour-illuminated mist, creating an instant sense of spatial density. The thick, almost physical blocks of coloured mist framed the space for the wandering or stationary observer, and formed an alternating sense of orientation and disorientation. It was interesting to experience one's own surprising shifts in mood and perception caused by the misty-colour-lit sensory zones. Another layer of the surreal experience was triggered by the ghostly presence of other visitors as they emerged and disappeared into the mist.

Since Virtual Reality aspires to simulate and replace our physical environment, it needs to create a fully artificial immersive experience via high-fidelity simulation. This is primarily achieved through the development of Head Mounted Devices [HMDs], or enclosed immersive environments, for example, the *Star Trek Holodeck* [and just to establish where I stand, *Star Trek* kicks *Star Wars'* ass]. This high-fidelity simulation needs to consider all the environmental and sensory aspects in order to offer a convincing immersive experience. This is perhaps the greatest challenge facing the development and implementation of the technology.

> **Even though our physical, virtual and augmented experiences still have different qualities, at some point [in the not so faraway future] we will achieve synergy between the way we apply and interact with all three.**

1.3 Oculus Rising

Virtual Reality simulation devices and technology have been developed and experimented with consistently since the 1960s. From Virtual Reality pioneer and cinematographer Morton Heilig, who created the electromechanical *Sensorama* in 1962, to computer graphics pioneer Ivan Sutherland's preliminary three-dimensional display experiments in 1966 and 1967 at MIT's Lincoln Laboratory. These devices, however, were cumbersome, and not fit for commercial use. Sutherland's 1968 head-tracking Virtual Reality display, for example, was so heavy that it had to be suspended from the ceiling. Research into basic Virtual Reality technology by military, aeronautical and space exploration bodies such as NASA– combined with Edward Thorp and Claude Shannon's 1955–1965 explorations and prototypes of wearable computing at MIT,[5] and the work of inventor, cyber-culture and wearable-tech pioneer Steven Mann since the 1970s – have resulted in the emergence of an increasing number of ergonomic and consumer-friendly Virtual Reality applications and devices.

The integration of Virtual Reality technology into fully immersive games really kicked off in the 1990's. Yet even the biggest technology and gaming corporations failed to develop a device that achieved commercial success and could penetrate the market. The *Sega VR* and *Atari Jaguar VR* Head Mounted Device prototypes take their place among dozens of other devices that were never brought to commercial development. Devices that did manage to hit the market – such as Nintendo's 1995 *Virtual Boy* handheld console and Sony's 1997 *Glasstron* Virtual Reality HMD– were taken off the shelves relatively quickly.

These products suffered from steep development and product costs, and failed to supply mass-market compatibility. A principal issue with their lack of success was the fact that these devices fell short of providing a truly immersive experience due to sub-optimal ergonomics, low-quality image and resolution, and physical side effects that left users "dizzy with disappointment, and just plain dizzy."[6]

Past failures with the diffusion and commercialisation of Virtual Reality HMDs may have discouraged many corporations and individuals from pursuing this area of innovation, but Oculus VR founder Palmer Luckey was not one of them. Frustrated with the inadequacy of the existing HMDs in his collection, Luckey created his first prototype in 2011 at age 18 [yep, in his parents' garage]. Luckey posted regular updates of his development work on a forum website frequented by Virtual Reality enthusiasts, using swarm creativity, and exchanging ideas and knowledge about the device and its technology. This example of what innovation leader Eric Von Hippel calls 'an innovation community',[7] was instrumental to the development of the *Oculus Rift* headset, since it marked the beginning of Luckey's collaboration with game development guru John Carmack.

This collaboration can only be compared with that of Apple's visionary duo Steve Jobs and Jonathan Ives. Luckey functions as the garage-entrepreneurial visionary, and Carmack as the development and design genius. Carmack modified the prototype, and demoed it at the 2012 Electronic Entertainment Expo, creating an instant industry buzz. As a result of growing interest, Luckey left college and focused on developing the *Oculus Rift*.

The diffusion strategy for the *Rift* system was radical for a technology development project of this magnitude, with a Kickstarter crowd-sourcing and crowd-funding campaign. Luckey and Carmack raised 974% of their original target, equating to a total of US$ 2.4 million. The Kickstarter campaign made the *Oculus Rift* develpment kit available in exchange for pledging a mere US$ 300. This strategy guaranteed a broad-based, multi-platform, trial-and-error development period via a Collaborative Innovation Network [COIN]. The open platform innovation approach enabled the 2014 public release of the *Rift DK1* [development kit 1], including the firmware, schematics, and mechanicals for the device.

Another advantage of this strategy was that it seeded the device to the most influential change agents in the gaming industry – multimedia and game designers, developers and innovators. Using crowd-sourcing, gaming conferences, vast media coverage and a unique development process, *Oculus Rift* had already ensured full innovation visibility and partial access to early adopter consumers. With its core target group being gamers – the natural early adopters – exposure and seeding of the technology was certainly achievable, and the commercial potential for the product was looking extremely encouraging with 100,000 developer kits sold.

1.0

Down the rabbit hole

In March 2014, Facebook purchased Oculus VR for a whopping US$ 2 billion. Boosting the market confidence in Virtual Reality technology and accelerating its development and investments, paving the way for other market introductions, such as the *Gear VR*[8] headset, which transforms the *Galaxy* smartphone into a portable VR device. An IP lawsuit against Oculus VR filed by ZeniMax Media, followed by Palmer's departure from the company in 2017 clouds the future of the company. Facebook Inc's decision to shut down the award-winning content unit Oculus' Story Studio and outsource content making,[9] also made many professional speculate whether the application of Virtual Reality would be as diffused as formerly predicted. However, we cannot undermine the influence that Oculus has had on the Virtual and Augmented Reality Market. As Luckey voiced himself – this is not just about the success story of Oculus.

> *In order for any Virtual Reality company to succeed, the entire 'virtual cycle' needs to become successful. Meaning that the number of VR units sold are less crucial to determine whether it would stick, but rather a frequent and constant use of the technology by end-consumers – "the dollars spent on content and hours spent in content."*[10]

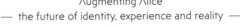
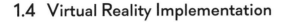

1.4 Virtual Reality Implementation

Even though its initial core development of the *Oculus Rift* was directed towards the gaming industry, its technology and device influenced Virtual Reality's integration in many sectors. In some cases, it amplified existing experimental systems [such as training techniques], and, in other industries, forming a foundation for a 'creative destruction' process, revolutionising entire interaction systems and applications.

Beyond current gaming and product simulation developments, Virtual Reality has already been successfully applied to educational development, methodology [think Virtual Reality class demos, or eLearning], and professional training through the use of simulation software and hardware.

> Virtual Reality simulation has not only improved professional medical treatment, it has also been used in mental rehabilitation therapy for amputees and stroke victims, as well as to support PTSD treatment. Making it possible for more caretakers and patients to improve the quality of and access to healthcare and psychological treatments.

> Virtual Reality also shows great promise and relevance for content delivery. With a decrease of 47% in film viewing and 48% in TV viewing due to gaming – the traditional entertainment industry has cause for concern.[11] Since the most popular *Rift* headset developer kit application is the Virtual Reality cinema,[12] Virtual Reality could actually manage to reverse that trend, offering a fully immersive entertainment experience for sporting events, concerts, film and television. It can also transform the role of the user during entertainment consumption to one that is more participatory – making even remote consumption an immersive experience.

Besides the need to overcome content issues, and the processing power that is required to create an immersive experience – consider that Virtual Reality games require up to x7 computing power versus a traditional PC game to create an immersive experience.[13] Virtual Reality's dependence on fully taking over the user's peripheral perceptions may cause a series of hindrances and side effects. The gaming and entertainment industry will need

to elevate traditional game design and immersion techniques to overcome the current issues, as well as those that have not yet been discovered. Physiological feedback and side effects such as headaches and motion sickness have already been directly triggered by Virtual Reality experiences using HMDs. Hardware design and simulations are constantly being adjusted to synchronise visual feedback to avoid participatory misalignment [and thus nausea] by:

» Limiting camera angles and creative techniques that don't register as 'natural' to normal vision

» Limiting head motion

» Maintaining low latency

» Maintaining a high frame rate

» Calibrating motion effectively

» Clean image rendering

Human vision is a fundamental experiential platform, which explains the massive focus on computer vision as a core research and development field within Augmented Reality and Virtual Reality. Yet, the ultimate challenge for Virtual Reality immersion will be to simulate a multisensory interaction to the most complex organic computer ever made – humans. Whereas Virtual Reality requires a complete sensory override by using isolated environments and sense-stimulating devices, Augmented Reality enjoys the advantage of building on existing environmental inputs and processing. Though the task at hand is still complex, it seems to be both more obtainable and more forgiving.

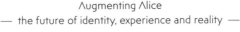

1.5   The Immaculate Augmented Birth

Although sensory enhancement and Virtual Reality simulation have been researched and developed since the 1960s, it took a couple more decades for Augmented Reality research and applications to emerge. One of the first pioneers of cyber and augmented space was the American interactive artist Myron Krueger, who explored human/digital/spatial interaction as early as the 1970s. Krueger tracked participants' movements inside a room. His *Psychic Space* used a sensory floor, whereas his *Videoplace lab* used gesture tracking to register how the participants moved around the environment, and transformed them into an interactive digital display or impression. Much of what we currently consider digital or interactive art is rooted in Krueger's early work. If we think about it, it is also the root of Augmented Reality, since it created a reactive, Real-Time digital impression manifested in a physical space.

Further developments in Augmented Reality focused mainly on the integration of Augmented Reality within a working environment, such as the previously mentioned Boeing Augmented Reality project, and Pierre Wellner's 1991 *Digital Desk* prototype, developed in the Xerox research lab. *Digital Desk* was a working prototype of a fully interactive [projected] computer interface, which enabled the user to use gesture tracking to input and edit physical-to-digital and digital content.[14]

Augmented work environments and Spatially Augmented Reality [SAR] became a core area of research for this technology.[15] In 1997, the MIT Tangible Media Group, led by Professor Hiroshi Ishii, started exploring the vision of Tangible Bits within the *ambientROOM* platform. They explored Tangible Augmented Reality, which combines "the enhanced display possibilities of Augmented Reality with the intuitive manipulation and interaction of physical objects or Tangible User Interfaces."[16]

In 1998, research conducted by Raskar, Welch and Fuchs – from the University of North Carolina at Chapel Hill and the NSF Science and Technology Center for Computer Graphics and Scientific Visualization – explored the office of the future via the application of image-based modeling and spatially immersive displays.[17]

Due to high costs and technical restrictions, Augmented Reality remained an experimental platform explored mainly by researchers. The *ARToolKit*, created by Hirokazu Kato at *HITLab*, changed that. *ARToolKit* is an open-source platform that provides video tracking, virtual object interaction, and 3D graphic models that can be overlaid on any OS platform.

The outcome was significant for interactive Augmented Reality applications such as *ARQuake* – the first outdoor mobile Augmented Reality game [2000], and the interactive *MagicBook* [2001] – which enabled readers to

> "move from the conventional form of the book to the immersion of Virtual Reality, [with the ability to] go in the other direction as well – from fully immersive to the Augmented or conventional forms."[18]

Research and development into augmented content did not reach a wider audience until the first real-world application of Augmented Reality via mobile devices. In 2008, an Augmented Reality travel guide launched with the *G1 Android* phone, followed by applications like *Wikitude* [an iPhone application that layers Wikipedia content over objects via the camera], and Layar [a mobile application that identifies geo-located points of interest in the vicinity of the user]. The *SixthSense* Augmented Reality prototype was presented at the 2009 TED conference, further extending the potential of Augmented Reality. Pattie Maes and Pranav Mistry demonstrated a wearable device that enabled a flexible application of Augmented Reality with multi-purpose output in communication, information and interaction. It wasn't until 2012, when Google announced the launch of *Glass*, that the industry became aware of the mass diffusion potential of Augmented Reality.

1.6   The Big Glass Hope

The most significant development in applied Augmented Reality was made by Augmented Reality and wearable tech pioneer Dr. Steve Mann. This Canadian inventor founded the MIT Media Lab's Wearable Computing group, and started exploring vision enhancement and registering devices in the 1970s. Mann wore his Wearable Wireless Webcam continuously, exploring notions of surveillance and reality augmentation. It is not surprising that Mann was often referred to as the 'world's first cyborg' – he even wears his HMD in his official passport photo.

In 1999, [together with James Fung] he invented the first Augmented Reality HMD, *EyeTap*. Shortly after, inventor and industrial designer Sir James Dyson started developing his own Augmented Reality headset, *Halo*, which was first unveiled more than a decade later in 2012. *Glass* has been described as "strikingly similar"[19] to both *EyeTap* and *Halo*.

Google announced the launch of its futuristic Augmented Reality product, Project Glass, on April 4, 2012. It was developed by the Google X innovation hub in New York, and featured the work of some of the industry's youngest and brightest UI, UX and product designers. The goal was to create a commercial wearable product, which would allow the user to access and display online information in Real-Time.

The commercialisation strategy for *Glass* demonstrated the need for an extensive supportive ecosystem for the product, including:

- » A commercial product
- » Better integration of interaction technology
  [UI, voice activation]
- » Extended compatibility with online infrastructure
  [apps and designated software]
- » An online community
- » Technical support
- » Product training

1.0

Down the rabbit hole

Although *Glass* offers some improvements over the *EyeTap* and *Halo* devices in terms of product design, user interface, features, and functional integration, its value lies in being a 'pure' technological invention. Mann defined Glass's core innovation value through the fact that it managed to translate the technology into a multi-functional device that could be used by the masses. "*Glass* is much less ambitious than the computer-mediated vision systems I constructed decades ago. What Google's involvement promises, though, is to popularize this kind of technology."[20]

The launch video was shot from the user's perspective, and showed what it would be like to go through one's daily functions with an information layer displayed in a user-friendly way. The launch video quickly went viral, proving to be an effective communication channel. Its influence on pop culture became evident when, a few months later, an anti-domestic violence campaign used the same 'day in the life via Glass' approach to provide the viewer with a first-hand account of what domestic violence victims go through.

Despite the high price-tag, the product received initial positive reactions from tech-savvy consumers, *Glass* was chosen by Time magazine as one of the inventions for 2012, as the device that will integrate Augmented Reality as part of our daily lives. It looked like all the ingredients for a successful launch and product integration were in place – futuristic technology, usability, and targeted marketing. The prototype was released to a select group of 'Glass Explorers' in 2013, and launched to the public in 2014.

While it may have seemed as though global consumers had adapted to wearable technology – with devices like step counters, smart watches, and Bluetooth headsets – Google's expectation of achieving seamless integration and mass diffusion of an eyewear-based HMD in the wearable tech category was premature at best, and perhaps completely wrong considering its lack of social acceptance.

There is no doubt that Google managed to shift the eyes of the industry toward the application of Augmented Reality. However, on a user level, it failed to generate long-term, widespread and meaningful adoption. This is rooted in Google's poor understanding of product positioning, societal shifts and trends.

The much anticipated *Glass* product was not successfully diffused; instead, its users were marginalised, targeted and even attacked while using the *Glass* device in the public domain.

> "I worry that Google and certain other companies are neglecting some important lessons," said Dr. Mann. "Their design decisions could make it hard for many folks to use these systems. Worse, poorly configured products might even damage some people's eyesight and set the movement back years."[21]

Consider the key reasons for *Glass*'s failure to achieve long-term adoption:

Over-layered interaction

The interface and voice activated commands were fairly simple to use and considered a positive and attractive feature of the device. However, the voice recognition [a technology that's still far from perfect today] and multi-touch trackpad on the temples failed to supply a fully intuitive and homogeneous control system.

Unclear added value

The advantage of Augmented Reality using an HMD was understood, however, it did not provide a clear-cut improvement over diffused mobile devices, such as smartphones.

Uber-exclusive

Google's launch strategy for *Glass* was based on creating high desirability by seeding it to a limited group of users. Unfortunately, the criteria chosen for the seed group was based more on their technological affinity rather than their role as a social influencer. This overly exclusive seeding limited the feedback and launch impact, affecting the product's initial social visibility and acceptance. Limited compatibility and content availability. The device was Android-based, which limited early adopters who use Apple devices. Google only released the *Mirror* API – enabling third-party developers to start making apps for the device – on April 25, 2013. And the device didn't offer compatibility with three key travel apps until May 2014, even though it positioned its users as explorers.

The uncool factor

The initial product design was heavily criticised. The sharp-edged display cube

1.0

Down the rabbit hole

was described as frightening and dangerous, and many wondered why Google ignored the obvious solution of a double lens device. The original product was not offered with prescription or tinted lenses, limiting its compatibility with potential users, such as those who already wear glasses and the visually impaired. "Think about it: for its *Glass* project, the company needed a screen on which to display the interface for its new computer platform. Attached to a head-born mounting system, the screen had to be positioned in front of the eye of a user. I'm wondering if any at the Google development team thought about whether you could just make *Glass* look like a regular pair of glasses."[22] The design was an odd choice considering the problems with the eyewear format. Glasses, as opposed to shades, are still considered an 'undesirable' accessory. The first design being painfully unfashionable, so the incentive to wear it was close to none. Attempts to improve desirability via a redesign, in collaboration with iconic fashion designer Diane Von Furstenberg, were futile, and users stayed away. Today we are finally witnessing launches of fashion-based HMD designs for Augmented Reality and image registration wearables, by social media and technology brands such as Microsoft, Facebook and Snap.

Glass failed to create a wide consumer base, or to lure existing users into making the product an integral part of their everyday lives. "After the initial testing, *Glass* has become an 'extra thing'. It's something I might wear if I know keen photos are a possibility, or if I'll need heads-up navigation, or just want to freak people out. It's nowhere near a part of my everyday life. Until it somehow breaks its chicken/egg lack of ubiquity, there will not be much demand to bring it along."[23] This is a problem shared by all wearable devices when attempting to impose an added functional value to pre-existing physiological, social and cultural aspects of the artifact.

We have witnessed the wave of designated health trackers and smartwatches being quickly adopted, and then left in desk drawers, because they failed to form a strong proposition that would compete with semi-wearables such as mobile phones. Instead, they rely on the proximity of a mobile phone to have a sufficient platform for display and interaction. As an autonomous input and output system, Augmented Reality has the potential to change that dynamic. Yet it will still have to do a much better job than the cultural and aesthetic approach of HMDs.

Glass was officially discontinued in 2015, and is currently in design revision. Its significance lay in signalling to the tech industry that Augmented Reality is here to stay. Google is heavily invested in Magic Leap – probably the most funded and valuable Augmented Reality start-up as of 2016. This is a clear indication that Google is rolling up its sleeves in preparation for the Augmented Reality battle between the tech and media conglomerates.

1.7   [Un]wearables

The deconstruction and reconstruction of computing systems has led to the creation of integrated – or invisible – computing. Miniaturisation of processors paved the way for mobile computing devices, and once graphic displays became freestanding objects in the 1960s [with the first commercial display being the IBM *2250 graphic terminal* in 1965], the path to wearable computing was inevitable.

We carry our mobile devices everywhere – tucked in a bag, a pocket, or placed on a surface only one vibration away from our attention. They have become commonplace, and a cause for a modern form of separation anxiety. We are all familiar with the sight of a highly alert adult frantically tapping their body parts as their eyes scan around the room in confusion and despair, attempting to locate their misplaced mobile device.

Wearables [as opposed to mobile devices] normally refers to objects that have direct contact with the body, and use various sensory input and output systems to mediate and communicate signals and data. Wearables are often designed as, or inspired by, existing decorative and/or functional wearable objects, such as necklaces, rings, bracelets, eyewear, headphones, and bras.

Gadi Amit, the designer behind the *FitBit* health tracker and the *Palm Zire* explains "We are humans, we interact with our eyes. The eyes are our representation of our soul, our emotion, our personality, much more than any element of our bodies. By putting something in front of the eye, you're obscuring your fellow from you. It is a major disruption from human communication."[24]
Digital wearable devices should elevate our use of mobile technology, as it ensures better proximity and gesture-based interaction with the device. Some digital wearables still have severe functional issues relating to size, weight,

WE ARE HUMANS,
WE INTERACT WITH OUR
EYES. THE EYES ARE OUR
REPRESENTATION OF OUR
SOUL, OUR EMOTION, OUR
PERSONALITY, MUCH MORE
THAN ANY ELEMENT OF
OUR BODIES. BY PUTTING
SOMETHING IN FRONT
OF THE EYE, YOU'RE
OBSCURING YOUR FELLOW
FROM YOU. IT IS A MAJOR
DISRUPTION FROM HUMAN
COMMUNICATION.

— Gadi Amit, 2014

and mainly battery supply which still effects their usability. In theory, however, this hypothesis often clashes with diffused behavioural and cultural perceptions. Even a proposal to slightly alter the proximity of the placed wearable versus a mobile device – from 'within the pocket' to 'against the skin' or as a gesture receptor and organ extension – should consider pre-existing social connotations, behavioural nuances, and individual preferences. Most notably:

» Culture-specific style

» Individual pre-existing style preferences [form over function]

» Peacocking [our need to display our possessions and adhere to trends]

» Physiological differences in fit, body shape and material sensibility

» Pre-existing usage [if I ain't wearing glasses, chances are I will be
» less likely to be wearing smart-glasses]

» Pre-existing usage patterns [irregular vs. permanent usage]

In the case of Glass, its initial unfashionable design was a definitive reason for its failure to achieve mainstream adoption. By the time more fashionable solutions were introduced, the social rejection of head-mounted registering devices became evident. The device and its users were already socially rejected and tagged as 'glassholes'. Various documented assaults on *Glass* wearers marked the lack of social readiness for input/output wearables in the public domain. Around the same period, Dr. Mann was also assaulted while wearing his own *EyeTap* device at a McDonald's restaurant in Paris in 2012.

The need to stick to complex fashion and usability systems inherent in the design of wearable technology makes for sometimes complicated ergonomics, production and distribution. This can greatly reduce the cost effectiveness of the product.

1.O

Down the rabbit hole

An effective solution for wearable technology success would be based on

Technology

Further miniaturisation and processing capabilities enhancements, allowing versatile application and effective integration within existing artifacts and usage rituals.

Design

Inoffensive or minimalist design, or an iconic design that will create mass desirability and a new style standard [think about how iPhone shifted the design evolution of all smartphones].

Culture

The understanding of a wearable artifact beyond a specific technological/functional aspect – its core cultural and social significance.

Integration

Development of biological imitating, second-skin and in-body wearables, transforming the category into a prosthetic-like enhancement.

1.8 AugMania

Currently, the easiest way to describe Augmented Reality is to say: "it's like *Pokémon Go*". This is quite curious when we consider that a technology that was first developed in the '70s, and has had functioning prototypes since the '90s, only became publicly known thanks to a yellow manga creature. It wasn't until July 2016 when an Augmented Reality application first gained mass popularity – albeit short-lived. *Pokémon Go* – a free, location-based app for mobile and wearable devices – was downloaded over 100 million times within six weeks of its launch, with an unprecedented 500+ million total downloads worldwide.[26] The app marked the beginning of the Augmented Reality Mania.

Pokémon was a group of mid-90s fictional Japanese anime characters that quickly became a global franchise including playing cards, films, a video game, TV series, theme park and musical. The *Pokémon* Go app was formed as a collaboration between Nintendo and Google-born development studio Niantic. Created as a geo-located quest game for iOS, Android, and Apple Watch devices, the game is free to download, with in-app purchases for digital assets and accessories.

Users engage with their physical environment to catch, train and battle various *Pokémon* creatures. The game's location-based tasks helped to position the game as an activity that promoted fitness and well-being. Eliminating work-arounds such as driving, geo-location and other game features like egg-hatching require physical motion, as their development is based on step count. The game was initially launched in selected territories, with phased launches in new regions to maintain a steady flow of new users and ongoing media hype.

Basing the game on the familiar and massively popular *Pokémon* franchise served as a nostalgic trigger for both new and former fans. This helped to create mass visibility for the product, and generated global curiosity. Building on existing mobile platforms made the application highly accessible, while also ensuring a quick adoption rate. Simple gameplay made the game compelling to a wide range of users, regardless of age or digital fluency.

1.0

Down the rabbit hole

Pokémon Go quickly became a social phenomenon. Social media was flooded with commentary about the app, with 15.3 million tweets in the first week alone.[27] At its peak, the application reached 45 million active users daily, yet within six weeks of its launch, 80% of its users stopped playing and/or deleted the app.[28] *Pokémon Go*'s hot-potato drop in users was triggered by several key factors:

#01 The unpredictable backlash against the viral, mass following of the application. *Pokémon Go* mania caused irrational personal and group behaviour, leading to disruptive social behaviours, endangerment, injuries and even death of participants and bystanders.[31] This resulted in mockery and partial social rejection of users.

#02 The massive following caused the second-hand experience to overshadow users' need to have a first-hand experience.

#03 The simplistic gameplay allowed immediate access, but failed to engage and create sustainable long-term value. The level of interactivity failed to create deep cognitive interaction or a rich experience. Users expressed disappointment and boredom caused by repetitive and unchallenging gameplay.

#04 The content was not reactive and responsive enough to users' behavioural patterns. Considering it was based on spatial and location-based experiences, it lacked long-term immersive value in terms of its adaptation to day-to-day rituals, resulting in 'flat' gameplay.

#05 Functional issues such as battery consumption were not considered, causing users to make a tough choice about their smartphone usage. Pragmatic functionality needs won out over the game's entertainment value.

#06 Issues of privacy and safety quickly alarmed existing and potential users. Between cases of *Pokémon Go* users lured to locations and robbed, or endangering their safety and those of others, the game's developers faced legal suits related to privacy violations, trespassing, and plain unsatisfied customers "complaining about the money they spent and what they received for that cash."[29]

#07 The augmented experience was a novelty rather than a true augmented experience. Although it related to physical locations, it failed to truly interact or be relevant to a specific spatial interactive experience.

▼

Pokémon Go's biggest value lay in the social phenomenon created by its massive media coverage, viral diffusion, and extreme level of user engagement. Despite mixed reviews and a number of weak features, its impact on the Augmented Reality industry and users' acceptance of the technology remains undisputed: "Pokémon Go is definitely setting the standard for Augmented Reality gaming, a niche that will only continue to grow."[30]

The app marked the awakening of the Augmented dragon, demonstrating how it could immediately be applied via widely diffused mobile devices rather than designated HMDs. We also witnessed how mass diffusion and easy access might fail to generate a long-term adoption pattern for Augmented Reality. Before augmented experiences raid our lands, we need to consider how to harness the true potential of augmentation as a valuable platform to elevate content and experience. It should be attuned to users' future and present needs, rather than being a disruptive experiential gadget that's abused, only serving to trap consumers in a monetary loop.

1.0

Down the rabbit hole

1.9   Why Augmenting Kicks Virtual's Butt

Facebook's 2014 acquisition of Oculus VR provided a hint towards the possibilities of the technology within virtual social media networks. But beyond the functional, development and cost aspects of Virtual Reality mass applications, another core aspect that needs addressing is Virtual Reality's Social Construction of Technology [SCOT].

Humans are inherently social beings. We have an innate need to create an emotional bond with and dependency on other humans. This was best proven by American psychologist Frederick Harlow's series of experiments using artificial surrogate mothers in a rhesus monkey nursery. The infant monkeys were offered a nourishing wired mother that fed them, and a comforting cloth mother that did not provide food. They spent the majority of their time with the cloth mother, repeatedly choosing nurturing over sustenance. These experiments demonstrate the importance of caregiving and companionship to cognitive development, while showing that social isolation and disconnection can have deep and lasting negative impacts, including emotional and mental disorders, and even death.

Virtual Reality is a synthetic layer that reaches a fully immersive experience only by isolating the individual from their existing physical reality. In other words – it is a closed system, whilst Augmented Reality permits a much more inclusive application. There are, of course, massive advantages to Virtual Reality in certain applications, including facilitation of new methods and paths for interaction and the creation of fully immersive experiences, which help in increased engagement and effectiveness in treatment in cases of autism, ADHD, and PTSD, for example. Yet even in a multiplayer or social context, Virtual Reality forms an artificial layer between a network of users. As social beings, humans eventually seek a solution that can include and support their normal social structure and environment, adding value to existing interactions and behaviours.

Virtual Reality has already pushed the gaming industry to develop new software and hardware to match the technology's potential. Although it has the capability of transforming the digital entertainment industry into a truly

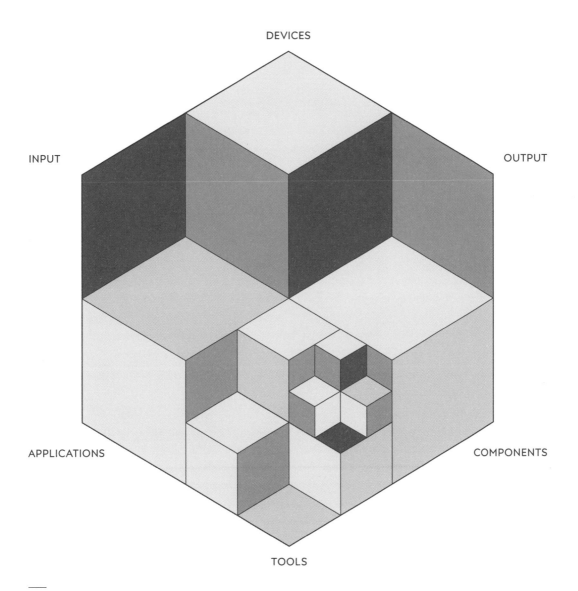

DEVICES

INPUT

OUTPUT

APPLICATIONS

COMPONENTS

TOOLS

The Augmented Reality landscape
Augmented Reality's success requires the
construction of an ecosystem that could generate
content and service the user and industry.
Author's Image, 2017.

immersive experience for the single user, it still needs to consider the social experience of users in online multiplayer narratives. Gaming and interactive storylines that provide gesture tracking and visual feedback, for example, provide the opportunity to develop unique forms of individual immersive expression, as well as an elevated multiplayer experience to establish a new sense of social immersion and new role playing opportunities.

In terms of resources, creating a full virtual environment raises bigger complications than augmentation since it requires developing a higher level of design in order to achieve realistic alternative virtual worlds. This includes forming a full virtual multisensory simulation with the technological and physiological complexities that comes with it. It is true though, that once these are achieved, Virtual Reality would have undeniable merits for the creation of alternative, fully controlled and fully immersive scenarios, and will establish its value from creating transcendental experiences that cannot be achieved by any other manner. Simulation [for professional or medical purposes] and interactive entertainment are probably the most relevant and beneficial industries for the application and user consumption of Virtual Reality content.

Virtual Reality is thus more prone to become a core tool for achieving immersion through simulation, rather than a tool to enhance existing experiences – when the narrative and value of engagement and interaction is detached from our physical reality. As creators and developers, we must remember that even if Augmentation might seem more limited in terms of content injection, the human mind is a beautiful machine capable of having the same, if not more engaging sensory triggering systems – if we build on an existing physical platform – such as reality. In fact, building on a physical layer might achieve the same, or even a more transcending experience. Leaving a gap for personal contextualisation and imagination can become a powerful bonding agent between users and the content, where impressiveness becomes an inseparable part of the experience. A simple example is how a great film might mesmerise you, where you are completely immersed in the narrative flow, only to emerge once the credits are rolling. No magic tricks, no special effects – just a great narrative that hooks you. Let's start there, and build experiences on top of that.

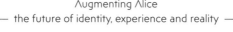

Pop culture often labels virtual-immersive futures and fully immersive alternatives to physical reality as a dystopian future. We see this in literature, TV series and full-feature films from *The Lawnmower Man* to *The Matrix* trilogy, where the fully immersive nature of a digital representation of reality results in disastrous personal, social and existential consequences. Ultimately, technology has the power to be a qualitative tool that we use to improve and enhance the reality we live in, rather than something that initiates escapism.

As opposed to Virtual Reality, Augmented Reality enhances the existing bond and interaction layer between user and environment, leaving the developer to focus on the add-on content that enriches the experience. After all, there is nothing more immersive or high-res than reality itself. If there is a single technology that will bridge the gap between the physiological, social and technological needs of its users, it will be environment-integrated Augmented Reality.

Core challenges in Virtual Reality diffusion

Technology

Virtual Reality still needs
to deal with serious functional
issues that cause negative
physiological reactions
from users.

Cost

Like any transformation
process Virtual Reality content
creation and consumption is
a costly investment for user
and industry alike.

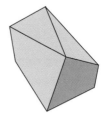

Hardware

Good luck getting the user
to keep them sexy goggles on.

Content

Missing breadth and depth
of content. Do not despair, there
is a development of Microsoft
Excel for Virtual Reality.
Shoot me now.

Social

Virtual Reality is a closed
system that is inherently socially
disconnected, limiting the user to
a confined virtual realm.

Experience

Requires a convincing
multisensory experience to
enable a fluid user experience.

Core challenges in Augmented Reality diffusion

1.0

Down the rabbit hole

Function

Better chance of reduced functional problems as it does not require fully immersive features.

Content

Augmented Reality layers have the potential to be integrated within a wide range of content creation and interaction platforms.

Hardware

Has a larger scope for interaction within a variety of wearables, Mobile, Spatial and Tangible User Interfaces.

Cost

Augmented Reality development and implementation costs would be lower than Virtual Reality's.

Social

Augmented Reality is an open system that is inherently spatially and socially connected.

Experience

Builds on existing [real-world, multisensory] experiences and interaction know-how.

"IT'S A POOR SORT OF MEMORY
THAT ONLY WORKS BACKWARDS'
SAYS THE WHITE QUEEN TO ALICE."

— Lewis Carroll, Alice's Adventures in Wonderland

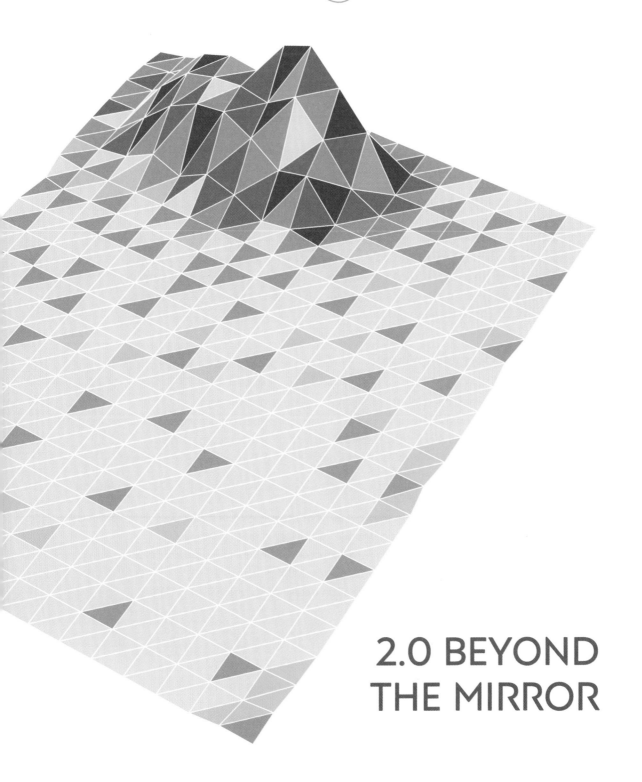

2.0 BEYOND THE MIRROR

Beyond the Mirror

Augmented Reality within a socio-demographic context

To understand the implementation of Augmented Reality, it's important to look at how social and demographic factors such as age, population density and habitat influence the interaction between users and technology. Especially as we are currently witnessing major social and demographic shifts on a global scale. There is a direct relationship between such shifts and the implementation of technology platforms – as sociodemographic conditions evolve, so does the nature of the user-technology interaction.

2.1   It's Gonna be Mega

Dense urban areas are catalysts for technology development and implementation, with cities built as a tight network of permanent and interim systems, societies and cultures. The rapid growth of urban spaces combine increased activity and interaction with a decrease in private space. This duality forces us to look for alternative systems that will enable growth.

> We are witnessing accelerated patterns of urbanisation in both established and emerging economies. With a constant 1.1% annual population growth, together with an increase of human life expectancy, the global population is estimated to reach 8.4 billion by 2030, with more than 60% of this population expected to reside in cities.[1]

According to the World Economic Forum, some 77 million people move from rural communities to urban areas each year. The population surge and increased rural-urban migration will see the developing world double the number of megacities [metropolitan areas with a population exceeding 10 million] from 14 megacities in 1995 to 29 in 2016.[2]

Global patterns of urbanisation
Author's Image, 2017.
[Based on World City Report, 2016]

2.0
Beyond the Mirror

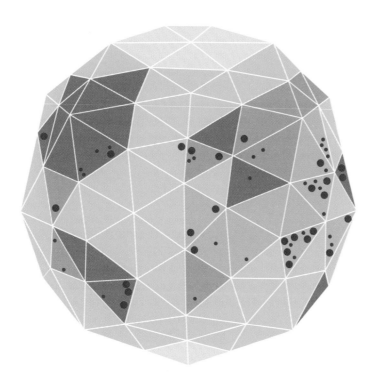

CITY POPULATION

+10 Million   +5 Million

URBANISATION %

80-100%   60-80%   40-60%

This has tremendous implications on both macro and micro levels. Social, economic, ecological and political adjustments will be necessary to deal with the ever-growing shifts in habitat density, and the resources required to support them. Forming layers of complexity as urban population densities increase. This will require solutions to infrastructure issues such as sanitation, traffic and pollution. There are severe implications for any glitches in grids of densely populated areas – tenfold in megacities – a power-cut during a heat wave, or water contamination that causes mass gastrointestinal upset – including tens of thousands of toilets flushing simultaneously, are not just public safety issues, but impact the economy and even national politics.

As cities grow into megacities, they consolidate the needs of millions of people, and mark the rise of new powers that will influence global social, political and economic objectives. The formation of global city coalitions ensure that shared causes and common interests are addressed at an international level. One of the most influential megacity groups is the C40 Cities Climate Leadership Group – a global alliance of cities aiming to drive urban action and even address climate change. Acknowledging the role cities play in global warming [already accounting for 75% of energy-related greenhouse gas emissions], C40 was a strong force in ensuring the 2015 Paris climate agreement addressed the substantial role cities would play in implementing green policies. The alliance also facilitated US$ 1 billion worth of green financing to support sustainable city infrastructure initiatives.[3]

> Megacities have distinctive ecosystems, cultures and sub-cultures that require the engagement of the municipalities to ensure long-term sustainable cohabitation on a social level. This means that we would need to develop solutions for more socially-focused functional issues, such as employment, public spaces and habitation.

When it comes to the use of space, municipal and private initiatives increasingly consider new ways of merging public and private spaces, with the creation of co-ops and residential cohabitation compounds in urban areas. Two of these exhibited at the 2016 London Design Biennale: *Common* – a co-living start-up[4], and Liu Xiaodu's *DenCity*[5] – a sustainable live/work environment in high-density areas. It's important to remember that

cohabitation communities might seem ideal on paper, but are extremely challenging in application. Look at the failure of the Israeli Kibbutz, which ultimately transformed into a very limited community model. Despite the fact there is much to resolve in co-ops and cohabitation models, the idea of shared resources and living spaces still seems like an inevitable option for high density, over-developed urban clusters.

Increased density in public spaces is already an issue in large cities, and will continue to be with the rapid growth of megacities. Such demographic swarming would effect us on several levels. On the human level, crowd density and traffic flow are critical to the operation of a city. On the environmental level, there is already an acute need to mitigate digital noise in public areas. As emerging technologies [like beacons] are implemented in public locations, we need to address the role technology can play in balancing content intrusion with accessibility. Particularly when we consider mechanisms of interaction, augmentation can be a partial solution to these issues – for example: aiding with filtering digital noise in dense urban areas might require the use of virtual and augmented [or even remote] presence in order to engage, as well as the use of spatially applied displays [holographic, projected or augmented] rather than a physical one within public and private spaces.

> Technology would not only play a role in the everyday functioning of city life, it would also facilitate social interaction. Since a city is also a social organisation, its growth will also influence social structures. Increased habitat density will lead to increased social friction, while simultaneously creating a sense of social isolation.

Even though social density ensures encounters with multiple individuals, it does not necessarily guarantee meaningful bonding and interaction. Futurist Alvin Toffler made the following observation back in the 1970s: "The average urban individual today probably comes into contact with more people in a week than the feudal villager did in a year, perhaps even a lifetime... The urban man may have a core group of people with whom his interactions are sustained over long periods of time, but he also interacts with hundreds, perhaps thousands of people whom he may see only once or twice and who then vanish into anonymity."[6] Toffler also refers to researchers like Columbia University's

economist Eli Ginzberg and psychologist Courtney Tall, who suggest that the combination of high mobility and urban density is shifting the nature of our relationships, conditioning them to be less stable and more short lived.

It is quite striking how relevant these statements are to urban society today. There is no doubt that issues of social interaction and isolation are a core concern in the delicate ecosystem of urban living, and more so as the systems expand. This sense of isolation triggered the development of geo-social network platforms, such as *Foursquare* and *Grindr*. I can see how augmented geo-social interaction platforms may become a potent tool in providing on- and off-site layers of social interaction in urban societies.

Digital layering embedded within high-density populations and spatial contexts [whether urban or otherwise] can act as an intensifier for the bright lights of the existing overbearing digital noise. Or it can act as a fantastic tool to amplify our urban environments – for the better or worse. Bringing cities to life via additional creative and data layering, giving notions of social activation and street art a completely different framing.

2.2 Location, Location, Location

Since the first territorial migration, the world has been getting 'virtually' smaller. Today, we can travel through places and spaces [both physical and virtual] with ease and speed. Our culture and society are more diversified than ever, and our social identities have become more flexible. Social identity is now a fluid concept, with interwoven ancestry lines, progressive concepts of gender, and even trans-species [including individuals who demand to be accepted as cats].

Globalisation has been achieved through trade and political treaties, but mainly by technological innovation, especially the creation of a global online platform with an ever-increasing number of users accessing it. The World Wide Web is a territory-free cyber space, allowing us to form new identity layers, social hierarchies and interactions, with Real-Time connectivity – heightened visibility and association with diverse cultures, societies and places. This leads to a more accessible community construction. If, in the past, communities were greatly defined by physical location, the boundless cyber space allows us to easily access and form a sense of identification with a social structure or a physical location, even if our relationship with it is brief or superficial. We now can have a sense of belonging, and understanding the culture of New York even if we haven't visited it, and join online groups and causes without contributing more than a 'like'. This is where online access enables a dynamic, multi-layered sociodemographic affiliation. One outcome of a connected world is that we are exposed to a wider variety of affordable travel destinations and experiences. We share our filter-perfect 'Wanderlust' online as we obsessively document our toes with the ocean panorama as a backdrop. As a result, we are witnessing more individuals self-identifying as 'citizens of the world' – a world with a less confined physical location, and a broader sense of community.

With Virtual Reality applications geared towards virtual travel, and Augmented Reality aspiring to add a new experiential level to a physical space, I do wonder if augmentation and virtualisation will shift our approach to leisure travel and nomadism. Will we be satisfied with being virtually 'transported' into new environments? Will our need for experiencing remote locations be satisfied by blending augmented foreign elements into our local physical environment? Can augmentation provide us with a true sense of a global experience without the need to set foot outside our door?

If, in the past, nomadism was restricted to specific cultures or circumstances, online accessibility and the miniaturisation of technology have helped to heighten mobility. As Toffler states, "the nomad of the past moved through blizzards and parching heat, always pursued by hunger, but he carried with him his buffalo-hide tent, his family and the rest of his tribe. He carried his social setting with him, and, as often as not, the physical structure that he called home. In contrast, the new nomads of today leave the physical structure behind."[7]

> Travelling has transformed from a leisure activity into a permanent nomadic lifestyle, creating a new breed of digital nomads. This new breed mixes work, travel and social interaction, operating from major cities and exotic destinations.

Digital nomadism is forming new mobile work/leisure norms and communities. New business initiatives based on the needs of digital nomads enable flexible

global spaces and social structures. "Demand for co-working communities, luxury hostels and ultra-portable products is spiking as growing numbers of young workers swap their nine-to-five lifestyle for a nomadic freelance career."[8] WeWork is a thriving co-working business, providing its members access to multiple locations in major global cities, as well as endorsing online community tools and on-site social activities. It is one of many of these 'types' of shared spaces cropping up around the globe.

Perhaps truly convincing, immersive virtual travel experiences could reduce unnecessary travel, for business and leisure alike, improving our carbon footprint and avoiding the horrors of suffering from jet lag in the middle of a board meeting. Virtual travel could create a new form of virtual nomadism. As a result, physical travel may once again become an exclusive vice for the adventurous and financially privileged. Yet simulation could never compare to the hidden experiences of physical travelling, for better and for worse. From the annoying passengers sharing outrageous conversations behind you, to chance encounters with kind strangers. Following a luring scent into a local eatery, or discovering a hidden urban gem as you wander through unfamiliar side streets. Real voyages include a sense of chaos that transforms travel into experiences. This is where augmented experience could add layers to our physical voyage, maintaining an authentic connection to the physical essence of mobility and location.

2.3 Digital Societies

For the most part, we live in a connected world. Civilisation, technology of one sort or another, and cross-cultural influences have reached and impacted almost every level of society. Whether we live in a developed or developing region, we are all exposed to global socioeconomic influences like never before. Even those who may not have direct accessibility through ownership of technological devices, still have unprecedented exposure to physical and digital content.

In his 1999 book *High Tech/High Touch*, John Naisbitt raises a strong concern that the imbalanced – somewhat obsessive – emphasis our society puts on high-tech [technology] qualities, overrides the value of high-touch [genuine] interaction. Naisbitt predicted that the influence of technological intoxication would have a wide influence on areas that are directly and indirectly related to technology usage, from religion to nutrition. Many of the shifting values he identified are very recognisable in technology's current influence on so¬ciety. In nutrition, we see that online visual culture and social media sharing have expanded the influence of global and local food cultures, leading to rapidly diffused nutritional trends, self-identification through dietary regimes, and shifts in body image and lifestyle trends. Naisbitt predicted several social shifts on behavioural and emotional levels, including:

#01

Superficiality

The favouring of a 'quick fix' for almost every level [from content consumption to interaction] and facet [from religion to nutrition] of our lives, which would make us develop a distant and distracted demeanour.[9]

#02

Ambiguity

The merging of the physical and cyber space, causing an increasingly blurred distinction between acceptable and unacceptable behaviours online and offline.

#03

Attachement

The development of a dual sense of attachment to technology, where we simultaneously fear and worship it.

Only a few decades later, these concerns have fully materialised. Our interest in technology has converged to an obsession, where most aspects of our everyday lives are influenced by or dependent on it. We have established complex, relationships with technology, where we attempt to amplify and control both the macro and micro aspects of our lives, while accepting its 'friendly intrusions' into our private space as a necessary evil.

Technology has become a core factor shaping the level, manner and frequency with which we communicate, consume, commute and interact in the world. And with that, it has become an inseparable part of our identity, so predominant in our society that it is now a key identifier in user archetypes

2.0

Beyond the Mirror

across all industries. However, in this current era of big data and consumer targeting, we need to consider a new way to segment digital users.

The key change is driven by the mobile, high-speed, multi-channel and social-media-driven access the Internet offers us today. This access provides users with independent, unmediated access to emerging technologies and goods. Online channels also provide multiple seeding opportunities for brands, users, content, services and products, with the potential for any of these to become [almost] instantly diffused to a global and/or targeted audience. Digital social networks, for example, represent a duality within social and personal identity. These are platforms that serve both individual emancipation and group affiliation. This enables us to form and join fluid digital tribes that are new, remote and nuanced.

While access creates new opportunities, it also has a reverse effect. As well as the ability to form and be exposed to cultural clusters, groups and individuals that we may not have encountered before, the wide exposure within the cyber world has created mass-uniformity. The over-diffusion of content and experiences instantly creates a 'flattened' experience, with a reduced emotional connection because of the overwhelming quantity of irrelevant content.

Mainstream marketing might still be effective and necessary for certain brands, but an increasing number of brands apply sophisticated algorithms to creating niche marketing strategies that offer tailored services and experiences. This approach provides a level of differentiation in a mass-user, over-saturated brand landscape.

New micro-targeted marketing strategies and supporting technologies are being developed to effectively predict and respond to the needs of users and small groups, providing users with a sense of personalisation and self-empowerment. Consumers, in turn, are encouraged to share intimate experiences and input, transforming their private moments into public ones. This is a bit of an odd cycle that plays on the duality of cyber space – offering interaction immediacy on a personal level with the option, and compulsion, to seed it back to the online public domain. The tension and balance between private and public will become a dominant factor in the

success of experience building, especially when we consider augmentation that embeds the potential to be simultaneously intimate, filtered and publicly shared. It remains to be seen how we will handle experiential layering and nuances.

This practice of participatory influence is, however, a double-edged sword. As brands deliver more micro-targeted content and services, consumer appetites and a sense of entitlement grows, demanding a heightened level of instant, fully responsive and personalised solutions from a product or service.

Technology has also become a predominant platform for unmediated social influence. In a society where technology is so dominant, it is key to constructing meaning and social narrative. Technology is the preferred and most immediate way for leaders to directly communicate with their public, as well as the general masses to express their support for [or discontent with] their leaders – this is how we can identify how open, restrictive or controlled a political regime is. What technology has created is access, and, beyond that, the ability for individuals and groups to influence cultural, social and political agendas, until it is no longer clear who is the dog and who is the tail in the social media wagging game. We saw the full expression of the new power balance between user, platform and traditional systems of media during the 2016 US elections. What became clear was that the result of the elections was driven by a strong desire and a sense of personal entitlement to individually influence the outcome.

Social media was strongly tied to the post-election triumph or defeat of the electorate. Sophisticated algorithms that had been customising users' feeds created echo chambers that presented a reality that matched the individual user's point of view. Complex and contradicting content does not feed well into our dopamine-seeking system. Our biology makes us seek satisfaction through confirmation bias in our social media feeds and technology use that may act against our evolutionary needs.

Or, perhaps we have reached an integration moment, where technology has become such an integral part of our ecosystem that it forms a new layer to our hierarchy of needs. Our problem is not that we want more. The problem is that the definition of 'more' currently means 'instant everything'. Will we

2.0

Beyond the Mirror

apply augmentation – the ultimate 'unlimited, instant everything' – to channel technology's potential into developing a sustainable biological, cultural and social approach, or will we apply it in a way that triggers an over-consumption and over-stimulated state of boredom?

2.4 Post-Social [Status]

In our fast-track, multi-channel society, we are already negotiating the balance between our authentic aspirations, our social status and our needs. We are constantly bombarded with both direct and indirect messaging that tells us that we need to adopt behaviours and consume goods and services that are necessary to our physical, social and mental well-being. This is a cynical, yet effective use of our irrational decision-making processes, and it underlines the value of a good emotional hook. For example, purchasing a Volvo is more than simply owning a car. It represents a person's true concern for their family's safety. Dove products represent self-esteem, self-acceptance, and a somewhat progressive view on materialistic society. Nike is targeted at people who 'just do it' - life's true warriors who make no excuses. Successful brands continuously demonstrate a deep understanding of creating and affirming emotional value.

Philosopher Alain de Botton first shared the idea that we have ongoing 'status anxiety' in 2004. The insight he tapped into was formed prior to online hyper-connectivity and viral videos, yet it perfectly explains our fixation with technology over the last decade. De Botton states that modern society places impossible hurdles in front of the average person:

> "Life seems to be a process of replacing one anxiety with another and substituting one desire for another," de Botton says. "Which is not to say that we should never strive to overcome any of our anxieties or fulfil any of our desires, but rather to suggest that we should perhaps build into our strivings an awareness of the way our goals promise us a respite and a resolution that they cannot, by definition, deliver." [10]

Mass and social media further elevates social and personal standards for behaviours, activities and consumption. We no longer consume to satisfy our needs, but to adhere to a projected social status, moving towards a binge cycle of consumption. The apparel industry is a sector that has soared because of status anxiety. During the 1930's Great Depression, the average wardrobe comprised fewer than 15 items. In 2008, the average American owned 92 items of clothing. Shopping has become a habit rather than a necessity. In 2015, it was estimated that British women spent around 100 hours a year on clothes shopping versus 95 hours for food shopping.[11] Looking at how we consume technology, we seem trapped in a loop where we are desperately striving to mend all of the gaps and flaws in our lives, constantly learning about new standards to adhere to, sharing our learnings online for mass-validation. This is a natural and noble aspiration, but are we truly elevating our situations, or are we merely replacing one flaw with another?

Advertising and marketing have successfully built on anxieties and basic emotional hooks to engage with consumers. These hooks can best be illustrated using Maslow's *Hierarchy of Needs*. The lower order relates to our physical survival and endurance, and the higher order relates to mental and social goals. This order applies to both individual and wider societal needs – especially in an age of instant gratification and content delivery.

Lower costs, better technological capabilities, and accelerating the pace of product development give us unprecedented access to a variety of goods and technology applications. We have long met the lower level needs of survival, and address our higher and emotional needs, yet it seems we have still not reached a state of gratification and happiness. Instead, we see high levels of depression because technology and online media keep us trapped in a vicious cycle of anxiety, where needs and values are continually updated, and once obtained quickly become irrelevant. Changing fashion, lifestyle and even health norms accelerate consumer trends in an endless pursuit of users to remain relevant.

Since advertising has used emotional triggers for centuries, it is only natural that technology utilises the same emotional hooks for its promotional strategies, promising to elevate our social and physical existence. A notable trigger is the aspiration to achieve self-actualisation

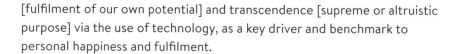

[fulfilment of our own potential] and transcendence [supreme or altruistic purpose] via the use of technology, as a key driver and benchmark to personal happiness and fulfilment.

Instead of being a window to completely new social horizons, the Internet and social media act as a mirror [somewhat distorted, but still a mirror] to existing social hierarchies and behaviours. Yet we also beautify and control the context of the imagery we use online, using image-enhancing apps, digital filters and rituals to portray an ideal reflection of reality. The expectation of maintaining an optimal digital image is quite stressful, creating a cycle in which users attempt to reflect their effortless, perfected realities within the online social sphere. This online social anxiety can lead to mental health conditions, such as Disconnect Anxiety, and the more diffused syndrome FoMO [Fear of Missing Out], where people are just too afraid to miss any fragment of the information stream.

Online emotional bonding and external affirmation of social status is further applied through the creation of feedback features, which shape a two-way online landscape, or the so-called 'web 2.0'. This was partially initiated by the massive amount of user-generated-content [UGC]. According to LinkedIn analysts, more than 4.6 billion pieces of online content were created daily in 2015 from social media platforms, blogs, websites and advertising campaigns.[12]

As users, our feeling of anxiety and frustration is enhanced by the variety of multi-platform media channels and emotional triggers we are exposed to. Now, more than ever as digital channels are streaming an overwhelming quantity of content where aspirational goals and perfected lifestyles are 'virtually' accessible with the slide of a fingertip. We are exposed to a 24/7 streaming of content that targets mass and niche consumers and knows no boundaries from mainstream to autonomous media sources, websites, social media, blogs, vlogs, health apps, travel guides and online trading – we are swayed, seduced and influenced by facts and lifestyles that we should follow.

This makes us feel compelled to portray a matching image of success, using online platforms and multimedia testimonials. A cycle generating a growing dependency on external assurances is reinforced by social media architecture, quantifying triggers [amounts of likes and followers] and content enhancing

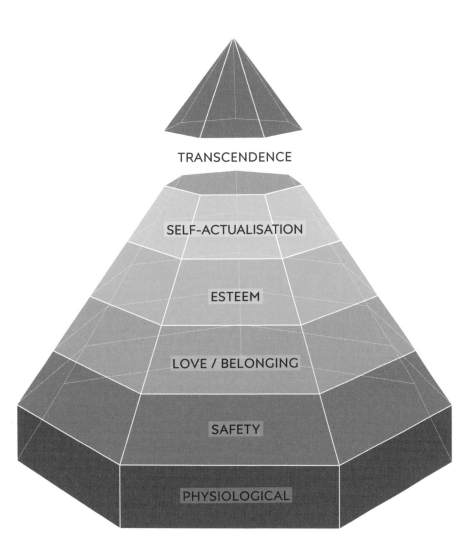

TRANSCENDENCE

SELF-ACTUALISATION

ESTEEM

LOVE / BELONGING

SAFETY

PHYSIOLOGICAL

Maslow's Hierarchy of Needs
Author's Image, 2017.
[Based on Maslow, 1962]

2.0

Beyond the Mirror

layers [suggested status updates, image enhancing filters] further perpetuating the need for external confirmation.

We go out of our way to document our lifestyle as aspirational, tightly curating our content for a targeted crowd and matching its 'appropriation' within a desired social context. The aspiration to achieve social acceptance causes us to adjust our online identities, as well as our offline behaviours, to maintain a specific image. Just think of how common it is for users to create multiple online accounts or filters – private, professional, public etc. – to monitor their own and their connections' online profiles [Yes Parents, your kids have figured you out. And, next to the account you're monitoring, they have another one too!].

But let's not blame technology for our social status anxiety. We do know that technology is never really the problem. Technology is a perfect system. The problem is that we create efficiency-targeted and quantity-based interaction which ads to users' anxiety as they futilely attempt to reach unachievable standards. Even cognitive computing seems to develop technologies that exploit human behaviours to 'maximise' the usage traction, rather than considering our actual needs.

> **Augmented Reality has the potential to become the platform that forms a whole new level of interaction. Since much of it would build on gesture-based interaction within a physical environment it could mark the transformation towards a uniformed high-touch/high-tech ecosystem – helping us construct a bio-digital society.**

This would be an opportunity for a new level of interaction. Rather than creating smart systems that are aimed at either substituting or exploiting human imperfection, we need to create a more human-centric interaction with a positive social effect on both virtual and physical world. A digital society doesn't need to be efficient to the level of inhuman, it can easily have a truly inclusive space. If you don't trust my opinion, ask Pope Francis. He shared, "How wonderful would it be if the growth of scientific and technological innovation would come along with more equality and social inclusion."[13]

2.5 Digital Tribes

As our personal and social identity embeds layers of digital expression, new social tribes are formed. These tribes may begin as casual online social groups, but have the potential to shift social hierarchies. States and borders have always defined societies and communities that were strongly rooted in the physical realm, but the emerging digital tribes will determine a new status and context of affiliation.

Affiliation with innovation has long been used to segment users in relation to accepting various product categories. In his 1962 book, *The Diffusion of Innovations*, Everett Rogers lays out the core factors that drive technology diffusion – such as innovation adopters' archetypes. Since we do not all adopt innovation at the same time, rate, or for the same motivations, Rogers categorises users in five core groups. These segmentations continue to be used widely to target consumers of emerging technologies, as well as other lifestyle products. The user archetypes according to Rogers are: innovators, early adopters, early majority, late majority and laggards. Rogers also draws an innovation adoption curve demonstrating the adoption flow from one user group to the next – from innovators to early adaptors, to early majority, and so on.

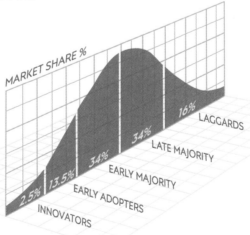

Rogers' Innovation Adoption Curve
Author's Image, 2017.
[Based on Rogers, 1962]

2.0

Beyond the Mirror

Although this theory has proven to be an effective tool for developing targeted and influence based marketing strategies, it no longer fully considers the breadth and depth of change that technology provides in terms of our access to products and services. The rate at which we adopt technologies and trends, and the way in which we apply them has changed dramatically since these models were first introduced.

As a result, these archetypes have become more fragmented and ambiguous. The adoption of technology and innovation has become a common practice that offers new, versatile positioning and segmentation opportunities. This is caused by a shift in mental state towards technology based on the users' digital fluency. Currently, we divide users into two core groups: digital migrants and digital natives.

Digital natives, or cyber natives, are native speakers of the digital language of computers, video games and the Internet.[14] They are technology fluent, and represent what is currently one of the biggest and most influential demographics – Millennials and Generation Z. Millennials [born between the early '80s and late '90s] are the first generation of digital natives, and an influential driving force in the global economy. Even though Generation Z [those born post 2000] are currently a lesser economic force, Generation Z expert Nancy Nessel describes them as "a large global generation with a loud global voice, a voice amplified and connected through technology". This generation "promises to be just as, if not more, influential than Millennials."[15]

Digital migrants are defined as 'those of us who were not born into the digital world, but have, at some later point in our lives, become fascinated by and adopted many or most aspects of the new technology.'[16] Of all digital migrants, Gen X has the most influential spending power, since it currently represents 25% of the US population and 31% of total US income.[17]

When I mentioned digital natives and digital migrants, you may have thought of them as two isolated groups, still defined by their access to and how frequently they use digital platforms. However, the digital access gap is rapidly narrowing – at least in developed economies. We are moving towards 100% access across a variety of age demographics. Research shows that close to 100% of people

under 45 are online, with high-majority percentages [84%-89%] in the 46-65 age category. Another interesting figure is the substantial increase of online access within the aging population, with a 53% online access of people aged 75 years or older in 2014 vs. 22% in 2008.[18] The increased rates of connectivity within digital migrants implies that we are fast evolving into a cross-generational digital fluency that will influence our interaction and identity formation.

> Digital accessibility is one facet of valuing digital fluency in a demographic level, yet we need to consider how this impacts the creation of new social structures and identities. This is defined more by how technology or new media is used, rather than the frequency of usage. This is especially notable in the digital natives group. Those poor souls who have never experienced a major phone-cord tangling accident, or who don't understand the connection between a pen and a cassette tape [a *what* tape?].

Researchers in the *Digital Youth Project* [19] found that contemporary social media platforms are becoming extremely dominant in digital natives' lives, "becoming one of the primary 'institutions' of peer culture for US teens, occupying the role that was previously dominated by the informal hanging out spaces of the school, mall, home, or street."[20]

As much as we might be tempted to describe such informal relationships as passive or consider the user as a social follower, the interaction between youth and digital media is actually based on multi-layered social and personal participation. It is true that such a platform can be more related to friendship-driven participation as a mainstream practice [I am there because everyone else is]. The research however, found that it is not the only driver. "An interest-driven genre of participation characterizes engagement with specialized activities, interests, or niche and marginalized identities. In contrast to friendship-driven participation, kids establish relationships that center on their interests, hobbies, and career aspirations rather than friendship per se."[21]

2.0

Beyond the Mirror

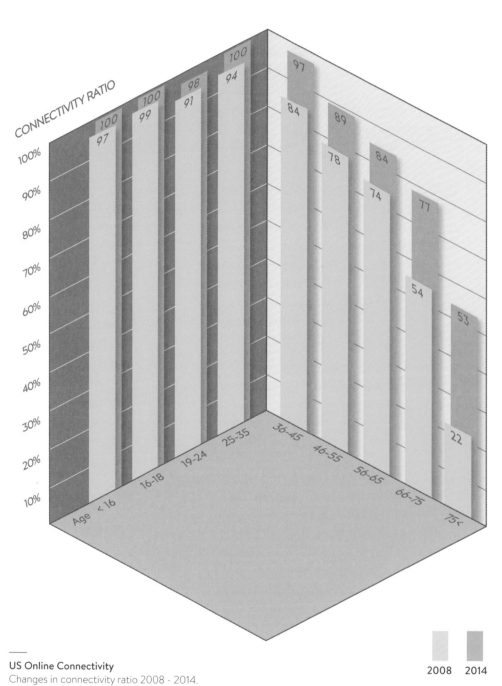

US Online Connectivity
Changes in connectivity ratio 2008 - 2014.
Author's Image, 2017.
[Based on Cole, 2015]

2008   2014

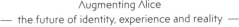
The level of interaction is represented through three different engagement practices that differ in channel usage, commitment and intensity. These practices are identified as 'hanging out', 'messing around' and 'geeking out'.

'Hanging out' mainly utilises traditional social networks and instant and text messaging, lightweight platforms that allow users to generate and share content, arrange social events, or participate in a casual activity, such as playing social games. This is also the engagement that is closest to family and home life.

'Messing around' represents a heightened level of engagement, where the user has a deeper interaction with the content and their own interests. This is a more participatory level of engagement, where the user is more actively exploring the digital realm for information, and has a transitional scope which is characterised with the user manipulating and creating multimedia content.

'Geeking out' is a more intense level of engagement, characterised by a more exploratory usage of technology, and a willingness to break social and technological boundaries. This involves more obscure media and a higher level of expertise and commitment.

This experimentation does not suggest an anti-social application of technology. In fact, the researchers found that even though new media tools were used to explore and expand social behaviours, social norms were not necessarily seen to erode while being online. "We did not find many youth who were engaging in any riskier behaviours than they did in offline contexts. Youth online communication is conducted in a context of public scrutiny and structured by well-developed norms of social appropriateness, a sense of reciprocity, and collective ethics."[22]

The research shows that we might want to have more appreciation for the contemporary engagement levels of young users, and adapt to the shifting values and norms for education, literacy, and public participation.

PERHAPS AUGMENTED
REALITY COULD BE
THE GENERATIONAL
BRIDGE BETWEEN THE
DIGITAL NATIVE AND
DIGITAL MIGRANT TRIBES,
REINTRODUCING FUTURE
KNOWLEDGE FOR THE
FIRST, AND HERITAGE
KNOWLEDGE TO
THE SECOND.

— *Galit Ariel, 2017*

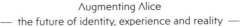

2.0

Beyond the Mirror

"Although questions about 'kids these days' have a familiar ring to them, the contemporary version is somewhat unusual in how strongly it equates generational identity with technology identity, an equation that is reinforced by telecommunications and digital media corporations that hope to capitalize on this close identification."[23] The researchers further urge educators and policy makers to understand the different nature of participation in the digital age, which is not restricted to 'serious' culture, but to more experimental, social and recreational, experiences. This applies to existing and future applications of digital interaction and perhaps Augmented Reality could be the generational bridge between the digital native and digital migrant tribes, reintroducing future knowledge for the first, and heritage knowledge to the second.

We are witnessing, now more than ever, the influence of technology applications on human evolution. New implementations, interactions and social affiliations are explored via the increased access and dialogue we have with technology. These can and should be utilised as tools that increase social interaction, build cultural bridges and create a society in which we can share common knowledge whilst practicing individual exploration.

"ALICE: 'WOULD YOU TELL ME, PLEASE, WHICH WAY I OUGHT TO GO FROM HERE?'

THE CHESHIRE CAT: 'THAT DEPENDS A GOOD DEAL ON WHERE YOU WANT TO GET TO.'"

— Lewis Carroll, Alice's Adventures in Wonderland

3.0 THE CHESHIRE ECONOMY

The Cheshire Economy

Reaching an Experience Ecosystem

We have had the privilege of viewing technology as our servant, summoned only to address our social and individual needs. Now, we need to acknowledge that technology is no longer a 'thing' that happens 'elsewhere', but an integral part of our everyday lives. The implementation of Augmented Reality will remove the final layer separating the physical and virtual experience, forming a fully embedded content and interaction system of data within our spatial realm.

3.1 Atoms, Bits, Data and Beyond

One of my favourite references regarding the relationship status between digital and physical space – is precisely 20 years old at the time of this book's publication. Ishii and Ullmar describe a divide between the bits and atoms worlds, within which we have a dual citizenship rather than a unified experience. Finally, I can confidently say that there's a technology that will shatter the barrier between the physical and the virtual – that is, of course, Augmented Reality. Reaching this point has been a long, ongoing, process.

In a way, moving toward implicit and virtual concepts that represent value is something unique to humans. From the moment we began to barter trade our goods [my two chickens equals your limping goat], through to developing currency systems [my two chickens equals one silver coin], the move from the atom economy to the bit economy became inevitable.

WE LIVE BETWEEN TWO REALMS: OUR PHYSICAL ENVIRONMENT AND CYBERSPACE. DESPITE OUR DUAL CITIZENSHIP, THE ABSENCE OF SEAMLESS COUPLINGS BETWEEN THESE PARALLEL EXISTENCES LEAVES A GREAT DIVIDE BETWEEN THE WORLDS OF BITS AND ATOM.

— Ishii & Ullmar, 1997 [1]

3.0

The Cheshire Economy

We created an independent value system that is adjusted and controlled by market forces, with the market determining the purchasing value of the currency, and therefore the value of the goods. This shift makes the value of goods an abstract concept, as nothing has a fixed and defined value. With the growth and standardisation of trading systems, banking and fiscal systems, a new industry has emerged, and with this our notions of trust and value. Financial worth is related to more than a physical ownership of wealth, it is a representation of present and future purchasing power. Technology has further promoted the relationships between the user and the financial system through online payments, credit cards, micro-transactions [in-app purchases] and the emergence of independent digital currencies such as the Bitcoin further reinforce the merging of currency, value and data; to become one and the same.

In 1999, Alan Cooper, a predominant pioneer in the field of user experience in software design and computer technology, spoke about the prominent shift from the atom economy to the bit economy:

> "The classic rules of business management are rooted in the manufacturing traditions of the industrial age. Unfortunately, they have yet to address the new realities of the information age, in which products are no longer made from atoms but are mostly software, made only from the arrangements of bits. And bits don't follow the same economic rules that atoms do."[2]

It is unlikely that our economic system will become completely atom-free, or based only on the digital exchange for goods. We humans just can't seem to overrule our need to have physical ownership of pretty, shiny things. Our economic systems aim to bring developing economies into the same production and consumption cycles as the developed economies, securing never-ending economic growth [and once we've discovered life on Mars, they're next]. The benefits of mass consumptions include reduced costs of consumer goods, increased manufacturer's profit and a competitive market with a larger variety. This also forms a vicious loop where increased offers inflate user consumption rates and in turn accelerates production, resulting in side-effects such as mass-urbanisation, over-consumption and environmental harm. Recent technology applications try to achieve more efficient mass production, through mass customisation and mass personalisation of manufacturing systems. This does not minimise consumption per se, but makes a more effective process – even if it does represents more of a symptomatic treatment than a cure.

Personalisation relies on technologies that combine supply-chain access, design and the use of local and even micro-production features, such as 3D printing machines and small scale manufacturing systems.[3] The idea of shifting product manufacturing back into small, or even household production is part of the vision for the Fourth Industrial Revolution - where technologies will fuse, and blur the lines between the physical, digital and biological spheres. We may be at the dawn of this new era, but we are far from having the infrastructure and applications that allow it to become a common practice in our everyday lives. It makes the current prototyping and manufacturing landscape more interesting and effective, yet 3D printing still lacks the quality, versatility and speed to become a household device and vehicle for consumption.[4]

To enable the diffusion of 3D printing, several key behavioural questions need to be addressed. On a pragmatic level, we need to enact regulations that cover design copyrights and health and safety issues, as well as ensuring that high-quality, versatile designs are available. One core question remains: Is there a fundamental need for the user to engage in the production and design of each and every consumed product? In the end, 3D printing appears to be another case of technology that misses the mark on its users' true needs and behavioural preferences, as well as its societal relevance.

Augmented Reality, on the other hand, may be the solution to enhance specific features – bringing the decoration and aesthetic features of a physical object into a new, interactive era. Imagine a perfectly fitted dress with an augmented seasonal print, or the space you could save in your tie drawer if one basic tie could be augmented to match any suit and colour combination. These might seem like superficial features, yet it is examples like this that may finally bring into balance our desires, commercial needs, and the availability of sustainable resources. As the Information Technology [IT] sector matures, we see a an evolution from bits to byte [data] value, and a clear shift towards a technology-based economic system. Technology companies have been consistently top-preforming brands, leading the industry and redefining the scope of innovation.

3.0

The Cheshire Economy

These companies also influence the atom world's demographics and social systems. Just as we have witnessed the rise in megacities, clustered tech industry areas – like Silicon Valley – have created new social structures, personal aspirations and global hierarchies. As knowledge industries grow, the influence of information-rich societies and individuals who know how to process it gain importance.

"We can recognize that it is not only the cost factor that leads to moving factories to a different country," says Alec Ross, author of *The Industries of the Future*. "The economic nomadism is increasingly perceivable in the fact that enterprises are present where they are most likely to find suitable and highly qualified employees and partners."[5]

Ross also makes an interesting observation about the changes within the bit economy. He states, "Data is the raw material of the information age. Advances in big data algorithms and processing represent a further shift in the high-tech industry business model and drive."[6] Marking the transformation from data being a by-product of technology to a core commodity. Software and hardware developers increase users' access to and dependence on technology by offering new business models that provide free access to platforms and services, instead generating revenues through data mining and targeted advertisements.

At the same time, smartphone payments, digital currencies and micro-transactions also provide new financial models. From crowd-funding to micro-loans, new financial initiatives are emerging everywhere. Bitcoin is one example of an alternative digital currency. Another example is the Israeli start-up *Colu*, which uses blockchain technology to create local currencies that encourage social and economic exchange in local communities.
There are those who hope that digital 'tokens' will be the tools that take over from centralised currencies and economic dogmas, allowing open-source, micro-financing ecosystems. Yet, even though digital currency may offer a compelling alternative for specific functional needs, it is not likely to become a global replacement that remains decentralised.[7] Since governments are so powerful in both the physical and virtual world, a controlled economic

ecosystem balanced by macro-level factors is ultimately inevitable, and probably beneficial to social stability.

As we move towards an information economy, creating traffic and a solid user base becomes vital for brands and content creation and curation becomes a key to achieving this. With the abundance of content on offer, brands striving to remain relevant need to create more meaningful and rewarding relationships with their consumers – forging a dynamic and multi-layered connection between consumer and brand. This is where the emergence of cognitive computing becomes a core tool in the facilitating of such processes, attempting to improve [and nudge] human/machine interaction and decision-making. Even though we would like to believe that we base our choices on rational processes, the tipping point for our decision-making is more emotional than rational. Daniel Kahneman and Dan Ariely are two notable behavioural economists who help mediate the notion of the irrational nature of our financial and life decisions. The truth is that we are unlikely to actually follow a framework for a predetermined decision. Retailers and service providers bank on our irrational decision-making by using advertisements and promotions that ride the emotional highway to consumer's hearts and pockets.

> This fact had been known for centuries – even Aristotle lists seven causes for human action: chance, nature, compulsion, habit, reason, anger and desire – out of which only one is related to a conscious, deliberate state. Most consumer engagement strategies try to ensure multiple action triggering strategies to encourage engagement [and to re-engage] with a brand. In 2008, scientists at the Max Planck Institute for Human Cognitive and Brain Sciences found that we make decisions up to ten seconds before we are consciously aware of them.[8] This means that understanding non-rational decision-making processes is more effective than trying to reason with ourselves regarding the choices we make.

Technology integration and the shift towards platform-based business models also means the leading role of content creation – through direct influence and actual content generation – has moved to the users. Social media platforms are a perfect example of user-generated content, where the platform mostly

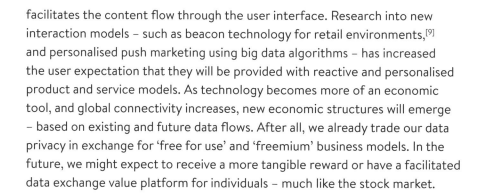

3.0 The Cheshire Economy

facilitates the content flow through the user interface. Research into new interaction models – such as beacon technology for retail environments,[9] and personalised push marketing using big data algorithms – has increased the user expectation that they will be provided with reactive and personalised product and service models. As technology becomes more of an economic tool, and global connectivity increases, new economic structures will emerge – based on existing and future data flows. After all, we already trade our data privacy in exchange for 'free for use' and 'freemium' business models. In the future, we might expect to receive a more tangible reward or have a facilitated data exchange value platform for individuals – much like the stock market.

The rise of entrepreneurial culture coincides with global efforts to drive economic development via innovation and high-tech industries. It is also fuelled by the role technology has within Western pop culture, including the glorification of success stories of technology entrepreneurs such as Steve Jobs, Mark Zuckerberg and Elon Musk. Generation Z is especially expected to keep the entrepreneurial wave soaring.

Currently, nearly 70% of Generation Z teens are self-employed, versus 12% holding traditional teen jobs. This ability to turn coveted skillsets into earning power will likely serve the Generation Z well as they enter the labour force. A survey by Northeastern University revealed that 42% of respondents expect to work for themselves one day, far more than the one in nine who are actually self-employed today.[10] Technology also significantly increases our access to online know-how and services, meaning that proactive users can quickly form new economic entities and facilitate a global transaction basis, regardless of demographic factors such as age and location.

> As the role of technology becomes more integrated and meaningful within our everyday lives and economic systems, we can expect future economic models will become more dynamic and in-sync with emerging users' needs and expectations.

We have seen the transition from the atom economy transforming into the data economy, leading to the content economy, and eventually the experience economy. This represents full transcendence of consumption hierarchies

3.0 The Cheshire Economy

and value systems, providing more and more emphasis on holistic value and experiences. Such transcendence will keep evolving as the intersection of social, technological and physical interactions tighten. Emerging technologies, and Augmented Reality in particular, will play an even more central role in forming complex and deep relationships between users, products, brands and experiences.

3.2 Augmented Storytelling

Storytelling has always been the only effective communication technique, enabling humans to contextualise and bond with information and values. It is also a great way to prime the user for engagement before, during and after the experience – that is if the story is authentic to the experience or product. *The Mast Brothers* chocolate brand demonstrates the value of storytelling. Two Iowa-born, Brooklyn-based brothers [bearded, of course] started with a genuine passion for chocolate making, experimented with artisanal bean-to-bar processes in their apartment, and eventually grew to achieve national and global distribution. The product was an ethical and transparent brand, with an artisanal, high-quality and beautifully packaged [and priced] product. The only issue with this lovely story was the eventual discovery that the early product was made from purchased and re-melted industrial chocolate bars.[11] Although the product seems to now follow the bean-to-bar process, it gained popularity in its early days, despite its pricey positioning versus a non-premium product quality. Clearly, its success is better attributed to the brand storytelling and the values, rather than the actual quality of the chocolate.

Legendary American salesman, Elmer Wheeler coined a fantastic sales principle in the '40s –"Don't sell the steak, sell the sizzle."[12] This transformed storytelling into a sales tool by putting an emphasis on a product's holistic benefits rather than its attributes. It has remained a favourite marketing element in the creative industry, and a value driver in an increasingly content-led landscape. The problem begins when the storytelling takes precedence over or conflicts with the actual value of the product or service.

3.0

The Cheshire Economy

Storytelling is the first step to affirming a brand narrative, laying the groundwork for a deeper and more complex affiliation by creating more emotional hooks between the user and the product or service. Of course, the danger in an online and transparent world is that the more elaborate the story, the more cracks that can be found. In this reality, brands need to ensure that their brand promise and its delivery are as close as possible.

Stefan Sagmeister's video *No F*ckhead, You Are Not a Storyteller*[13] created for the 2014 'Future. Innovation. Technology. Creativity [FITC]' Toronto conference illustrated the contempt for the widespread abuse of the word 'storytelling', as a means to claim added value where there is none. This over-use occurs at both the commercial and personal level, as we see more micro-stories, snaps and in-between moments used to project a certain persona and maintain the [accelerated] cycle of new-content generation, aligning with the user's craving for continuous stimuli.

The fantastic *Kenzo World* commercial,[14] written and directed by Spike Jonze, captures the voice of a generation aspiring to express and display uniqueness through spontaneous, quirky and sometimes awkward self-expression. Digital platforms liberate content creation from brands and entities. Even though co-creation might be a popular solution for brands, it also places the user in a new 'paradox of choice', which already exists due to the vast quantity of content, products and services. An overload of choice and decision-making leads to eventual anxiety – ultimately driving a need to de-clutter and simplify our lives. The new paradox of choice relates to content creation which places the user in a constant state of anxiety because they wish to produce [and consume] content and experiences that are valuable and meaningful to the observer – AKA anyone with a screen. As augmentation becomes more diffused and accessible, the question remains, will it add value or become a new layer of digital noise?

Storytelling is a relatively easy path to immersion, which is why many brands build identities and marketing strategies around it. Branding professional Cheryl Swanson, who approaches branding from a cultural context, describes a brand as a "product with a compelling story". [15] What brands offer the user is a connection to qualities and experiences that may or may not be obtainable. Successful exercises embed brand presence

and usage rituals to make the brand experience inseparable from the targeted individual and social context. What Augmented Reality does is to combine brand storytelling with physical and digital platforms, interlacing multidisciplinary methodologies to create a rich narrative.

> The challenge will be figuring out how to transfer storytelling into narrative landscapes, and finding the right balance between control and choice-making. This means creating a complex narrative and reactive system based on deep knowledge, and triggers for user and social behaviours. Creating these storytelling scenarios will need to consider global, local, community, tribal, and individual perceptions of multi-layer concepts, ideologies and points of view. Applying these practices within tailored narratives will be highly effective in creating an initial hook, yet might be less effective in the long-term. The ongoing need for the user to create, select and control their experience is exhausting – they are constantly placed in the driver's seat.

Ultimately, users will want entities and brands to take a stand, and clearly represent specific and distinctive values and approaches. Even when consumers will be creating augmented experiences, it will be the tools and engagement systems that differentiate augmented content and hardware platforms.

3.3 Rethinking Narrative

Creating interactive engagement while maintaining a level of narrative control presents a dilemma for developers in 'experience-scaping' – which one should lead, and how can they be balanced? Constructing smart narrative/interaction hierarchies will become a core factor in successful experience building, and will require a deep understanding in human cognitive engagement. Traditional storytelling techniques will evolve, and probably adopt a lot of their mechanics from gaming and interactive industries, brands will actually benefit by adopting an open 'storyworld' model, rather than attempting to maintain a defined brand narrative.

Companies that wish to use Augmented Reality will need to consider its physical and technical implementation, as well as having a vision for content creation or facilitation. In the new Cinematic Reality, they will need to consider the balance between unique narrative-based content [where the content moderator/designer can have more influence on the artistic elements], versus a more interaction-based simulation [linked to the user's feedback].

A wise path forward would be to gradually integrate the implementation of Augmented Reality, since it will involve new pathways to integrate and develop content. However, this will require:

#01 Calibrating and coordinating entire physical environments to ensure digital layering fidelity.

#02 Overcoming disconnect challenges, including unresolved conflict between real and virtual input and output mapping and behaviours.

Artificial Intelligence researcher, Andreas Dengel presents an interesting modern paradox, he discusses the increasing amount, velocity and variety of data which forces us to optimise knowledge management. Western society requires individuals to accelerate and enhance their data processing skills, and change the manner in which we acquire knowledge and gain expertise. Dengel envisions a co-creative system for a cyber-social environment, in such a system Augmented Reality is an ideal tool to enhance cognitive processes, resulting in improved user interaction, leading to better knowledge acquisition and decision-making.[16] The idea of co-creation within education,

closely ties to the notion of a socio-technological community, where technology becomes a tool for co-creation, rather than an end product. Institutes and business would be platforms that enable the user's creation, rather than defining the outcome.

Game designer, Chris Crawford shares his thoughts on the conflict between narrative and interactivity: "Abstraction is how we can transcend distracting arguments over plot versus interactivity. Instead of thinking about a specific instance [a plot], we must learn to think in terms of something more abstract."[17] Although his solution was to create 'storyworlds' that enable users to explore and implement multiple or an endless number of plotlines, the future holds a much broader spectrum of narrative types. Complex narratives will require a reactive, flexible system, perhaps Artificial Intelligence-led. Alternatively, we might see how new professions would emerge, requiring narrative creative teams and control systems. Such systems would focus on maintaining balance and tightly monitoring the interaction, as the augmented narrative would influence actions and behaviours in a Real-Time, physical world. This obviously raises copyright, legal, liability and moral issues about the control and monitoring of these narratives. These issues need to be clearly defined and communicated by creators, facilitators and consumers.

> Even if these issues are resolved, and a safe system of context and control for the user is created, imagine the potential impact of having the ability to create an augmentation layer that might include a parallel or overriding narrative in your life.

For a small monthly subscription, your everyday experiences would be elevated – with encounters, people and objects that you may have been unable to experience in the purely physical world. Imagine a simulated reality where you are simultaneously the hero and the narrator. This could easily become a source of isolation and escapism, depending on how much of this intimate narrative you share. 'Narrative surfing' could become a new method of social participation, and a surprisingly intimate form of inclusion. When positively applied, augmented narratives could induce a user-centric, highly intimate experience, as well as inclusive multicultural experiences

3.0

The Cheshire Economy

that expand the mind and creativity. Imagine the colliding, competing and interweaving relationships between different 'storyworlds', Emo kids versus cheerleaders, surfers versus wall-street executives, Augmented Reality could be a new lens to experience worlds and narratives of any social paradigm.

3.4 'Say "Hello" to My Little Experience!'

What do we mean when we say 'experience'? It quickly emerges as yet another buzzword that can be used to describe a vague value in the digital realm, and in the marketing of, well, almost everything. If we want to understand experience better, we need to understand what it entails.

Moving from a product value economy to a service economy, today's brands, services and content makers are becoming an intertwined part of our everyday lives and lifestyles. In many ways, brands become as influential as traditional social structures. As the market shifts toward more emotional and behavioural feedback systems, we are moving toward a deeper experience-based ecosystem and economy.

Experience is based on the evolving interaction within a space – whether it is physical, virtual, or holistic. An experience transcends the functional, and gravitates into behavioural and social layers and values, creating a unique space between the user and a brand, an object or an activity. From comfort eating to being a football fan, emotional bonds and rituals are formed out of unique experiences. Successful experiences form successful relationships - however these are challenging to artificially orchestrate. Like any relationship, a mutual alignment of intent and desired outcome are crucial. Another consideration in creating a lasting experience is reaching a high-quality immersive level during the interaction, forming a high-quality relationship after the actual engagement moment. All of this while competing with an increasingly stimuli saturated environment.

Play theorist Brian Sutton-Smith developed a model specifying the five elements of game experience. I have translated his ideas into a holistic view of experience building, consisting of:

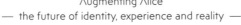

Experience definition

Defining quality and level of
interactive feedback and delivery.

Gameplay

Defining user and
system dynamics.

Multisensory

Integrating perceptual cognition
and sensory feedback, including visual,
auditory, scent and haptic.

Multi-layered

A variety of individual and social
interaction which allow unique and
shared layers of interaction.

Delivery

Achieving successful experience delivery.

There are many variables within and outside the system that may either guide
or derail an experience outcome from its original goal. These could also lead to
happy accidents or experiential nightmares. Woodstock was a happy accident
– it exceeded its original goal of being a local musical happening, transcending
into a spontaneous experience and a cultural beacon for generations to come.

3.5 Experiential Value Generation

Experience is the ultimate method to differentiate, create and add value to a product, platform or service. It forms a multi-layered intrinsic bond with the user, triggering multiple nodes that link and bring the user back. As we discuss the 'value' of 'things', let's quickly explore what we mean by 'value'.

> The estimation of value is traditionally related to access, uniqueness, quality and how elaborate the product is. This helps us to categorise products as having luxury, premium or entry-level value. The ownership experience and its usage creates an emotional-value bond. Whether you look at spices or artisanal products, their value shifts as their [real and perceived] accessibility and craft evolve. As our production, mobility and transportation abilities have developed, we have noticed the shifting value of products, and the emergence of a value system based on intrinsic and non-tangible value [that is, more brand and service focused].

In the past, value and influence were measured via net worth, class system, intrinsic value, or the possession of a skill. Moving from the atom economy to the bit economy changes the value chain. In the digital realm, function [including accessibility and relevant features] and user experience determine the value of digital products. The novelty of digital content value lies within the nature of the digital experience. The data economy perceives users as both a source for data mining and consumption subjects. We have moved away from a one-off digital transaction economy, to an ongoing data-monetisation system. Content platforms use big data analysis to form new products and services which build on user behaviours. In turn these systems utilise the users' interaction with the platform to mine data that would be traded and/or implemented back into the platform development, and so on.

Today, online access seems to be the core criteria for individuals and groups to influence and create value. Opinion blogs, talkbacks, tweets, Facebook likes and Instagram following are redefining power and social hierarchies. We are irreversibly connected – making data the new currency of value and power.

But does this hive mindset guarantee an elevated qualitative value? Is the sum greater than the parts, or are our experiences – even new ones – so formulaic and familiar that we eventually lose individualism and the ability to experience true intimacy. Transmitting your inner thoughts online makes a wider recognition of human emotions, but also trivialises them – sometimes to a mere emoji.

A service or product can be defined by various value levels, defined by product features through to price/positioning [value for money], brand values, unique delivery or a new business model. We are entering an era where experience will become a core value driver of brands and services. Augmentation will further transform all systems and brands into boundless experience entities, allowing brands to elevate the value of products and services, offering a reactive, personalised and versatile layered experience.

> Orchestrating successful experiences is challenging, it requires providing the user with an initial engagement hook, and maintaining engagement by building dynamic interactions, and balancing the embedded experience goal through the user's actions. As immediacy and accessibility increase, the less forgiving users will reject any brand experience 'glitches'.

Virtual and Augmented Reality would make the experience economy extremely influential. Bank of America and Merrill Lynch predicted in their 2016 Thematic Investing report that there will be "250-300mn users by the early 2020s, with the long-term potential to capture 2/3 of our leisure time, and 50% of our leisure dollars."[18] We are already in the situation where we are surgically targeted by our demonstrated preferences, allowing the seeding of tailored activation hooks. Tailored experiences and the services will further quantify users' engagement to form an ongoing interaction that will trigger behaviours and consumption patterns. Eventually resulting in a digital/physical engagement level that would be seamlessly implemented to form hyper-experiences.

3.0

The Cheshire Economy

3.6 Sustainable Technology

Within the context of an atom economy the capitalist system pushes us to consume more physical goods. Together with the surge in global population and accelerated production and consumption patterns, this push to consume more is creating a world of depleted natural resources and extreme climate shifts. In the short-term, the solution lies in lower energy consumption and efficient resource distribution. We have already seen how demographic shifts, in combination with bit and experience economy changed traditional retail and industries landscapes. A shift of mindsets and the search for efficient, alternative uses of natural resources and experience-led value, would complete this cycle and transform the way we consume goods and services.

Digital experiences also require increased amounts of resources, and consumption will grow for three simple reasons: Consumption of physical goods is subject to severe diminishing returns at some point on the wealth curve [you can only have so many goods around you], IT and automation increases the proportion and polarisation between the wealthy [owning and utilising data and algorithms for wealth generation], and the less wealthy [whose job has been automated] – the latter prone to use technology and since they are simply more affordable experiences.

Consumers have come to expect a transparent, sustainable and innovative product and value chain. For example – Tesla's value proposition marries ecological vision with product performance. We are already noticing the implementation of concepts such as the circle economy and the shared economy. This approach would require a substantial revision of political, social and economic systems, to make way for ideological consuming, manufacturing and servicing frameworks [and nations].

There is no wonder that sourcing alternative energy sources would keep on being a core driver within technology and innovation. Following the success of the electric car, energy entrepreneur and Tesla CEO Elon Musk aims to change "the fundamental energy infrastructure of the world."[19] Through additional initiatives such as Solar City and Tesla Energy – Musk

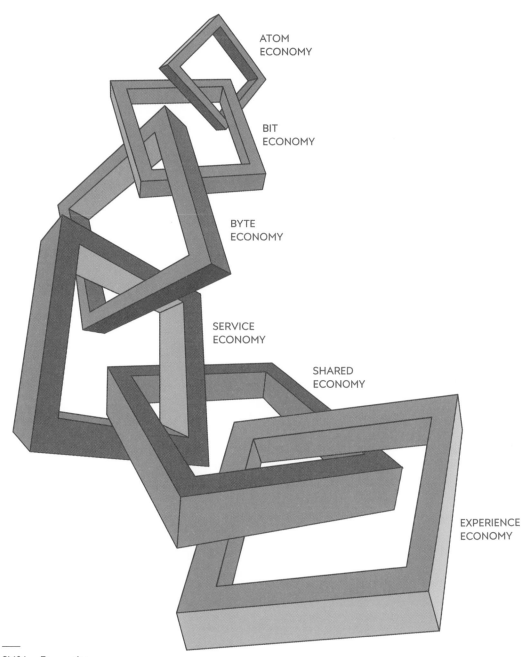

ATOM
ECONOMY

BIT
ECONOMY

BYTE
ECONOMY

SERVICE
ECONOMY

SHARED
ECONOMY

EXPERIENCE
ECONOMY

Shifting Economies
From atom to experiential economy.
Author's Image, 2017.

3.0

The Cheshire Economy

challenges traditional concepts of energy supply and storage systems
for homes and commercial spaces.

Technology is expected to provide innovative solutions for a cleaner
supply chain. Global legislation has played a big part in facilitating that,
not only in terms of introducing and enforcing green production standards
and corporate social responsibility [CSR], but also through the creation
of financial incentives for companies that promote and research
ecological innovation.

Alec Ross, foresees the prospective role of green technology in leading
agricultural innovation, "as temperatures rise and potable water becomes
an ever-scarcer resource [70% of freshwater used globally goes toward
agriculture]. The best hope for feeding our more populated world comes from
the combination of big data and agriculture — precision agriculture."[20]
Since global population growth is not likely to stop or decline, our
behaviours and consumption rates need to undergo more drastic changes.
Basic resources such as space, energy, water and air will have to be used
efficiently [and even rationed] in order to allow the future survival of
the human race. It is also clear that humanity will have to re-evaluate its
consumption and lifestyles as a preventative step.

Augmented Reality might relieve us from our need to balance our
ownership of physical goods, via the enriching the experiential 'value'
of the product. Perhaps partially solving the diminishing resources
caused by over-consumption and over-production, and maintaining the
object's relevance and experiential value through a dynamic digital layer.
Environmental concerns caused by extensive commuting could also be
partially compensated for by augmented and virtual presence. We must
further explore the potential of the experience economy to act as an
alternative that would enable us to build experiences on top of our
valuable resources, rather than consuming them in their entirety.

Even though augmented experiences might help us in reducing physical
consumption, we need to be weary of not replacing one addiction with
another. The application of interaction-triggering features, within an

experiential platform might end up creating an infinite experience consumption loop, pushing the user to constantly interact, and creating superficial and artificial needs. As Mihaly Csikszentmihalyi stated:

> "There is another serious problem with using extrinsic rewards as the only incentive for reaching desirable goals. Extrinsic rewards are by their nature either scarce or expensive to attain in terms of human energy. Money and the material possessions it can buy require the exploitation of natural resources and labour – If everything we do is done to get material rewards, we shall exhaust the planet and each other." [21]

3.7 Bring On the Big Boys

One of the biggest challenges in developing emerging technologies, is how to maintain a sustainable cycle that is user-focused, especially when the user is one of the data economy's resources. There are some notable independent key players in the Augmented Reality market such as Meta – with Dr. Steve Mann as chief scientist and advisor, and Magic Leap, which single-handedly boosted the Augmented Reality market through unprecedented financing and the captivating visualisation of its product/experience. However, it will most likely be the technology conglomerates that will ultimately lead the mass augmented revolution. The keys for success will not be handed to those who 'only' provide great technology, but to those who can create a heterogeneous augmentation system that includes affordable hardware, rich content, access to a broad base of users, resulting in a seamless digital/physical user experience. Apple, Microsoft, Facebook, Amazon and Alphabet are the strongest candidates to lead, and eventually dominate the augmented landscape. Each of these companies offer a different approach to the augmented market.

Facebook made social media into a core interaction platform, achieving unparalleled reach since it was founded in 2004. Initially focusing on social media platform extensions, it acquired popular competitors such as Instagram and WhatsApp. Facebook showed signs of looking into new interaction platforms, and becoming highly invested in computer vision technology with its acquisition of Oculus VR, Pebbles, Surreal Vision and

3.0

The Cheshire Economy

MSQRD. The value of Facebook lies in its social platform, which constantly increases users' engagement rituals, and as a consequence increasing the amount of time spent on the platform.[22] Despite Zuckerberg's faith in a Virtual Reality social engagement, Oculus VR has been the biggest setback in Facebook's path to create an immersive social network platform. If Facebook is planning to spend a few more billions[23] in betting on a technology that could lead a new socially immersive behaviour Augmented Reality would do a better job of blending online and offline social interaction. I believe even Mark is starting to realise that now.

Another key player is Apple. This technology brand spent six straight years as Forbes' #1 for brand market value, and profitability.[24] Worth US$ 586 billion as of May 2016[25] it is also considered the world's biggest company. As a market leader in the innovation and sales of smart devices [including multimedia players, mobile devices and smartwatches], as well as building its reputation as experts at honing-in on its innovation-driven hard-core consumer base, Apple is likely to implement augmentation applications via the most natural seeding path to the market – mobile devices.

As Fortune magazine identifies:

"design, not function, is the most important factor for AR to make the leap from a smartphone feature to the computing interface of the future."[26]

In the past, Apple successfully launched emerging technology applications through deciphering behaviour-based interactions and user needs. The design and marketing of the iPod as the device that delivers '1000 songs in your pocket' is a perfect example. This approach may give Apple the edge it needs to lead in Augmented Reality implementation.

Apple CEO, Tim Cook, had been a long-time, avid advocate of Augmented Reality. Their interest and investment in integrating Augmented Reality into mobile devices and wearables could be the tipping point for this technology's diffusion. Apple had introduced the ARKit framework enabling developers to harness Apple's mobile processing and operating systems into creating [and embedding] high-end augmentation in apps. Despite some past design hick-ups, Apple is still leading in making Augmented Reality appeal to consumers through their user-centric, slick product and system design.

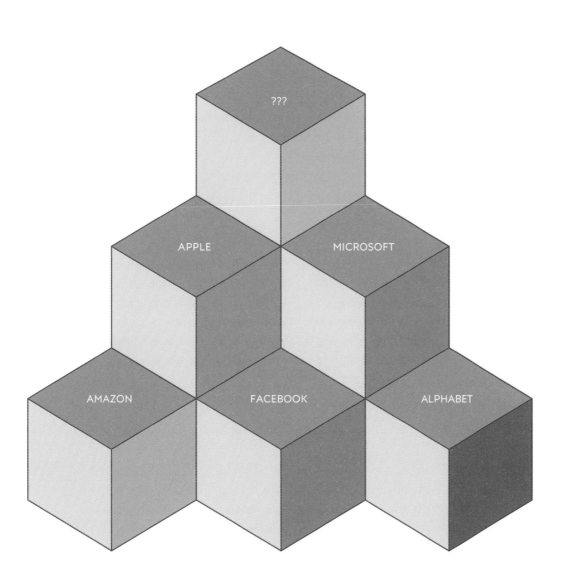

Augmented Reality Big Players
Combining advanced technology, unprecedented
financial resources and access to a global user pool [and data base].
Author's Image, 2017.

3.0

The Cheshire Economy

Even Microsoft – once considered an archaic white elephant – is regaining a leadership position through innovation and quality design. It started playing a dominant role in the Augmented Reality scape with its HMD development [the *HoloLens*] and content development. Its strategic partnership with Adobe and Netflix completes a strategic move towards the creation of a unified hardware, software, content creation and social network system. Microsoft demonstrates a clear focus on Augmented Reality, as well as its learnings from its *Xbox kinect* interactive console, the *roomAlive* Mixed Reality prototype to the View Mixed Reality educational platform that operates on any *Windows 10* device through a webcam. With the launch Augmented Reality shades and their collaboration with Netflix in building a content app for the *HoloLens* Augmented Reality headset, this also marks the strides they are making in creating a widely diffused product and entertainment content base.

Google has become the generic term for online searching, yet its income comes from data mining and analysis. Despite being a free-for-use platform, it monetises targeted advertisements [via *Adwords*] through what Investopedia describes as "Taming the Sea of Information."[27] Alphabet – the umbrella company that owns Google, YouTube, DoubleClick, Calico, Waze and Nest Labs – is heavily focused on Artificial Intelligence applications for smarthomes, wearables and vehicles, and is set to create "a Manhattan project of AI."[28] It has purchased nearly all machine learning and robotics companies in the market. This includes Boston Dynamics, the firm that produces spectacular yet terrifying life-like military robots, for an undisclosed but undoubtedly massive sum. It spent US$ 3.2 billion to buy the smarthome appliances maker Nest Labs. It also purchased the secretive and cutting-edge British Artificial Intelligence start-up DeepMind. As well as acquiring Bot & Dolly, Meka Robotics, Holomni, Redwood, Robotics and Schaft, and DNNresearch. Peter Norvig, Google's research director, recently said the company employs less than 50% but certainly more than 5% of the world's leading experts on machine learning. He [being one of those leaders] is not wrong. The Google 'A team' includes Regina Dugan – who headed the Defence Advanced Research Projects Agency [DARPA], the secretive US military agency that funded the development of *BigDog* rough terrain robot; British computer scientist Geoffrey Hinton – who is probably the world's leading expert on neural networks; and [drum roll...] Ray Kurzweil– one of the world's most notable Artificial Intelligence visionaries,[29] who Bill Gates

described as "the best person I know at predicting the future of artificial intelligence."[30] Implying its superior potential to enable the much needed integration of Artificial Intelligence engagement systems with Augmented Reality interaction. Through the Google's *Tango* platform, the company already demonstrates its ambition to embed Augmented Reality technology within Android-based mobile devices. Combining it with their robotics and Artificial Intelligence capabilities, might form a powerful application.

Amazon and other online retailers such as eBay, Ali-Baba, may not have entered the Augmented Reality realm [directly] yet, but those who have access to data would inavitably bcome an inseparable part of the experience economy. With Amazon accounting for 50% of all dollars spent in the US by 2017, their influence With Amazon accounting for 50% of all dollars spent in the US by 2017, their influence and access to the most precious resource would place it in an advantageous position. As stated in The Economist magazine:

> "The giants' surveillance systems span the entire economy: Google can see what people search for, Facebook what they share, Amazon what they buy."[31]

These technology moguls curate information systems, and therefore hold the key to the most lucrative commodity – information. They thrive because of users' predisposition to access and comfort and gain power through market reach, quickly surpassing traditional sectors and even countries of influence and revenue. Add to the equation the fact that governments, unable to develop in-house technology capabilities at the same rate of the free market, become core B2B customers.

As Artificial Intelligence and the Internet of Things are further integrated into everyday life, we will witness more situations where environments and products record and analyse our activities. Transferring normal activity into data, which equals power. This creates moral and ethical issues about the nature and use of personal data by tech companies and the authorities. We have already seen this start to happen, with the incident where Amazon's smart assistant *Alexa* was the only potential witness to a murder,[32] leaving us to ask what would a smart device, with an integrated sensory and behavioural feedback systems, be able to do?

3.0

The Cheshire Economy

The leading tech companies are making so much money, and are expected to make so much money, that their market value is enormous. At the same time they fear each other and most of all missing the 'next big thing'. These companies actively use their cash and market value to purchase any technology that seems promising and any company that can become a threat. This is ultimately driving a start-up acquisition bubble and culture, accelerating the development rate, yet not allowing technologies and platforms to mature, as start-ups create market hype to attract investors or acquirers for partially developed technologies and concepts, and everyone keeps riding the wave of emerging technology.

We should not perceive that these tech titans are not a conniving enemy, nor are they empowered by mere market monopoly. However, users need to be aware of their motivations, since they would certainly determine the faith and focus of Augmented Reality, and as a result a big portion of our experience world. It is possible that they will pick up on an approach that focuses on the better-good rather than self-interest. The digital hippie in me can at least dream of such things. We must review who holds the keys to this information kingdom – the user, the platform builder, or the governments. The answer to that will determine whether we become an information society, or have our big brothers and sisters monitoring and shaping society for us.

3.8 Econo-Me

The notion of 'supply and demand' is not only an economic term. It is deeply connected to a mental state of mind. In his 1776 book *The Wealth of Nations*, Scottish philosopher and political economist Adam Smith links this economic principle to individualism. The rise of 'me' culture is part of a bigger system fuelled by consumerism. In turn, it refuels our need to assert our sense of self via external means. In fact, technology has helped to channel our self-obsession into a valuable currency.

Over the last few decades, we have witnessed how consumerism, and the technology that facilitates it, has reshaped values and social structures. This is further supported by mainstream entertainment, which is predominantly aimed at gratifying a mass audience rather than debating the more complex aspects of our existence. Both mainstream and social media tend to create a complex combination of high success standards. Conveying 'success' as the ultimate aspiration, one that needs to be achieved and constantly nurtured and mirrored back to the social sphere.

We feel compelled to maintain the upper hand in everything, all the time – a condition that is hard to sustain on both a mental and practical level, unless you can keep acquiring it by goods and appearances. This is not a new condition. Each generation curls their lips and raises their eyebrows at the following generation, questioning their values and value.

> "The children now love luxury; they have bad manners, contempt for authority; they show disrespect for elders and love chatter in place of exercise. Children are now tyrants, not the servants of their households. They no longer rise when elders enter the room. They contradict their parents, chatter before company, gobble up dainties at the table, cross their legs, and tyrannize their teachers."[33] Yep, this is what Greek philosopher Plato, living 400 years BC, thought about the youth of his generation.

Now, it seems that we are reaching new heights [or lows?] of encouraging self-importance. The drive to achieve instant gratification throughout our lifetime, is a cross-generational issue. As screens and corporations replace

THE CHILDREN NOW LOVE LUXURY; THEY HAVE BAD MANNERS, CONTEMPT FOR AUTHORITY; THEY SHOW DISRESPECT FOR ELDERS AND LOVE CHATTER IN PLACE OF EXERCISE. CHILDREN ARE NOW TYRANTS. ...THEY CONTRADICT THEIR PARENTS, CHATTER BEFORE COMPANY, GOBBLE UP DAINTIES AT THE TABLE, CROSS THEIR LEGS, AND TYRANNIZE THEIR TEACHERS.

— Plato, 400 BC

society's role in educating, it is challenging to reassert an independent sense of self or a deep communal engagement. As a society of individuals, we have the tendency to override moral and social needs once our personal convenience has been satisfied. Placing individual needs in the centre of the engagement is precisely the focus of many technology platforms. At what cost, and with which consequences, we don't discuss.

Despite alarming red flags about the impact of a consumerism-focused culture on societal, environmental and moral levels, it is hard to implement or impose morality standards within the technology industry [beyond the marketing slogans]. There seems to be very little space to debate how we as society would like to shape our physical and technological reality. Interestingly enough, the creative experimentation that built Silicon Valley was very much intertwined with hippie ideals, building on values such as open-source, creativity and sharing. In fact, some of the most powerful technology moguls built their empires based on these ideologies, from, Apple's 'Think different' to Google's 'Don't be evil'.

As these companies have grown, their slogans remained – more as a veneer than a core value. I had hoped to see them continue towards establishing platforms and applications focused on societal values to truly maintain these ideologies. Since technology has been incorporated into almost every aspect of our lives, and on every level of our hierarchy of needs, we cannot [and should not] reverse its dominance. Our crops, climate control, travel, shipping, manufacturing, health, communication, social interaction, status, knowledge acquisition, and education all rely heavily on technology. However, we can apply it in a better way, as a positive force in our global culture that can balance personal benefit within wider social value. Call me naïve, but I believe that a vision for positive long-term impact makes for good business.

Creating a path towards transforming the 'me economy' to the 'we economy' is vital to the future of human society.
The responsibility of changing the inward spiral to an outwards action lies with both developers and users – with the users demanding it. After all, it is all about supply and demand, right?

"ALICE: I KNEW WHO I WAS THIS MORNING, BUT I'VE CHANGED A FEW TIMES SINCE THEN."

— Lewis Carroll, Alice's Adventures in Wonderland

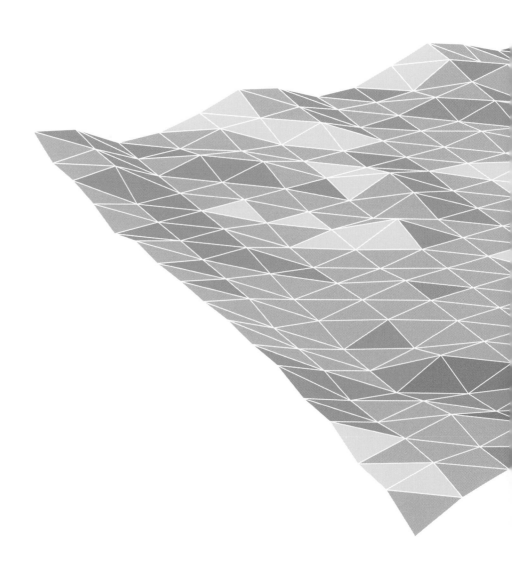

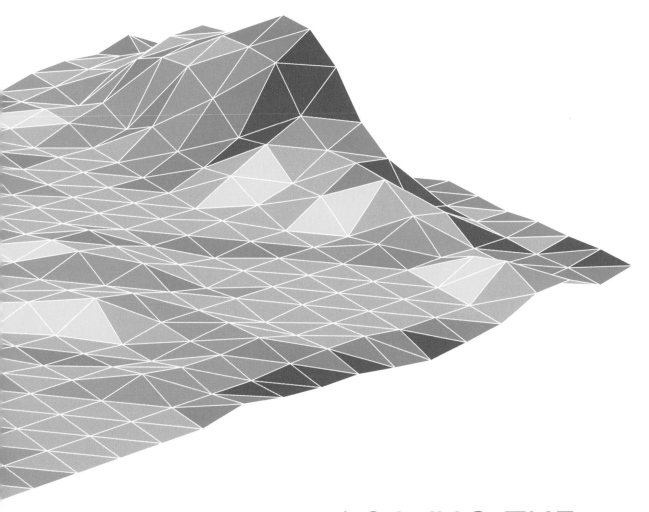

4.0 WHO THE
F*&K IS ΛLICE?

Who the F*&k is Alice?

Redefining Identities in the Augmented Age

We decipher reality through our physical senses, and our social perceptions – shaped by our life experiences and sense of identity. Our personal experience of reality is ultimately subjective. This relationship between reality and identity is interconnected – a shift in one of them influences our perception of the other. Augmentation technologies will enable us to extend our perception and sense of self. Whether we explore inwards [looking at intimate mental processes], or outwards [constructing an augmented shell around us] will be up to us.

4.1 The Digital Identity Crisis

The digital realm has become an inseparable element that helps to define our personal and social status. The constant stream of information, the rise of social media and the 'always on' culture, constantly modifies online and offline etiquette, relationships and social interaction. We use technology to define ourselves via digital access privileges, online influence, and the sense of control we get through technology usage. Armed with portable multimedia registration technology, we explore social conventions and personal boundaries. Technology is used to track and display every aspect of our lives – including personal preferences, physical state, mood, relationship and social status – via a variety of applications and devices. The dynamic use of digital media for creating and editing our existence and experience in our daily lives constantly blends remote experiences within an intimate context.

Our public and private self are fused into one identity, as sociologist Eva Illouz observes:

> "The process of making the self into an emotional and public matter finds its most potent expression in the technology of the Internet, a technology which presupposes and enacts a public emotional self and in fact even makes the public emotional self-precede private interactions and constitute them."[1]

We have already witnessed social media profiling for commercial purposes – including job applicant vetting, insurance risk assessments, and security profiling. The demand to be up-to-date and constantly online has affected both our personal and professional worlds, from professional social networks to employers using instant personal messaging apps to communicate with employees, expecting 24/7 availability and instant responses. This is just one element that causes a loss of differentiation between private and professional identities. Recognising the issues with this lack of separation, French legislators passed new laws that provide the right for employees to make better choices about their life/work balance and connectivity.

Technology has become a tool for the continuous [somewhat compulsive] documentation, affirmation and construction of identity. Mobile devices and online platforms deliver, store and archive our interaction streams and online relationships. As a result, we are witnessing unprecedented levels of global anxiety about the portrayal of personal identity and status through digital and online media. While the solution might seem banal – one can simply disconnect from technology to regain a sense of relief – in practice this option is not really viable in our connected culture. What we may have missed in our transference to the digital realm is to have a more critical look at and understanding of how we differentiate or integrate our physical and virtual identities. This distinction is already difficult to make, as we conveniently share [consciously and unconsciously] data directly and indirectly, constructing a behavioural profile and data based that reflect our personality and identity.

The source for this is the fact that digital feedback systems are heavily reliant on social engagement to recruit a wide user base, and they create a range of tools and 'nudging' systems to sustain interest and content creation.

4.0

Who the f*&k is Alice?

Platforms build on engagement and gratification mechanics that push us to control, affirm and receive feedback on a quantitative and qualitative level. This conditions us to constantly interact with our devices and platforms in an attempt to balance the push-pull system that defines our identity, privacy and status. Digital natives, as oppose to a novice, accept online interaction as a primary channel for connectivity. These users are no longer blinded by such mechanisms and are aspiring for more meaningful, intense and unmediated interaction platforms. Look at the second wave of social media platforms, which have shifted to instant messaging platforms, such as WhatsApp and Snapchat. "With no way for users to 'fave' or 'share' them, Snaps never go viral. There's less pressure to be perfect."[2] The tension lies between our need for a unique and intimate identity and interaction, and our ever-growing need for digital affirmation – how many likes and views, and from whom they come – to feed our digital-status beast.

> This search for a deeper connection is partially due to the sheer quantity of online content causes a 'flattening' effect of the digital landscape. A partial expression of that is the reproduction of a common visual language. A desirable effect at first – memes and content sharing were a way to have a communal understanding of the digital landscape. Yet it seems that these days interior, product and graphic design trends are instantly homogenising the aesthetic zeitgeist, as we wonder through from one perfectly curated eclectic interior [which I like to call 'Pinterest interiors'] to another, with a sense of 'déjà vu'.

Such visual overexposure creates a counter-reaction. In a post-viral society, the aspiration is to form an authentic identity and establish a strong sense of meaning that would override the shared content influence. Digital natives are using technology to independently explore online expressions, hack and redefine their identities. We can only imagine how more immersive digital/physical hybrid experiences could aid in forming new intimacies within the social realms. Augmentation will launch a third wave of social media platforms that will intensify physical and virtual feedback systems. The outcome of embedding digital User Interface within the physical environment will be the creation of hybrid emotive behaviours, rituals and identities that will place a layer over intimacy and public expression in new and exciting ways.

4.2 Me, Myself, and the Digital I

Even without considering the added virtual layer, the perception of identity is a challenging notion. In the digital realm, it is dual and complex. In an augmented world, it's a totally new ball game. Our 'sense' of self can be in a constant fluid state as it is shaped by external perceptions and influences, while our 'real' self remains intact and constant.

As much as we would like to believe that each of us hones an individual and independent sense of self, our identity is heavily based on our social interactions, shaped by the exploration of similarities and differences, and the formation of identification and empathy. It is a dynamic process.
As Nietzsche stated:

> "We ourselves keep growing, keep changing, we shed our old bark, we shed our skins every spring. We keep becoming younger, fuller of future, taller, stronger."[3]

Similar to the way Harry F. Harlow established the need for social bonding, John Bowlby [one of the pioneers in the development of attachment theory] identified a similar evolutionary construct that triggers human babies to seek attachment as a safety measure. This need is strengthened when babies begin to move independently and explore their surroundings. It is initially triggered through the interaction with the primary caregiver, and as a child's world and social circle expands, so does his/her interaction netting, influencing and shaping the attachment mechanism further. A secure attachment has a positive effect on the formation of one's behavioural patterns, personality structure, and sense of self, while an insecure attachment is likely to have a negative effect.

The most distinctive transition point between the social and personal identity arrives [drumroll...] during adolescence – a period in which we are exposed to an increasing number of external influences. Adolescence is a perfect storm of hormones rushing through our bodies and brain, as we explore new intimacies and behaviours within new and existing social systems. As we emerge the other side of this stage of mental 'plasticity' and acne-prone skin, we supposedly have a pretty established sense of identity. However, we are now witnessing

4.0 Who the f*&k is Alice?

a growing phenomenon within the developed world of delayed adulthood. Today's young adults are more likely to extend their studies, travel and delay financial independence compared to previous generations. Psychology professor Laurence Steinberg thinks it might not be such a negative thing, stating that:

> "Evolution no doubt placed a biological upper limit on how long the brain can retain the malleability of adolescence. But people who can prolong adolescent brain plasticity for even a short time enjoy intellectual advantages over their more fixed counterparts." [4]

Psychologist Barry Schwartz argues that we are already trapped in a 'choice paradox,'[5] where the abundance of choices we are facing in the consumer society – with supermarket aisles overflowing with cereal brands competing for our attention – leaves us feeling anxious and in a paralysis of choice. With the profusion of digital content that is being created, we are close to a 'choice crisis.' which has possibly contributed to the arrested emotional development of many.

The identity crisis is also driven by the conflicting messages we receive in a connected society. We are presented with the notion that we are part of a truly global community with a shared value system, and at the same time we receive constant triggers to differentiate ourselves by formulating a unique identity. The hipster phenomenon that crossed borders and cultures perfectly portrayed this urge to create a community and a cultural movement, meshing nostalgic notions of unity with an authentic expression of self. Whilst the original intention could be seen as admirable, the 'new authentic' resulted in a fairly uniform expression of visual and cultural narratives, and has instead resulted in a gentrified expression of the 'authentic' environment and the context it was aspiring to channel. This is another symptom of the 'flattening' effect where not only the quality of information is simplified, but so is the representation of a unique identity.

In the digital age, where all is shared and duplicated, uniqueness and authenticity are becoming fleeting concepts – where external features, fashions, behaviours and diets are becoming viral. That can perhaps only be regained by creating less inclusive – and more exclusive formats. We are

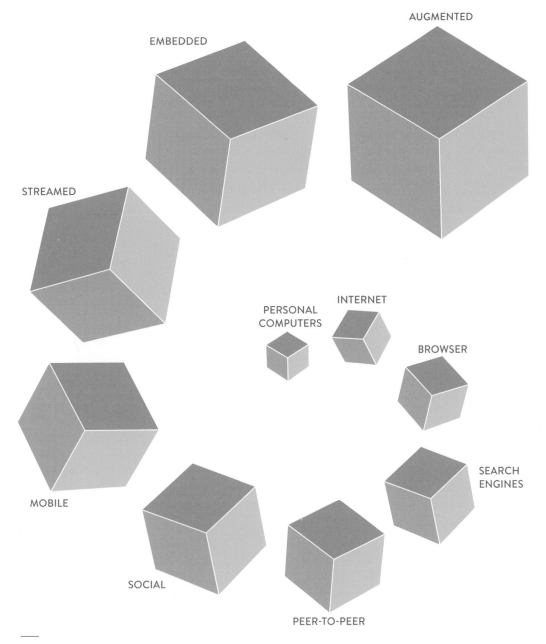

Digital Interaction Evolution
Technology advancements effect our social interaction and activities.
As a result our experience of the world and sense of self evolve.
Author's Image, 2017.

already witnessing the formation of exclusive online networks and groups, which begins as instant messaging interest-focused groups and targeted social online platforms, but evolve with the need for a more private [and secure] environment on both a physical and digital level.

It is already proving challenging to separate our actions and identity within the 'digital world' from our 'real world' identity. Once augmentation becomes a diffused interaction platform, added digital features will be common place in our everyday narratives. Since augmentation will merge the two worlds, the representation of our identity will be even more intertwined. Augmented Reality will be tested on the balance it can provide us in defining our social and private identity, hopefully allowing us to navigate better between the two, and perhaps also enable us to explore a constant state of 'becoming'.

4.3 Right Here

The core element that defines our perception of reality is presence – 'being' in a certain space and time. Let's break down this idea of 'being' in Spacetime. Our embodiment and navigation in space is very much related to our sense of presence. How we move, navigate and interact with the world around us is directly related to our physical embodiment and [private and social] identity.

In an autonomous virtual sphere, one should be free to represent an abstract identity in form and context, yet the digital sphere poses a level of duality. The World Wide Web symbolised a new realm for identity and self-expression, users becoming their own Digital Gods, forging and exploring identities that are free from physical and embodiment constraints. But very quickly we experience how online identities were appropriated to existing social and mental dogmas and purposes. Aligning one digital self and existence with the physical representation. After all, we are 'trained' to express our individuality through our unique physical features and our physical interaction.

Even during the early days of 'virtuality', we could see how this has an effect on our interaction within cyberspace. One of the earliest platforms to use avatars in a virtual and societal context was *Second Life*. Given complete freedom to

explore new levels of interaction as a different representation of the self, the majority of users chose to create an avatar with the same gender, ethnicity and even similar features to their physical presence. Many users upgraded and modified some features – choosing an edgier haircut, a more sculptured physique – but in almost all cases the virtual avatar and the physical user could easily be linked together. Think about that – instead of making a different body type or being, even a disembodied avatar with the form of a pink cloud – we still choose to explore the virtual world as, more or less, ourselves.

René Descartes' "I think, therefore I am"[6] is a higher perception of consciousness as an indicator for existence, but consciousness is only one aspect of identity. Our identity is still strongly defined by the main tool we use to interact with reality – our physical body – and consequently we strongly attach our identity to our physicality. We use our reflection in the mirror to identify and evaluate ourselves. We are one of only a few species that can pass the Mirror Self Recognition test, alongside some species of apes, dolphins, orcas, one type of bird, and a single elephant – named 'Happy'. Bodily self-awareness is an important social aspect that allows us to differentiate ourselves from others as a physical entity, and also to compare and imitate behaviours and traits.

The natural selection results in physical features that improve the survival rate of the species and projects on the individual's attractiveness. This is of course also conditioned by cultural or periodic biases. From height, weight to hair and even skin colour, humans have used various methods [and a lot of mirror staring] to embed and enhance our physical traits in order to portray a modified identity. Non-intrusive external modifications include ornaments, fashion garments, body modifying fashion [from heels to bras] and makeup. Physiologically intrusive modifications are longer lasting – they include exercises to shape the body, tattoos and piercings, and even cosmetic surgery. Some religions forbid intrusive bodily modification and enforce a unifying dress code – including clothing that camouflages the body features [more often where the female body is concerned]. We are indeed a species apart in terms of the importance of our physical identity within social and cultural hierarchies.

This is where the Third Space Theory becomes related to our formation of identity. The Third Space relates to how one's unique interaction within the physical [First Space] and the remote [Second Space], influence the sense of self and vice versa. The physical [First Space] and the remote [Second Space] used to be two distinctively separated realms. With new communication methods and devices, the virtual forms an ultra-space that allows us to bridge those. Augmented Reality would elevate this notion on a multisensory and perceptual level, eliminating the differentiation between the two. Eventually it would blend them into a new experiential layer – the Third Space. Where the tangible, remote, physical and virtual become an integral aspect of one's identity.

> Several Augmented Reality implementations would even shift our entire perception of Spacetime. Telepresence would even stretch our time/space perception. We would be able to send or 'summon' a convincing representation of one's physical presence across a remote space. In a further future with incorporated interactive spatial mapping and mixed reality gesture sensors the virtual representation would be able to form new output and interaction systems embedded in our physical environment. One could simply Telepresence oneself to check on the kids, read them a bedtime story and remotely turn on their night light.

Besides pragmatic applications related to the functional aspects of 'augmented presence', we might want to consider how it could change our social interactions and relationships: could bigamy, infidelity or social isolation truly exist in a Third Space world? Much of it would depend on the level of impressiveness and interaction these experiences would offer. Access and regulation would present another conflict related to Telepresence and Third Spaces – whether Telepresence be a privilege of the few or the right of the many – and as we tend to cross digital boundaries much quicker than physical ones, as they pose a less threatening implication towards our physical survival, how would it dent our respect and perception of social and private spaces.

Another notion that relates to identity and presence related to the fourth wall concept. This refers to early performance and entertainment practice, relying on the existence and creation of an 'invisible' wall between the deliverers

of content and the audience. Experimental theatre and film making tried to break the stage/audience barrier and form a more intimate relationship between the performer/content and the audience. The notion of interactivity, especially within the context of video games, disassembled the fourth wall paradigm altogether. Interactivity aspires to interlace the interaction between the user, platform and interface to achieve immersion. Moving away from the observational level to the Overworld [mostly used in role-playing games] created a major shift in this respect. As the user experienced top-down or third person perspective video-game interactivity, the player was elevated from a control level to an immersive level. Another significant step was the introduction of Open World games – also called Sandbox games – where the participants can independently shape interaction, behaviours, goals and value systems. Common examples include World of Warcraft, Eve Online and Minecraft. The freedom rendered through these games, enables self-expression and a strong emotional bonding of the user with the platform, as well the formation of collaborative and profound social interaction.

> As consequence of applying Augmented Reality our physical environment [and reality] would become a Sandbox platform – allowing users to freely manipulate and apply digital content within it.

This would effect several levels of users' perception of reality – and even the perception of time. Since a state of immersion manipulates our perception of time, an ongoing immersive state would ultimately alter our cognitive state. The question that needs to be asked is how would a constant augmentation state interfere with this embedded ability on a short term and evolutionary level. Other challenges that would need to be solved to make the experience realistic, yet unique, would be to consider collision detection of augmented objects, gesture control, as well as considering environment alteration such as non-static objects.

4.4 Right Now

Let's proceed with the 'time' aspect in relation to 'presence', time is the fourth dimension we use to define our experience and interaction in the physical world. The concept of time is important to our perception of reality and presence, and we tend to consider it as having a fixed value. There are many reasons that support our belief of this – for example, we have universal units to measure time, including seconds, minutes and hours. "Humans once lived without any concept of time at all. In this early, hunter-gatherer existence, information was exchanged physically, either orally or with gestures, in person. People lived in an eternal present, without any notion of before or after, much less history or progress. Things just were. The passage of time was not recorded or measured, but rather experienced in its various cycles."[7]

> Time, like any other value, is a state we experience via cerebral activity. Since we are discussing our perception of reality, and in order to avoid an in-depth discussion about the nature of time and absolute value, let's just say that scientists, philosophers, and thinkers have all debated whether time is a concept or a measurable unit, and whether it has an absolute value. Einstein linked time to space through his famous theory of special relativity [$E=MC2$], referring to the Spacetime continuum as a fourth dimension. But relativity also means that time can be experienced differently in relation to mass and energy. What this means is that Spacetime is a 'fabric' that can be manipulated, eventually enabling us to bend time.

String Theory replaces the idea of point-like particles as the building blocks of the universe with strings [which are, in fact, filaments of energy]. These strings vibrate in different patterns and those vibrations produce particles – or matter – that creates the universe around us. Kaluza also introduced a hypothetical additional dimension to Einstein's theory which revealed the theory of electromagnetic fields. The String Theory is basically saying that all matter and all forces within the universe are made up by different frequencies of vibrating energy, and that means that time and space bending is possible, as well as the Parallel Universe Theory that suggests that our reality is only one representation within a limitless multi-dimension and multi-timeline existence.[8]

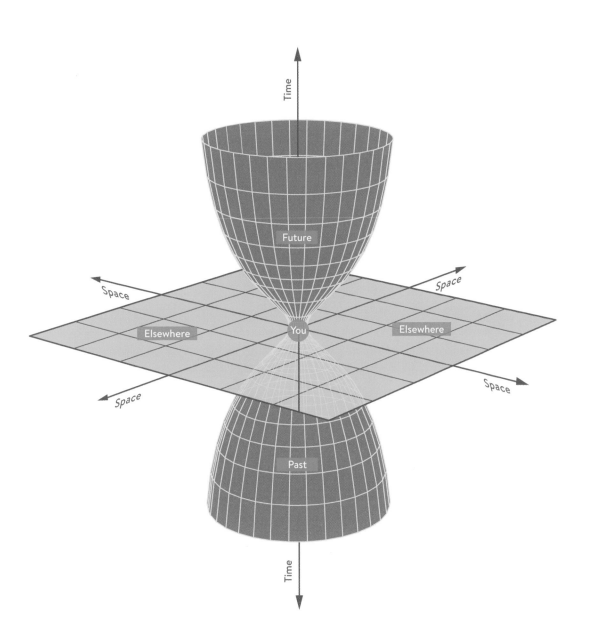

The Spacetime Continuum
Space and time are intertwined. The fabric of space is flat unless it is
introduced to the presence of matter, which allows space and time 'bending'.
Author's Image, 2017.

4.0

Who the f*&k is Alice?

On our little blue planet, time is generally measured on a steady continuum. Our experience of time is still subjective – even when we argue that it can be measured accurately. We perceive time via defined processes that are responsible for encoding flow and the sequence of events within a linear time context. Our brains have mechanisms that act as internal 'pacers', allowing us to track and coordinate an independent sense of time. Yet these mechanisms can be distorted by a variety of factors – physiological, neurological, mental and even cultural – that can influence our relative and absolute perception of time-flow and its quality. We often relate a quality value to time, suggesting that we have attached a value to it that can change. We are actually describing the quality of the experience we had within the timeframe:

'I had a lousy time'

'Time flies when you're having fun'

'Today was a slow day'

Much of our definition and perception of time is related to the quality of an immersive or flow state. The more we are immersed in an activity, the more our perception of time flow and relevance change. 'I lost track of time', is one expression we use to describe the state when our activity is so engaging that it alters our time and task hierarchy. This can be related to negative or positive experiences. Many trauma victims can describe in detail the instance of the traumatic experience describing it as if 'time stood still', allowing them to observe different layers of the experience.

Time cycles and seasons have been fundamental in defining cultural and religious rituals, as well as indicating social relationships and hierarchies in society. Time has become a basic concept in the cultural and human experience. In the Old Testament's *Story of Creation*, God's first action is to define matter [creating Heaven and Earth]. The second is to create light, and then "God called the light Day, and the darkness he called Night. And there was evening and there was morning, the first day."[Genesis 1:5][9]

On an individual level, frequency, accuracy and timespan define and shape the nature and depth of our relationships with people, things and spaces. We often quantify and qualify them as things we would or would not like to 'spend time' on. Thus, time has become a fluid concept that evolves and changes with our

perception and context. It is highly influenced by technological advancements, and although we consider it as consistent in quality it is often argued to be neither. Since time directly reflects and defines our perception and our interaction with reality, reality itself must be a fluid notion that evolves and changes with our individual and social perception.

We accept clocks as a universal measurement tool, and use time to quantify and measure other values, such as motion and velocity. Time is also a determining factor in our activities and lifestyle – we use it to define societal interaction and values, the balance between work and leisure, the value system for income and salaries, to quantify relationships, and to define achievements and progress. In James Gleick's book *Faster* [1999], he explores the difference between our casual reference to the notion of time, versus time's shifting value in respect to the acceleration of technology. One of the reasons for our transcending sense of time relates to the change within time measurement systems and the massive cultural and mental shift moving from the sundial to International Atomic Time. Gleick, an American author and historian of science who uses cultural observation to view the impact of technology, notes that, in the past, we would consider a watch to be accurate when it would run behind by 'only' a few hours a month, than a few minutes. In order to achieve precision, clocks and wristwatches needed to be taken to expert watchmakers to be adjusted. In fact, it was only in 1920 did wristwatches had their own self-winding mechanism. Now that we have incredibly precise and globally synchronised digital and atomic systems to measure time fragments [even though the increments are imperceptible by human senses], our individual and cultural perception of time changes. With it, cultural values such as immediacy, productivity and effect also change.

Transportation is another technological advance that has changed our cultural and social interaction in relation to time. The technological progress supporting transportation systems, allows things [people and goods] to move from A to B in a quick, safe, and now trackable manner. A third technological advance is communication velocity, allowing us to stream and instantly deliver rich multimedia content. All these factors change our cultural perception and interaction with time. Now that we are able to measure time in nanoseconds, we expect immediacy as a basic standard of quality and service.

HUMANS ONCE LIVED
WITHOUT ANY CONCEPT
OF TIME AT ALL...
IN AN ETERNAL PRESENT,
WITHOUT ANY NOTION
OF BEFORE OR AFTER,
MUCH LESS HISTORY OR
PROGRESS. THINGS JUST
WERE. THE PASSAGE OF
TIME WAS NOT RECORDED
OR MEASURED, BUT
RATHER EXPERIENCED IN
ITS VARIOUS CYCLES.

— Douglas Rushkoff, 2013

The pace of living is accelerating, and the amount of activity and interaction we fit into one day may be more than we could have achieved in a week, or a month, only a few decades ago. Even though we see the provision in time measuring as a sign of progress, some question its social value: "Who decides when acceleration is 'good' for society and when it is 'bad'? Or do we simply place our trust in the combination of technology and the free market?"[10]

The immersive nature of technology increasingly [and intentionally] forms gaps between our physical perception of time and our 'high tech' perception of time. Our connection to nature and its cycles is replaced by a modern, more efficient rhythm.

Whether it's by alarm clocks, artificial lighting, high-velocity commuting or information streaming, we are driven to override our physiological rhythm and needs, and to be present and functioning 'on demand'. Such a transition creates the means and context to condition and facilitate control over individuals and society, and to this end utilises technology and the notion of performance [and time] to gain power and profit. It's no wonder that modern anxiety and 'Fear of Missing Out' are leading to increased numbers of work-related burn-outs and even death from self-harm or exhaustion [the Japanese coined the term 'Karōshi' – 'overwork death']. Whereas certain aspects of Augmented Reality, such as Telepresence, are aimed at reducing the need for time consuming commutes to afford us more free time. We are not however, always able to translate technological advantages into a balanced lifestyle. After all, binge watching our newest favourite show is completely irrational, considering we have constant on-demand access to it. The overload of products, options and experiences does not clear our calendar, but fills the gaps with more content and interaction.

4.0

Who the f*&k is Alice?

4.5 Instant Identities

> If the revolution were to be televised, human evolution would
> be streamed. The digital revolution has dramatically impacted
> content consumption, behaviours and the entire market landscape.
> Digital immediacy has been transformed into a commodity, a
> content channel and a business model. As a result, multimedia
> content requires more storage space, and better data compression
> algorithms, data synchronisation systems, and security.

Once robots and Artificial Intelligence can manage our mundane chores, we
will be free to explore the more enjoyable aspects of reality. Since leisure
activities trigger a flow state, the value of time on a social level may change.
Without the obligation of having a task related obligation, we may use time as
an experience-logging system that synchs our timeframes and rhythms to a
social/leisure framework.

Content sharing platforms such as Vimeo, WeTransfer, and Dropbox have
transformed the way we share content and collaborate across the globe.
Video conferencing platforms such as Skype, FaceTime, Google Hangouts,
GoToMeeting and GoToWebinar have provided global reach to individuals and
businesses. Content streaming has changed the way we consume and deliver
entertainment, shifting from traditional production houses and channels to
digital content creation and delivery.

Netflix has led the way in tapping into the consumers' need to balance access
and control, steering away from traditional content distribution and endorsing
the binge-watching phenomenon. However, our expectation of having instant
access all the time has created a new perspective on the value of experience
and content creation. Over accessibility risks compromising the sense of
exclusivity or true intimacy. Social media platforms such as Facebook function
as an experience archive [via the user's wall and timeline], yet they restrict the
user to a linear expression and experience of events. Facebook uses several
features that nudge us to repost past events and post compilations, but it was
Snapchat that found the key to the digital natives' hearts.

Originally launched under the name Picaboo in July 2011, Snapchat gained mass popularity with Gen Z and Millennials alike by building on selfie culture while offering user control over image manipulation and distribution. Snapchat is a social media platform focused on instant sharing of multimedia content referred to as 'snaps'. Snaps are made by self-capturing stills and videos, and can be added to with filters and layers. The application creates a balance between private/public and instant/heritage content creation. Snaps are sent as a private message, while your 'story' is a semi-public feature where content can be viewed by the receiver for a limited amount of time [a few seconds] before disappearing. The immediate nature of the platform, combined with its quirky attitude, has enabled it to establish a targeted user base [young adults], while maintaining an edgy image and relevance. Mainstream media was initially baffled by Snapchat, attempting to dismiss it:

> "[it] doesn't look or feel like any normal form of communication…
> [It is] The people's champ of smartphone peep shows."[12]

The success of Snapchat is partly due to its intuitive, user-friendly interface [for digital natives], and maintaining relevance with reactive feature updates. Another success factor is the interactive social engagement the platform encourages, using multi-user filters and group messaging models. The most innovative feature of the application is its Real-Time facial recognition and mapping algorithm, which enables the application of individual and group filters [since September 2015]. This is probably one of the most used and undervalued Augmented Reality applications. Neither users nor professionals consider the application's lenses [i.e. face effects], filters [face-swapping, digital stickers, emojis, text] and drawing feature as Augmented Reality. This is great news, since it suggests a seamless integration of the technology as a foundation for future adoption.

CNN, ESPN, Cosmopolitan, BuzzFeed, Spotify, National Geographic, Vice, Vevo, and People Magazine officially created active accounts in 2015. The application is available for all mobile platforms, with wide accessibility via a free-to-use purchase model. It monetises its popularity through a feature purchase model, and by allowing companies to sponsor customised filters.

Following the introduction of the face lenses in 2015, Snapchat's data stream reached 10 billion daily video views, up from 2 billion, surpassing even Twitter's daily usage.[13] By the end of 2016 the platform had 150 million daily registered users. Growth is expected within its specific user demographic, assuming the platform will maintain its targeted user group strategy of addressing its consumers in an engaging and relevant manner. The success of this platform is built on selective social inclusion and interaction. Snapchat is a social catalyst – certain filters inherit a social meaning within certain user groups [so please, tell your mother that the dog filter = the slut filter in Gen Z visual lingo]. While the use context remained confined to the original target group at the beginning, the user base is diffusing, decreasing the relevance for and participation of the core consumer.

In September 2016, the company officially changed its name to Snap Inc, and announced the launch of a wearable device called *Spectacles* [aimed at live-streaming content, rather than augmenting imagery]. There remain mixed opinions about its failure and success.[14] What is certain is that it will test the social readiness for head mounted data-capturing devices, either accepting it within a general social consensus or creating a user base of 'Snapholes'.

4.6   Real-Time Time

Why are we using the term 'Real-Time', and what is the difference between that and [real] time? The phrase first appears in the 1953 American Mathematical Society publication, in relation to computing: "With the advent of large-scale high-speed digital computers, there arises the question of their possible use in the solution of problems in 'Real-Time', i.e., in conjunction with instruments receiving and responding to stimuli from the external environment."

Real-Time relates to the technology enhanced perception of time, ignoring and disrupting cycles within nature, culture, and systems. It causes the urge to be 'first to market', pushing developers and marketers to work to quick development cycles and implementations justified by agile processes that allow limited feedback. It feeds the consumer's ever-growing desire [created by the industry itself] for new product and new stimulation.

"Despite the bastardization, the concept of Real-Time is a genuine addition to our understanding of haste. And not just haste. Real-Time implies communication. To understand any Real-Time process, we expand our sense of pace to include side-by-side time scales."[16] In this reference Gleick points out that despite its deceivingly simple meaning, Real-Time suggests a different perception of reality. "Not long ago, all time was Real-Time, but Real-Time is no longer a redundancy. Some authorities call it a retronym, like snail mail, acoustic guitar and rotary-dial telephone: an old thing's new name, made necessary by the branching progress of innovation [E-mail and electric guitars and Touch Tone phones – and, what, artificial time? Imaginary time? Virtual time?]. But Real-Time is not an old thing. Real-Time might be a limit we approach asymptotically, or it might be a state of mind."[17]

Today we experience Real-Time content creation and delivery as a given that shapes our interaction and behaviours. "Our society has reoriented itself to the present moment. Everything is live, Real-Time, and always-on. It's not a mere speeding up, however much our lifestyles and technologies have accelerated the rate at which we attempt to do things. It's more of a diminishment of anything that isn't happening right now – and the onslaught of everything that supposedly is."[18]

Value is very much related to the idea of exclusivity; the trick is in balancing desirability and accessibility. Product and service mark-ups rely on the user's [true or perceived] sense of having access to exclusive distribution, availability and service. The concept of supply and demand is ancient, but in modern marketing it is a simple exercise in increasing demand by orchestrating limited supply. If humans are mortal, the time limit is what enhances value. Time limited offers and content achieve that value enhancement, and seasonal cycles and limited editions are another way to maintain consumer interest. Real-Time delivery of content lets the user maintain a sense of immediacy, and a unique experience that fully engages the user.

As a brand, *Monocle* goes against the grain by avoiding social media content, instead choosing live content streaming to maintain an exclusive brand image and limit user access. Launched in February 2007, Canadian publisher Tyler Brûlé's Monocle magazine has built a print, web, broadcast and retail

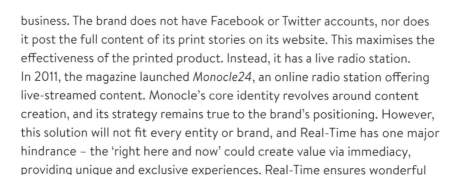

4.0

Who the f*&k is Alice?

business. The brand does not have Facebook or Twitter accounts, nor does it post the full content of its print stories on its website. This maximises the effectiveness of the printed product. Instead, it has a live radio station. In 2011, the magazine launched *Monocle24*, an online radio station offering live-streamed content. Monocle's core identity revolves around content creation, and its strategy remains true to the brand's positioning. However, this solution will not fit every entity or brand, and Real-Time has one major hindrance – the 'right here and now' could create value via immediacy, providing unique and exclusive experiences. Real-Time ensures wonderful accidents, but also unfortunate coincidences [just like life!], melding into the experience. This makes it difficult to deliver a specific and consistent level of experience and content quality.

In an era of Real-Time and cross platform content creation and delivery, storytelling strategy gurus Gaston Legorburu and Darren McColl suggest shifting away from focusing on price, story or experience-based differentiation to 'storyscaping' differentiation[19] – this concept is aligned with our future technological landscape. Brands and content will need to play a different role where they are intertwined with the user's identity on a tangible experiential level, playing a more complex role in the user's value system and perception of reality. The shifting nature and immediacy of interaction will lead to a fluid perception of time and reality, and most certainly a period of adjusting social values. Delivery of instant interactive experiences and a new stream of consciousness creates a new concept of Hyper Reality, where reality itself can be orchestrated, controlled, and manipulated.

The last part of the equation is the new meaning that 'being in the present' would have. Augmented Reality, and especially Mixed Reality, enables a new type of 'in'. We are no longer the participants that are present in the environment – we have a far more dominant role. We are creators and manipulators of reality. This will change our relationships with people, places and things.

4.7 Augmented Intimacies

Technology advancements influence many aspects of our social interaction. We seek to enhance our communication via technology, and as we craft new digital communication tools, it affects us in unexpected ways. Our overloaded digital mailboxes testify to an increasing volume of content exchange, but do not necessarily guarantee better productivity. In fact, it has become a distracting factor that interferes with work efficiency, while new applications and digital assistants are being built to help us declutter our ever-inflating inboxes.

The Internet has had a positive initial impact in other functional areas, such as job searching, yet with both recruiters and applicants using the same formulas to both screen candidates and beat the screening bots, there seems to be no constructive benefit to using online algorithms to match jobs and applicants over using old-school personal networks to find candidates. Yet, digital tools play a significant role in areas more related to social and intimate behaviour, such as forming relationships. Stanford professors Michael J. Rosenfeld and Reuben J. Thomas,[20] researched the influence of the Internet as a rising social arena for relationship creation among heterosexual Americans. They found a substantial peak in encountering a romantic mate encountering from the '90s onward, becoming the most likely method leading to romantic pairing by 2009. This is the result of several factors, including increased access and mobility, improved search algorithms, the emergence of designated and non-designated social and dating platforms, as well as the social acceptance of online interaction and dating.

While there has been a decline in couple pairing in traditional structures such as primary and secondary schools, religion and family, Internet coupling has been accelerating. This is not to undermine the Internet's role as a tool that complements other ways of meeting. Traditional structures and physical locations remain influential for relationship first encounters. The Internet might be an effective platform, yet certain behavioural and physical factors [such as proximity] are still essential to form and initiate relationships, even when initiated via digital means.

The research finds no difference in quality or stability of relationships formed online versus those formed elsewhere. However, online relationships are

characterised by having more racial and cultural versatility than traditionally formed relationships, indicating that the Internet plays an important role in cultural diversification – perhaps not as an initiator, but certainly as an enabler. The conclusion is that technology is fundamentally a behavioural lens that reflects social shifts. It may intensify certain behaviours, but even when new rituals are built they are based on existing needs, aspirations and dogmas.

> Relationships and emotions come in all shapes and formats. In
> *The Book of Human Emotions*, Tiffany Watt Smith[21] talks about the
> histories of 156 human feelings, from common guilt to rarer emotions
> including 'basorexia' [the sudden urge to kiss someone]. At their
> core, relationships are based on reliance and intimacy. They are not
> restricted to humans – we develop emotional attachment to pets,
> objects, places and situations.

Our emotional attachment to animals seems natural, since we can identify similar emotions and interaction hierarchies in them, such as loyalty, affection and dependence. When it comes to objects, we constantly define our relationships with objects and spaces through emotional narrative, which theoretically should be reserved for living beings. People depend on trust, and even express romantic [and obsessive] notions towards brands, objects and environments. When you reflect on it, it is quite a bizarre notion, since it implies we have a mutual, 'two-sided' relationship with them. The reality is that we only really have a one-sided relationship, with the attachment based on a projection from the user layering emotional meanings on non-living entities. Let's face it, until our phones and computers reach singularity, they don't really 'care' who operates them. Perhaps they will even have a 'find my human' feature once they do.

The source of this emotional bond is twofold. First, ownership is a big part of our social structures, which support the development of deep affiliations and rituals with the 'things' that surround us. Ownership on its own creates an 'endowment effect' which intensifies an objects' perceived value… and so the cycle continues. The second part related to how we use objects and spaces for solace and as emotional surrogates – it is a part of the natural human condition.

The Rise of Online Intimacy
Online romantic and social platform had enabled a new way to interact on
a romantic level, replacing traditional social frameworks and hierarchies.
Author's Image, 2017.
[Adapted from Rosenfeld and Thomas, 2012]

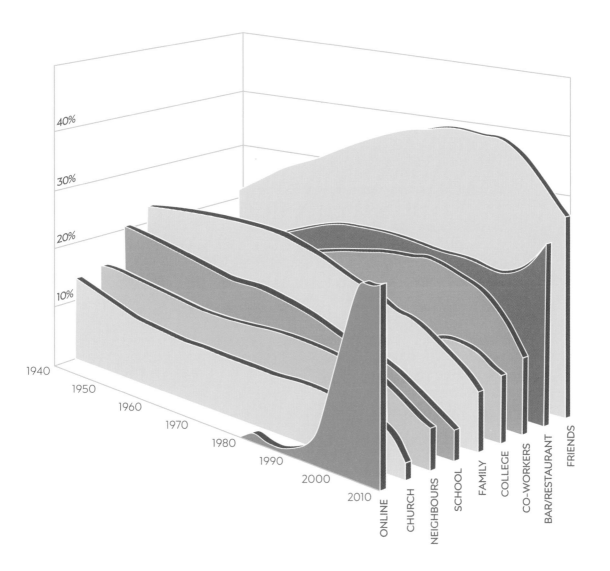

4.0 Who the f*&k is Alice?

The Italian neurophysiologist, Giacomo Rizoletti implies in his research that this bond leads us to perceive objects as an actual extension of ourselves – both on a physical and mental level. The anthropology of object usage reveals the shifting context of artifacts in terms of social hierarchies [from military to 'civilian' fashion uniforms], social status [from crowns to engagement rings], and wealth [from mansions to the latest smartphone].

In some cases, object-bonding might be viewed as 'on the edge' of bizarre. Look at hoarders, who cannot separate and detach from objects, and fetishists, who get aroused by objects [now exchange the word 'object' for 'technology content', and suddenly it is socially acceptable]. Some people develop deep emotions for inanimate objects, to the level of displacing relationships and even wanting to marry them [with actual wedding ceremonies that have included marrying the Eiffel Tower and even a rock].

> The term for fixation with objects or body parts is 'fetishism', though the term is mostly used in a sexual connotation. Humans often use substitute objects to enhance sexual performance and create intimacy, and technology plays a dominant role in using machines to replicate intimacy and sexuality. Our sexual identity is a complex notion that has been equally explored and suppressed across cultures and throughout human history.

The *RealDoll* company 'upped' the role-playing by providing a detailed and highly humanoid sex doll. These dolls replicate human physiology with hyper-realistic touch and movement functions, and are custom-made to the user's preferences for body type, skin colour and detailing. Although they are fundamentally made for sexual purposes [and are anatomically correct through and through], they are marketed as 'love dolls', and indeed some individuals develop deep romantic feelings and relationships with them – as portrayed in the excellent movie Lars and the Real Girl. The manufacturer is exploring integrating Artificial Intelligence into the dolls, however creating an animated version may prove tricky in terms of achieving a convincing experience.

Roxxxy TrueCompanion, the first sex robot equipped with a variety of integrated sensors that evoke reactions, used the assistance of a psychologist to construct

bond-forming mechanisms in the development of its Artificial Intelligence-based intimate experience. The doll has several modes that reflect different personalities and trigger different reactions and interactions. However, relatively high costs, the lack of a sophisticated Artificial Reality system, and independent motion and function still leave plenty of gaps to be filled between the user and the love-bots. Augmented Reality can provide a different level of intimacy, as it will utilise existing environments and partners.

Pornography is a key accelerator industry for all emerging technologies [and we should be grateful for its live streaming, online payments and popular diffusion], since it is truly reliant on tapping into the user's most fundamental needs, while providing an elevated experience and seamless service to ensure a healthy commercial revenue.

Pornography consumption is heavily related to the way we treat sexuality as a society. The experience and visibility of human sexuality adhere to communal norms, moral and religious codes and legislation.

> The intensified nature of 'virtuality' and augmentation technology would undoubtedly expand moral and social values of sexuality. The more sophisticated the technology, the more we move away from a detached fantasy and into a tangible experience. The confined environment of Virtual Reality is perhaps an easier pathway to contain this shift, while augmentation would need to consider more complex issues because of the blending of private, intimate and public realm.

How would our sexual identity change if we augment the sexual organs, appearances and locations of our partners and ourselves? Where do fantasy and privacy clash if we choose to add a non-consenting person's presence, face or body to a physical sexual act? It's safe to assume that we would further explore our sexual identities via our augmented selves. Having the ability to experience what some cultures may consider 'unacceptable' sexual behaviour while participating in a 'culturally accepted' act, may represent a sense of mental liberation, but is also somewhat repressive, as socially unacceptable activities would not be 'physically' played out. There is also a concern about developing dependency on, or an actual relationship with, an augmented avatar

that may replace or reduce our opportunities for exploring interaction and intimacy with another human being – as imperfect and challenging as we are. Augmented presence and long-distance relationships may even become an alternative lifestyle, providing a controlled way to participate in another person's life via your representation rather than your physical self. Imagine a relationship where you skip to the good bits without having to show up, dress up, or handle someone else's snoring or unpleasant body odours.

Besides heightened risks of porn viewing addiction and [binge] compulsive masturbation practices, leading to male sexual dysfunction and psychological distress, such engagement unveils a new mental state with an obscure standard towards impulse control. Even though the value of augmentation within recreational and commercial sexuality is clear, the impact would stretch beyond the sexual context to the broader context of accessing a mode of 'fantasy actualisation'. The ability to access and explore fantasies, boundaries and creativity in the broader context would inevitably explore the line between personal desire and social limitations/ dogmas, the manifestation of the individual identity, and the need to maintain balance and the status quo within social structures. The boundless intensification of experiences via Virtual Reality and Augmented Reality will precipitate changes to the nature of our desire-driven experience and values, especially once we reach a fully immersive sensory feedback. We could fulfil our desires without getting off the sofa [or out of bed] – a 'reality-couch-surfing' taken literally. The risk here is that we become stuck in an endless loop of pleasure-seeking or the numbing-out of stimuli.

4.8 When Wonderlands Cross Over

Augmentation will add a new experiential layer to our spaces and environments, perhaps acting as living memories and emotional triggers, and altering our interaction with and within our environment to eventually create new behavioural patterns and rituals.

Facilitating individual actions is an instrumental part of forming common social etiquette, regulations and laws. Even evolutionary and survival-driven

behaviours such as eating and procreation are subject to moderation and control that reflect on personal and social identities. For societies and entities, sustaining structures and hierarchies is connected to their ability to impose rules and regulations. For this to be effective a moral/personal/ behavioural code of conduct needs to be established in a way where it is rooted in personal intent and mind. "Thou shalt not covet" is not randomly placed within the Ten Commandments – it is one of the first expressions that demonstrate the understanding that controlling desire is the first step to controlling whether you act on the desire or not.

Controlling desires and fantasies results in controlling cultural, social mindsets and perceptions, eventually shaping broader social behaviours and hierarchies. Desire-driven entertainment may be a new narrative/content trope that would evolve because of this tension and need, which could dial into a variety of personal, sub-cultural and clusters of fantasy exploration and augmented preferences to form experience-based tribes. Augmented amusement, rituals and exploration spaces could easily be formed for social and personal exploration – much like the concept portrayed in the *Westworld* television show, but allowing a more accessible, cost effective and versatile experience. These augmented exploration spaces would be shared across local and remote groups, resolving the need to travel to a simulation space – your desired simulation would blend into your existing environment.

Blending and adapting storyline narration to the physical realm could become a core Augmented Reality business model, allowing users to stream various personalised or 'growing' experiences to fit within their everyday life. This would be intensified once Augmented Reality seamlessly incorporates gesture, haptic, and Real-Time feedback. The combination would provide a targeted and curated deep layer of intimacy and feedback. While the augmented experience would be tailored to your preferences, it would intensify deviations, learnings, and adaptations while you are using it.

Using augmentation to mix a fantasy layer on top of the 'ordinary' reality has immense potential for creating a bond with the user and achieving intrinsic emotional hooks, hopefully widening the use of the technology. Finding the 'sweet spot' between forming fantasy hooks and not overtaking or undermining existing and aspirational relationships within the physical word is vital.

Importance of Balancing Emotional Triggering

#01

Behavioural
Nudging

Content creators that would have access to one's fantasy layer creation would influence deep emotional bonds within the user's mind. This would allow them to nudge, shape and suggest personal and social behaviours in a deep manner.

#02

Simulated
Interactions

Another certain impact would be on a personal level - the oversimplification and unconditional access to alternative yet realistic [enough] experiences would enable us to be satisfied with artificial entities and simulated interaction and relationships.

#03

Creative
Exploration

The actualisation of fantasy, whether generated by users themselves, platform makers or entities would mean the reinforcement of a defined sensory perception [whether visual or multisensory] great benefits in terms of expressing and exploring but also means the facilitation of imagination which might restrict certain aspects of abstract values and creativity.

#04

Societal

On a societal level - the lack of [virtual or augmented] 'forbidden fruits' might mean losing our conditioned self-control thresholds. Effecting our decision-making, interaction and relationships and interactions inside and outside the augmented experience. Altering wider notions of morals, intimacies and social etiquette in a broad context.

#05

Desire Value

Our [already] reduced impulse and gratification cycles could diminish altogether, changing our perception towards desire and as consequence their value.

4.9 In Your Face

Social etiquette relates directly to physical gestures, rituals and representation in both the public and private space. Since the nature and expression of intimacies and relationships would be affected by augmentation, it would in turn shape broader behavioural and social interactions. Social etiquette is a tool that transforms cultural signals into behavioural norms to facilitate and maintain social hierarchies.

We alter our appearance or presence to manifest our identity, our cultural and social affiliations. The extent of such alteration reaffirms our level of affiliation – the more complete and permanent, the more we suggest commitment – there is a difference between donning your favourite team's cap, a full uniform or tattoo. In structured societies [from military and religious regimes to societies], the nuances of your religious outfit will signify precise affiliations, including internal hierarchy and personal status from details such as pins and marks, uniform colour and material, and even the tilt of your hat. Thus, our physical appearance and our preparation ritual to achieve it signify a certain commitment to our status and the message we want to portray – at least in public.

Once we add an augmented layer to our appearance, modifying and even altering it instantly, it would challenge how attached and committed we are to our identity. After all, we could easily create specific filters that would simultaneously represent different personas within different groups and contexts – for example, a dignified office manager to co-workers, and a pierced rock star to anyone else. The ability to easily maintain a split identity would be interesting to explore, in terms of whether users maintain understated physical features, layering an outspoken identity on top, or vice versa. And it leaves us to wonder what shape the 'coming out' to the true self would take.

Augmentation would allow us to explore gender, religious and social dogmas. For example, should an augmented burka be applied by the female user or – since the issue is really related to patriarchal control, would it be the responsibility or role of the male viewer? The same goes for augmented bodily enhancements. The idea of allowing users to capture and augment other people's presence is one that might be considered amusing – especially based on conversations I have

had with Snapchat users who already [ab]use facial recognition to capture and augment a stranger's image, and distribute it on social media. They understand that it is perhaps not socially acceptable, and try to do it discreetly [since they are using mobile phone devices to capture it, the gesture is easily exposed], but they don't consider it to be an issue. A person's presence for them is an image captured on their device, and thus within their partial ownership and right to manipulate.

This can become a dangerous precedent since it is about an individual's presence as a subject and object. What is probable is that people's augmented tagging might be an interesting new way to interact in the physical environment, though I wonder how comfortable users would be with strangers objectifying and mocking them without their knowledge or consent. In this context, augmentation in public spaces should allow protections that limit or prohibit augmentation of others, considering such acts as digital assault.

Much of the success of Augmented Reality would depend on how well it would remediate, and integrate existing social behaviours, etiquettes and gestures. Apple excelled in diffusing its multimedia devices due to in gesture and navigation from the iPod wheel to graphic effects and representation incorporated in their User Interface. The remediation and usage of gestures in augmented interaction and recognition, would influence mass social behaviour and appropriation. The use of mobile devices already changed social interaction within public spaces, Sony's Walkman was perhaps the first device that was designed to give an experience that physically forms a distant sensory separation between the user and the environment.[22]

Mass application of augmentation within the public domain may alter our social rituals and interaction, perhaps resulting in a unified universal system, much like emojis re-established a universal visual language, as did certain gesture interactions, such as mouse clicking and screen swiping. Gesture-based activation experiences could become a great tool to intensify experiences – using crowd and individual gesture interaction to trigger, mirror and intensify experiences. However, cross-cultural variables must be considered to permit and design overrides. From my personal experience, I can tell you that the Middle Eastern gesture for 'wait up' [gathering your fingertips and wagging your hands

in an up-and-down motion] is precisely the same as the Italian gesture for 'what the hell do you want/are you talking about' [bordering 'f&#k off']. This is clearly not something you should use casually – an incident with a lost train ticket almost landed me in jail.

Gesture-rich communication cultures, individual nuances and physical disabilities could all form an interaction bottleneck in the application of Augmented Reality. I would advise that developers anticipate gesture recognition to prevent interactive environments and systems from crashing within a few minutes of mass usage.

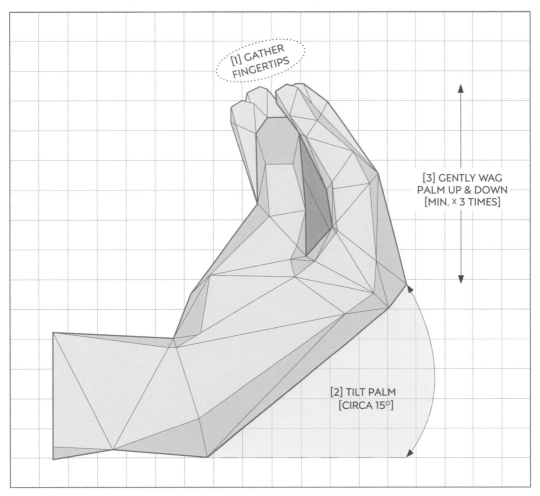

Gestures can be tricky
The same one means both 'wait up' or 'what the hell do you want/are you talking about'
Author's Image, 2017. [Inspired by Munari, 1963].

"IF I HAD A WORLD OF MY OWN,
EVERYTHING WOULD BE
NONSENSE. NOTHING WOULD BE
WHAT IT IS, BECAUSE EVERYTHING
WOULD BE WHAT IT ISN'T,"
SAID ALICE.

— Lewis Carroll, Alice's Adventures in Wonderland

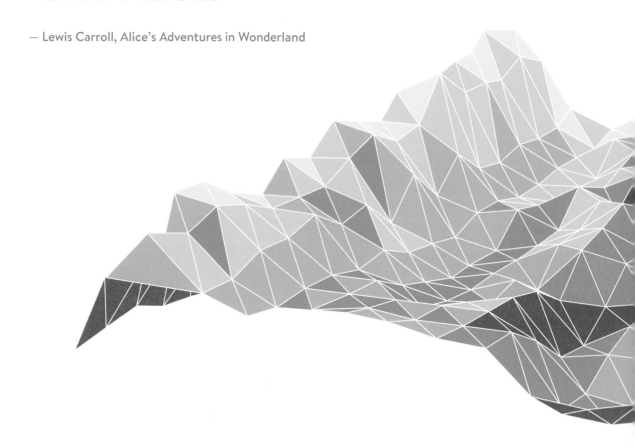

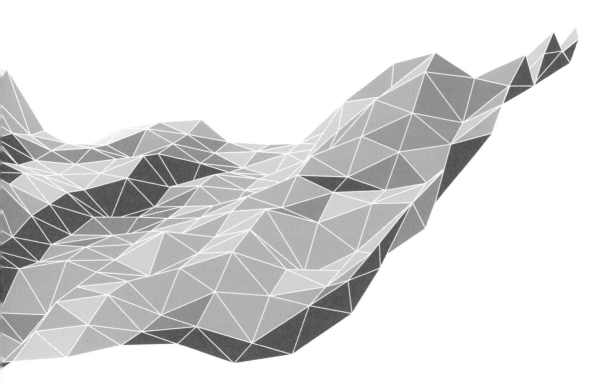

5.0 OFF WITH
THEIR HEADS

Off With Their Heads

Data Queens & Citizens of the Augmented World

Once augmentation becomes the standard for content and experience creation, those who hold the keys to the technology will have unlimited access and influence in constructing realities, social interaction and behaviours. We need to understand who will be the ones who would truly control augmented content, what the implications are, and which means of constraint we should put in place to ensure that Augmented Reality application is balanced and ethical.

Consider the potential of Augmented Reality as an immersive advocacy platform. Where digital and physical experiences intertwine, control and manipulation of behaviours will be driven by the experience creators. Makers of realities. Market drivers. Gods.

5.1 Information Politics

In *The Condition of Postmodernity*, David Harvey talks about how the post-war Fordism should not be seen as a mass production system, but as a representation of a total way of life: "Mass production meant standardisation of product as well as mass consumption; and meant a whole new aesthetic and a commodification of culture."[1] Capitalism had enabled the rise of technology as a geographical and cultural expansion, "in order to seek new markets, new sources of raw material, and new sources of labour, and to create more accumulated capital. This logic develops its own cycle that continues endlessly."[2] Economic and political systems are firmly intertwined, and as tech corporations become an economic force – with entities like Apple worth double the budget of the state of California in 2016 – so grows their political influence.

We have already seen how their expansion into multinational entities, and seeking of fiscal benefits overseas, have turned taxation and financial regulation into a political issue on a global scale. Tech entities have an unprecedented impact on industry, knowledge and economics. Technology-influenced and eventually technology-led governance [or Technocracy] is not a far-fetched idea.

> "The political and the economic realms are closely intertwined. There existed [and still exists] a definite interaction [dialectic] between the political and the economic, where one helps to shape and form the developmental contours of the other."

In this sense Held's emphasis on the term 'capacity' is insightful. Capacity in this sense connotes a form of power, the power to change either [or both] the political environment or the economic realms."[3] The tech [bit] and data [byte] economies become more dominant, as multinational tech conglomerates gain more data access, user base and fortune [exceeding that of many developed nations]. An inevitable future where politics and tech are intertwined is rapidly catching up with us. The option of having digital citizenship is not an unlikely proposal as they come into power. In fact, Denmark has already reached this conclusion by being the first country intending to appoint a diplomatic liaison to the tech industry in 2017.

Governance is not only about holding an official political position, it's also about shaping the public narrative on the level of content, morals and ethics. As the reach of technology conglomerates grows – across hardware, software and content creation – so will their influence grow on the public narrative. There is a reason why social media is highly restricted, if not banned, by centralised political systems [think China, Turkey, and India], and is becoming more and more regulated in progressive political systems. It's because mass communication platforms provide direct access to the user, bypassing official regulations, channels and hierarchies. Digital communities and affiliations are becoming increasingly relevant to user identity, and thus political, national and demographic structures lose meaning and power. The builders of these platforms of course aspire to gain more access in order to have more influence. Facebook, Google and Twitter are becoming more and more exposed to public and political backlash due to their contribution to, or lack of prevention

5.0 Off With Their Heads

of criminal or discriminatory content, 'fake news', and breaching privacy via borderline illegal [or at least unethical] information gathering techniques.[4]

The implementation of augmented content is potentially an even more powerful tool to influence and track public narrative. According to Radio Free Asia, the Chinese government banned Augmented Reality applications in January 2017 due to concerns about users, and national privacy and security issues. "In view of these national security considerations, as well as a sense of responsibility for the safety of people and property... the administration will not be approving this type of game for the time being."[5] These concerns are more related, in my mind, to issues of content control, due to possible future implications of augmented interaction and diffusion.

The online space may have started out as neutral, and is perhaps still marketed as a user-based democracy, but it is very much controlled by political and commercial forces that take advantage of legal loopholes and security gaps. The race started with legislative and regulatory authorities lagging behind the pace of technology development. Jane E. Fontaine, Director of the JFK School of Government, talks about the future 'virtual state', derived from the digitalisation of governance, and the governance of digital entities. Governance is based on legislation and regulations, however government entities are far slower to react to the changing digital landscape. Legislation is reflective of community and social standards – think about the different opinions held regarding the legislative approach to homosexuality, age of consent, cannabis and alcohol consumption, and gun possession. While technology entities are becoming boundary-free organisations, legislation is still limited by different approaches across territories, regimes and religious societies.

Net neutrality regulation is only now under consideration, with actions toward imposing it starting mainly in the EU. Since the impact of Augmented Reality has the potential to be far deeper and more immersive, we may want to establish a social code and regulation framework prior to its implementation and diffusion.

The question of whether or not to use technology is no longer relevant, unless you live in complete isolation, it is embedded within the everyday lives of first, second, and third world citizens. It is *how* we use it that defines us as individuals, and as parts of a social and political hierarchy. As our economic system weaves into an information system – and as the physical and digital means of control and communication blur – we can expect to see the rise of self-governing digital entities. Whether they are formalised as an integral part of a political system or via the creation of a parallel system, we will become digital citizens.

In a 'virtual state', status and influence will be determined by one's access to technology. "With the digital haves better connected than the digital have-nots, gated communities have found their online equivalents with the like-minded and the well positioned increasingly talking amongst themselves and traditionally vulnerable groups such as immigrants, the lower classes or senior citizens simply dropping off the digital map."[6] The 'have-nots' will be the citizens that either cannot physically access, or lack the capacity to manipulate, digital content.

As digital interaction becomes an embedded feature within our physical environment, the meaning of staying 'off the augmented grid' – will have an influence that goes beyond a private preference for either content consumption or privacy. Being disconnected would mean having one's access to an entire interaction layer denied, and limiting the opportunity to connect to one's common culture, social structures and even civil status.

5.0

Off With Their Heads

5.2 Whose Story Is It, Anyway?

Augmented content and interaction will put into play ideas about possession and ownership that were clear when we only needed to consider the physical realm. Creation and possession used to be a straightforward matter – a simple ownership transaction or a creation process. As consumption moved away from tangible goods into services, experiences and interactions – what philosopher Vilém Flusser refers to as "Non Things" – marked a change in our understanding of ownership. Consider content consumption as an example – even within the digital category, it was a simple process when we still needed a physical asset [DVD, vinyl, cassette, etc.] to establish access, ownership and value. Through the use of direct digital channels, we have traded physical ownership for data ownership, and beyond that we have progressed to subscription and free-for-use models. What we are actually witnessing is that purchasing is not the content itself, but it is about access, matched content features, or service. In other words, we now acquire the experience of consuming the content.

Content ownership models will be pushed further, delivering new types of innovation and value where users' creation and sharing of assets trigger new interactions and social behaviours. Lead users and influencers could receive rewards for testing, developing and sharing augmented content and experiences. Or perhaps they will be allowed to use the augmented platform freely if they allow content and product placement within their physical reality, enticing them to purchase the actual service or product. In any case, users must remember that high-level and high-value experiential and interactive augmented content is [and will remain] a costly process. Since nothing [that can be monetised] is free, someone will be paying the augmented bill – most likely the user's privacy.

Most free-to-use service models are not charities. Sooner or later, they impose a revenue structure for their use, either directly via limitations and fees, or indirectly through targeted advertising and data mining. Regardless of the user myth that posting a pseudo-legal declaration will protect their rights and privacy, social media and free-model platforms can block, monitor, censor or

delete users' data and content without repercussion. It's all in the fine print of the Terms & Conditions agreements we never read. On a more calming note, irrational and unfair conditions – whether we clicked 'I agree' or not – do not hold up in court.

Our laissez-faire attitude to sharing our data has become a cultural norm. As data accumulates in the servers of tech moguls, they have access to an unprecedented amount of information and insights at the individual and social level, giving them more control to set moral standards. Digital content platforms often block and monitor access, and eliminate content deemed morally offensive or inappropriate by the audience, governments and regimes. Even within the free, modern society, platforms mostly adhere to legal and moral codes and consensus – leaning towards a more conservative approach. The Free the Nipple campaign challenged social media platforms' prohibition of any representation of the female areola, regardless of its context. It highlighted that nipples were only deemed sexual and offensive when tied to the female gender [male nipples are not censored]. It also highlighted that, in many cases, one could not easily differentiate whether the nipples belonged to a male or female body, which begs the question, what was so offensive to begin with? This was especially absurd when the censorship was blindly imposed on images of any nipple, regardless of the execution method, whether a print, an art piece or an iconic image.

Ethical and philosophical debates are still evolving, examining notions such as ownership of digital assets. In 2012, Bruce Willis sparked public debate when he threatened to sue Apple Inc. to maintain the right to leave his iTunes library to his daughter in the event of his death. Digital dust is an online blog created by Vered Shavit dealing with *Death in the Digital Era & Life After Death on the Net: The Digital, Virtual and Online Aspects of Current Death*,[7] which asks questions such as "What does it mean, death in the digital era? Death in the virtual era? Life after death on the net?" and "What Happens Online When You Die?"[8] Indeed, the concept of digital as an artificial layer – and as such unbound from our physical existence – will further evolve, especially at the dawn of singularity and the creation of an augmented existence. Will our augmented worlds be a public or a private possession? Do they belong to the continuum of the physical world they are bound to, or to our physical mortal entity?

Second Life provides an ideal opportunity to explore the differences between physical and virtual ownership. A multi-user 3D virtual world developed by Linden Lab and launched in 2003, the platform enables users to choose and edit their avatars, as well as navigate, shape and interact with the virtual world around them. *Second Life* is an open-world platform rather than a game, since it does not have a defined goal besides being an open framework for virtual creations. It also has its own internal currency –Linden dollars – that enables users to own and create digital content and trade it [including in-game assets, property and activations]. Since its early days, *Second Life* has been an interesting laboratory and case study for human interaction and identity in the virtual realm. One interesting case looks at users' ownership of their built digital assets. There are several cases,[9] where Linden Lab was sued by users for suspending their accounts [due to breach of terms and conditions]. The users demanded to retrieve their digital assets, and were eventually compensated [in US$] because Linden dollars had real-life value, and it was clearly stated the creator of the digital content was the owner.

Our relationship with ownership is not derived from the transaction process alone, but also the creation process. Whereas, in the past, access to the tools needed for content creation was limited to royals and priests, today users have access to the tools to print, post, podcast and literally manufacture content with hardly any technical knowledge. The importance of this within the context of technology and innovation is undeniable. The democratisation of technology and innovation has been driven by the changing role of the user within the tech industry: "Users had developed 77% of the innovations in the scientific instruments field and 67% of the innovations in semiconductors and printed circuit boards."[10] User-developed products and content are proving to be vital to sustaining innovation, and the basis for the existence of many platforms. Users have transcended from passive consumers to content drivers, from co-creators to autonomous creators. This is true of all types of content and products, beyond communications and social media. Consider the Maker Movement, where users want to design and create their own physical content and world. This active user shifts the creation and production value chain so facilitation, platform building, and experience architecture become crucial to defining the business model and product value.

Von Hippel already referenced the shift from users who are influencers [marketing-led] to lead users [innovation-led] who create new products and processes. Whereas, in the past, identifying these users was pivotal to innovation and the ability to maintain relevance, today artificial intelligence helps us to identify patterns and tendencies that go beyond their face value. Where the power play shifts again will be from the balance between hive data mining [looking at crowd behaviour and patterns], and queen bee data analysis [transforming core user needs and actions into a strategic platform].

Whether the user is a worker bee or a queen bee, they expect to be heard, respected, considered and influential. This power was handed to them by their ability to consume and distribute content in a limitless, effortless capacity with little or no [direct] cost. The service economy – which focuses on the value of service innovation rather than product innovation – only reinforces the dominance of the user. This relationship becomes complicated when the illusion of user ownership and complete control fades – being denied access to the cloud or your online account/content helps users suddenly realise the difference between access and ownership, much like the difference between having hard cash in your pocket versus just having a credit line.

As content creation and representation become part of a user-forged reality, we are introduced to a new user mindset, where everyone is a self-proclaimed creator, and the value of the content is measured by diffusion and populist consensus rather than cultural standards. The first outcome is content overload, and the forging of new quality standards. Eventually, content overload leads to a desire to curate content, establishing new content 'leaders' and hierarchies. Much of the future of Augmented Reality will be based on how organic or facilitated these content-filtering, quality and hierarchy structures and relationships are.

What should we expect in terms of user/content relationship once augmentation applies the interaction layer on an even more intimate level? Since augmented content will be an integral part of users' physical presence, connecting directly to their rituals and emotive experiences, influencing augmented content would literally mean interfering and intruding upon a layer of the user's direct experience of reality. Thus, any act of removing,

censoring and limiting augmented access would cause a severe imbalance in the user's interaction with the functional and mental aspect of reality.

Consider the fact that the 'mere' loss of our mobile phone triggers an actual sense of grief. Beyond the loss of the artifact, the user is dependent on the phone as a communication and content device. Smart devices are now an integral part of our digital [and hence physical] identity. Consider the effect caused by the removal of interaction layers that are directly placed onto your physical reality and existence. This would create a greater feeling of distress, with a disorienting experience in our physical, spatial interaction. Augmentation could trigger a new debate relating to content control and ownership, especially within a spatial context. Since augmented assets would be more closely related to a physical space manifestation, perhaps would we finally accept a hybrid ownership value/model of digital assets and entities. Perhaps the future divorce would include a shared custody of the augmented pet, artwork or the right to maintain the augmented tattoo that marked the couple's first anniversary.

5.3 Get Out of My Reality

We have already discussed issues about augmented presence and content, trapped between the increasing density of public spaces, diminishing private space, and shifting intimate space – both physically and digitally.
When we consider public space, we generally expect legislative regulations and social consensus to secure certain boundaries and standards governing our interaction within the public space, preventing offensive and invasive behaviours towards individuals and groups. While some protection has been offered for minors since the early days of the Internet – such as the Children's Online Privacy Protection Act of 1998 [COPPA], a US federal law – adult use and exposure to online privacy violations remain an issue that requires more reactive legislation and enforcement than currently supplied by governments and international policing bodies.

The concept of ownership relates to both legal proof of ownership and physical presence or possession. We still treat digital presence and ownership

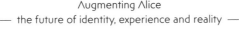

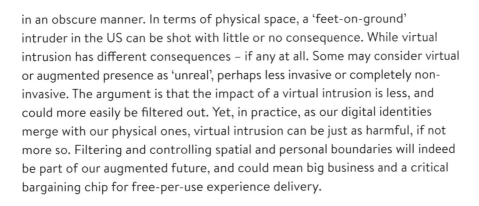

5.0 Off With Their Heads

in an obscure manner. In terms of physical space, a 'feet-on-ground' intruder in the US can be shot with little or no consequence. While virtual intrusion has different consequences – if any at all. Some may consider virtual or augmented presence as 'unreal', perhaps less invasive or completely non-invasive. The argument is that the impact of a virtual intrusion is less, and could more easily be filtered out. Yet, in practice, as our digital identities merge with our physical ones, virtual intrusion can be just as harmful, if not more so. Filtering and controlling spatial and personal boundaries will indeed be part of our augmented future, and could mean big business and a critical bargaining chip for free-per-use experience delivery.

> As we gallop towards a data and experience economy, we must give consideration and regulation to the definition of ownership and experience appropriation within public and private spaces. However, much like online advertising, imposed augmented content and 'behavioural interaction mining' may simply be 'the price of doing business' – an integrated feature you would not be able to block out completely. We are already using an increasing number of integrated applications and devices to monitor and manage almost every aspect of our lives. We manage and synchronise our private and business calendars, finances, health and well-being activities, communication, and even simply tracking time.

Enhancing usability encapsulates a paradox. In the process of making computers truly 'invisible', we transform the user interface into an intuitive and graphic, gesture, or verbal input/feedback system, while gradually losing our ability to directly control and influence the computer itself. The oversimplification of data representation also carries some cognitive risks. It plays into our tendency to 'flatten' and ignore complexities. This doesn't necessarily make things simpler, or better. In his excellent essay, *The Cognitive Style of PowerPoint*, information design pioneer Edward Tufte discusses the role PowerPoint templates play in compromising verbal and spatial reasoning – they may even directly cause corrupt and compromised data representation. Tufte even argues that the use of PowerPoint presentations might have indirectly caused the *Challenger Space Shuttle* disaster. [11]

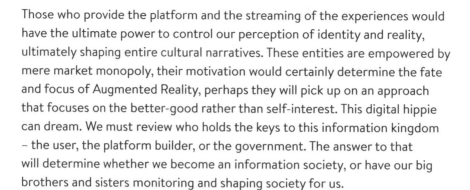

5.0 Off With Their Heads

Those who provide the platform and the streaming of the experiences would have the ultimate power to control our perception of identity and reality, ultimately shaping entire cultural narratives. These entities are empowered by mere market monopoly, their motivation would certainly determine the fate and focus of Augmented Reality, perhaps they will pick up on an approach that focuses on the better-good rather than self-interest. This digital hippie can dream. We must review who holds the keys to this information kingdom – the user, the platform builder, or the government. The answer to that will determine whether we become an information society, or have our big brothers and sisters monitoring and shaping society for us.

The expansion of having a diffused digital experiential layering through mobile or spatial interaction would be the expansion of user behavioural surveillance via governments and corporate bodies and the 'Sousveillance' – coined by Mann – referring to the registration of actions by the users [via mobile devices and wearables]. The more our experiences rely on digital mediation, the more they can be monitored, hacked into and controlled, making us more vulnerable to be exploited by governments, commercial interest groups, and hackers.

Augmented Reality also gives us the power to filter-out content and 'things'. We could edit-out or create 'undesirable reality blockers' against negative and undesirable elements. As Dr. Mann defines it as Augmediated Reality: "[Augmediated is] a port-manteau of augmented and mediated, referring to an ability not merely to add overlays [augment] but also to subtract [e.g. deliberately diminish] or modify."[12]

> All our problems could literally, disappear 'Ex boyfriends – never to be seen again', 'Carbs? What carbs? I don't see any carbs in my reality', 'Assholes, be gone!'

An existence truly coloured by rose-tinted glasses! Augmentation in the public space may also pose an interesting alternative to imposing certain restrictions, such as dress codes for females within orthodox religious societies, or built-in modesty filters for those who cannot deal with temptation.
If it sounds like a far-fetched application – you're wrong. Mann & Fung's *EyeTap* could remove elements in the physical environment in Real-Time. This application can be used for ad blocking, allowing users to regain control over

the augmented content pushed into their physical space. This, in turn, could provide a heightened sense of personal liberation through the application of content filtering, but what may be seen as a recipe for control could quickly become a tool of avoidance and divisiveness. This option could too easily be turned into an offensive and discriminative act, where undesired realities, conflicting notions or undesirable elements of society are simply eliminated. The notion of Augmented Architecture in terms of the construction of physical and experiential layering and elimination within a spatial and social context, would become a core concern as well as an experiential opportunity.

> Well, we can't all be coders and programmers, but becoming completely reliant on smart systems also makes us reliant on the developer, platform builder, and device to make judgement calls regarding our privacy and safety. What happens when it streams or purges data we may not intend to share or delete, miscommunicates content, overrides our decision-making, or actually takes control over us? Consider that, in an augmented world, data and interaction would be directly embedded into our physical space. As ubiquitous computing systems develop, applications, devices and interfaces are being built to streamline and anticipate our actions and choices in a fraction of a second. In return, we trust them to protect our data and make the right choices for us. As the barrier between the physical and the virtual breaks, how dependent will we be, and how invasive will these digital hiccups become?

Another 9-11 tragedy doesn't need to physically occur if all users simultaneously experience it happening via their augmented systems. Issues of privacy and security need to be considered throughout the implementation of Augmented Reality. Even less drastic intrusions into our augmented space, such as cyber-bullying or identity theft, could carry devastating consequences. The emergence of protective services will be inevitable, including anti-surveillance and off-switch devices, sophisticated data and identity back-up systems, protective garments, establishing tech-free zones to regain control against content hacking, and filtering third-party streaming content.

Besides the protective solutions we need to take preventative actions. Not having legislative restrictions for the application of Augmented Reality may

enable our physical environment to become the ultimate 'sandbox' platform, where literally anything can digitally happen to us. Endless possibilities may sound exciting, however this also means accepting the possibility that our reality may be taken over without our being able to control it – the wet dream of any marketeer, tyrant or terror organisation.

5.4 Resist the Disruption

So here we are, with the possibility to make all our dreams come [digitally] true. Will we be able to harness this creative platform for the better, or will our human nature abuse this new technology to offend, control and disrupt our environment? In fact – can we scrap the 'disruption' trend? 'Anti-disruptive' researchers like MIT's Cyborg Anthropologist Amber Case call for the creation of human-centric and calming technology – or as I like to call it, 'Constructive Innovation'.

I would love to believe that Augmented Reality will mostly bring [or only bring] positive impact. Yet, to achieve that, we must learn from previous mistakes, and assume the worst to design the best. During my Industrial Design studies, one of my professors encouraged us to hand over our prototypes to another random student, and ask them to use it – or, more accurately, abuse it – in any way they choose to test the durability and usability of our designs. When I expressed concern about the fate of my model, he simply said,

> "You can't control all the idiots, but statistically you will have a few doing all sorts of stuff you didn't want them to with your design. It is your role as a designer to anticipate and prevent this as much as possible."

This advice holds true for technology as it does physical products. Technology is **not** the issue – it is perfect. Humans are the ones that are flawed. We are flawed because of our diverse needs, our irrational behaviours, and our endless attempts to break things and disassemble in new ways. This is how we create technology to begin with.

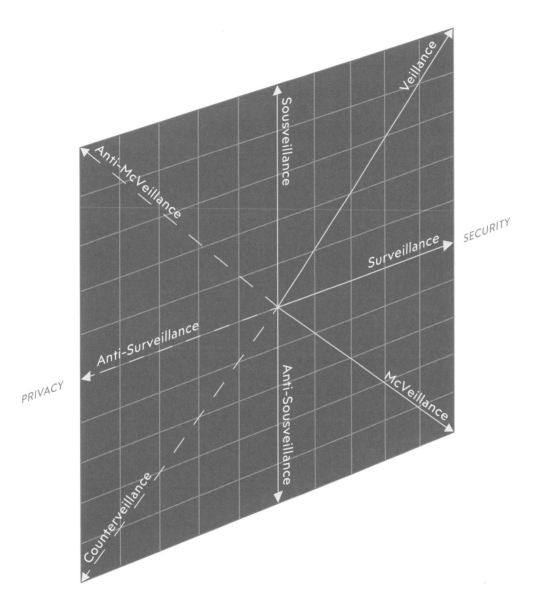

The 8 Veillances
Author's Image 2017.
[Adaptation from Mann, 2012]

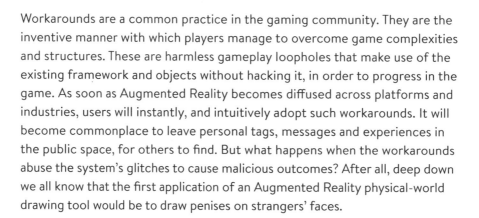

5.0

Off With Their Heads

Workarounds are a common practice in the gaming community. They are the inventive manner with which players manage to overcome game complexities and structures. These are harmless gameplay loopholes that make use of the existing framework and objects without hacking it, in order to progress in the game. As soon as Augmented Reality becomes diffused across platforms and industries, users will instantly, and intuitively adopt such workarounds. It will become commonplace to leave personal tags, messages and experiences in the public space, for others to find. But what happens when the workarounds abuse the system's glitches to cause malicious outcomes? After all, deep down we all know that the first application of an Augmented Reality physical-world drawing tool would be to draw penises on strangers' faces.

The dark web was initially constructed to allow privacy and anonymity. This platform serves as a safety blanket in a Big Brother world. Slowly but surely, it has evolved into a 'safe haven' for digital freedom seekers, anti-establishment activists, and, naturally, criminal activity. Yet we need not go so far as the dark web. The World Wide Web, social media and instant messaging apps have made the virtual and digital space dense with information, and easy to manipulate. Digital communication enables messaging and recruiting for criminal acts and terrorist activity. Isis commonly uses the Telegram and Twitter messaging apps to preach, recruit and activate followers, demonstrating how an open communication framework enables free rein use for the best and the worst of us. American families of Isis attack victims in France, Belgium, and Orlando have gone as far as filing lawsuits against Twitter for enabling this activity and playing "a uniquely essential role in the development of ISIS's image, its success in recruiting members from around the world, and its ability to carry out attacks and intimidate its enemies."[13]

This is one of the first signs of users beginning to shift away from the idealised view of open-source content, instead looking to platform facilitators to provide community rules, etiquette and standards. This tendency accounts for issues such as identity and safety, but also when looking at the quality and trustworthiness of the content itself. Social media feeds have become main information streams, and users' first instincts were to follow, like, share and believe the digital stories easily, especially since they supply a Real-Time stream of information, and the ability to instantly participate or provide feedback.

This has caused two polarising effects. It has severely reduced the role and authority of the mainstream media in certain segments of the population, and, at the same time, the overwhelming quantity of fake news content is creating a new need for verification and control.

> Within the augmented context, we will have a greater need for guidance since the experience of the Augmediated world could potentially be more personalised, more intense and more invasive. Restrictions – especially due to the inability to control head mounted and haptic devices – may leave users exposed to anything from hacking to inappropriate and misleading information. With many applications targeting gaming, education, and entertainment for kids and teens, will we be able to control the content flow to ensure it adheres to an appropriate standard?

Digital platforms help us to communicate and express our identities in new ways. They are built to provide easier access and information delivery, which makes them more user-friendly, but also aids in flattening the representation of the user as the accelerated digital stream flow sublimely encourages content curation versus genuine content creation. This, in turn, manifests a digital identity that, in a way, is not fully authentic or representative of our physical persona and behaviour. We may portray a different or better version of ourselves, but whether we like it or not our digital and physical identity are intertwined. Cyber-bullying, catfishing [forming an online relationship with someone by creating a fictional online persona], and identity theft all reinforce the fact that we are as vulnerable to misrepresentation of our digital identity as we are to misrepresentation of our physical identity – maybe even more so.

As our augmenting options expand, so too would the ways augmentation modifies our physical presence and identity. Using Real-Time face tracking and projection mapping, Nobumichi Asai created *Omote*[14] and *Kagami*,[15] to superimpose interactive images as digital 'makeup'. Interestingly titled 'Real-Time Face Generator', it raises fantastic possibilities for our presence as a new art form, where augmentation and interactive media transform our physical being.

5.0 Off With Their Heads

But how far do we go with altering our identity, and what happens when someone invades, duplicates or abuses your augmented or physical identity? Knowing how problematic identity theft is today, imagine how terrible it would feel to have someone out in the world augmenting into you? Augmented physical enhancement is easier and safer to reproduce and reverse than physical alterations. Imagine someone walking into your house or workplace with your face on. Or maybe they don't choose to use your face, but they might take other aspects of your identity – your speech pattern, your scent, your bum.

Another famous legal dispute within the *Second Life* virtual universe is the case of Anshe Chung, a *Second Life* avatar and business mogul who managed to earn a high monetary value and a business empire, both within and outside the virtual space, based on the creation and trade of virtual assets and experiences. Chung [the avatar] was featured on the cover of Business Week, and in several other leading business media, including CNN, Fortune magazine and the Red Herring. Chung's influence had become so great that 'she' was literally a legislative or 'ruling' force within her 'Dreamland' regions.

Yet she is most famous for being the target of the first live virtual sexual assault, conducted during a live virtual interview, where she was attacked by animated genitalia. This attack may seem like a harmless prank, however the virtual realm is connected to and reflective of the physical world, and we must have clear definitions about what constitutes assault and damage. Even if a physical persona was not harmed, sexual harassment or verbal assault causes trauma and distress – just as in the physical world – and should be punishable by law in the same way. But who would police the cyber world? While many governments are building cyber task forces and units, they are mainly aimed at preventing people from breaking existing 'physical world' laws online – with a specific focus on topics such as online sexual luring of minors, illegal online transactions and identity theft.

The superimposed digital layer over our physical world will change our perspective on the idea that 'what happens in digital, stays in digital'. That separation between the physical and the digital will no longer be relevant, and we may see physical laws and law enforcement applied to and interpreted in our digital existence. This will require the institution of more dominant cyber legislation and law enforcement units, an area in which we are lagging.

Privacy is a key issue that will need to be addressed prior to the widespread diffusion of augmentation. Having a device that streams [personalised] content and interaction is a great feature, but it includes private data and unique usage patterns. How can we protect ourselves from unlawful data access? The truth is, we can't. At least not completely. It's a scary notion, but if our information stream is accessed by a third party. Any person or entity with access to our augmented stream would gain insight into our most intimate conscious and subconscious cognitive and behavioural drives. They would gain insight and access to our triggers, intentions and actions.

Data gathering and trading within an information economy could lead to severe issues related to surveillance and control, including intrusive targeted marketing. Those abilities and strategies hold a highly disturbing scope, whether they are generated by platform developers, content creators, bullies or hackers. Whereas the use of smart devices for collecting data was intended to provide positive impact and improve our lives, even in crime solving. However, this was not the case for *Alexa*, Amazon's digital IoT assistant, that had been questioned about a murder 'it' might have witnessed.[16] The idea of having devices and entities that enable complete access and the ability to quantify our everyday behaviours, without the users' knowledge, feedback or control, regarding its storage and usage is somewhat disturbing. Consider *My best friend Cayla*,[17] a Bluetooth interactive toy designed to

5.0 Off With Their Heads

conduct simple Q&A conversation with a child, via a child safe web search. This toy is far from a fully developed Artificial intelligence algorithm that is close to singularity. In fact, complex/ambitious questions are asked via a human operator who controls the device [remotely] to provide the appropriate answers, while gathering valuable user data. Even such a device has already been hacked, and repurposed to read aloud the best-selling erotica novel *Fifty Shades of Grey*.[18] **Not quite** the fine bedtime literature you want for your child.

It becomes pretty tricky when we consider Augmented Reality's specific features – a technology where optimisation relies on Real-Time, location-based, sensory-based interactive content delivery and an interaction device.

> As an interface, Augmented Reality is a data goldmine that can analyse behavioural patterns, psychological drives and actions. The combination of big and deep data mining with behavioural interaction means the exploitation of the technology to apply targeted marketing, 'push' behavioural tactics and data-based classification.

It is somewhat disheartening, since this may cause a data-based polarisation of society via algorithm-based behavioural content, quantifying us as data streams, subverting content and context of behaviour in order to compartment our content stream rather than building on organic qualities and independent interaction flow. This creates an awkward situation where humans are truly being classified, quantified and even discriminated based on the 'sum' of their data. Something not completely new, we see this applied via credit rating in the US, insurance companies that track data to evaluate risks.

Social and civil protection laws are inevitable. China has already made steps towards banning the *Pokémon GO* app because of 'concern for users' personal safety'.[19] Since access to other online platforms and social media are restricted, this might be a first step in controlling augmented and virtual content on a wider scale. And let's not forget that technology works both ways – security and privacy protection applications will be in high demand. Today, demand for ad blockers and paid platforms that enable privacy, such as VPNs, is on the rise for a reason.

We are no strangers to attacks, bullying and even sexual assaults in the virtual realm. Yet can the use of an offensive augmented tag, sexual slur or virtual action be prevented, avoided or even considered a crime, since it did not 'actually' happen? As cyber laws tighten for online platforms, so would a moral and criminal code for augmented content. Since we would regard augmented reality as an extension of our reality and physical identities, augmented crimes may end up being prosecuted and treated similarly to physical crimes.

Users may have become complacent about digital and privacy threats, however cyber security is a growing segment in the tech industry. Security protocols, software and hardware advancements are constantly being developed to balance usability with security. New identity and behavioural verification protocols allow access – including biometrics and Security Information and Event Management [SIEM] technology[20] – while elevating security. Anti-surveillance techniques are already being developed with the sole purpose of protecting the user's privacy. These include secure devices, digital blocking stickers, and print designs incorporated into garments [such as *HyperFace*][21] that provide camouflage from facial recognition and user tracking. As we develop more of these technologies, we may find we have the capability to be somewhat or completely digitally anonymous while navigating augmented spaces.

5.0

Off With Their Heads

5.5 Hacking Reality

We learn about our reality through exploration, observation and play. Play is one of our earliest social interactions. As we grow older, we are expected to demonstrate these learnings, showing more meaningful and purposeful context and narrative, and shifting play from an open platform to a game that includes distinctive rules and outcomes. Games teach us about reward systems, social hierarchies and cultural boundaries – everything we need to integrate and function within society. At a certain point, we are expected to completely separate the serious reality from the playful fantasy. As adults, we are expected to approach our work and studies in a meaningful way – meaning not by the path of playfulness. As time passes, we discover that the assumption that these activities should be detached from playfulness has proven to be incorrect. Integrating playful and 'purposeless' activities, features and systems can add a layer of intrinsic bonding that has the potential to increase engagement, creativity, and productivity. It supports skill and knowledge acquisition, triggering various brain functions that aid in processing and linking information in a richer manner. The term 'serious play' was developed to describe an array of methodologies that aspire to integrate playfulness and meaningful action/knowledge acquisition.

> The role of technology as a facilitator of play, knowledge acquisition and serious play also changes. If, in the past, it took 'a village to raise a child', today it takes an online app. The role of the adult caretaker and educator has been handed over, and streamed via digital media.

Televised programmes, such as Sesame Street and Dora the Explorer help children to acquire basic skills, knowledge and values. We learn to build the foundations for our perception of reality using media and digital aids. The long-term physical and sensory effects of increased exposure to interactive streaming are being researched, but the most interesting of these is the evolving perception of reality. How will the augmented-native child experience reality? In a sense, they will find a non-digital reality incomplete. Will it sharpen the difference between 'realness' and 'fakeness'? We may be witnessing a post-realism generation, that is not interested in the bare reality, or a post-digital generation, that would have a clear distinction between the

THE DIFFERENCE CAN BE SUMMED UP IN ONE WORD: AUTHORIZATION. I DON'T NEED AUTHORIZATION TO GET IN. IT'S THE WORD THAT INSTANTLY TRANSFORMS ME FROM THE WORLD'S MOST WANTED HACKER TO ONE OF THE MOST WANTED SECURITY EXPERTS IN THE WORLD. JUST LIKE MAGIC.

— Kevin Mitnick, 2011 [22]

5.0 Off With Their Heads

digital and physical layer, valuing the physical layer more for its authenticity. Most likely, reality and Augmented Reality would become two sides of the same coin, one defined and complemented by the other.

Intrinsic motivation is becoming increasingly important in our society. Within work environments, employers are looking for systems that keep employees engaged and eager to actively contribute to the organisation's activities and success. Monetary reward and professional progress are important, but as the lines between personal and professional identities blur [count how many times a person self-identifies by name and immediately after by their profession], the more frequently we encounter intrinsic motivation as a key factor for work aspirations. Personal ambition and gaining influence. Alignment between organisational goals, and personal vision and conviction. A sense of belonging. General enjoyment.

> Whereas previous generations may have been satisfied with having and keeping a job, we are increasingly looking for meaning and gratification. This is partially because having a purposeful task alone does not sufficiently engage us. We require intrinsic gratification to keep engaging in the game. The other reason is that we have increasingly been conditioned to look for gratification everywhere. These intrinsic motivations and embedded triggers become a common tactic used in marketing, advertising and media. Of course, due to commercial needs or true conviction of their necessity, developers and makers will look towards built-in systems that maintain the user's interest and engagement longer, deeper and more frequently.

The application of Augmented Reality will undoubtedly be used for commercial and retail purposes quite quickly. Retail marketing experts are eager to use Augmented Reality to boost the declining retail landscape. It's a fantastic tool to improve in-store experience, advertise product, and ultimately for data analysis. Sadly, within the free platform model, direct and indirect advertisements and behavioural triggers would be layered on top. Our public landscape might be flooded with pop-up banners, infomercials and advertisements. It may well be that the physical landscape would have to tone down on physical visual input to become a 'white space' for digital layering.

After all, this could always be updated and accessed to serve as interactive content and an entertainment platform. We might witness our cities and public spaces turn into white spaces, blocks and blocks of neutral facades that enable a better application of digital content.

> In this age of hyper-connected digital and content environment, an expanded level of experience has already stretched beyond our physical reality, consuming surreal and extreme experiences that bend our perception and stimulation level. In our not-so-distant future, Augmented Reality will sit at the tip of our noses or our senses, yet this same vicinity to our perceptual and physical identity may mean that we would lose substantial cognitive filters and processes, allowing platform makers, corporations and hackers to have access to our realities.

I can already see the modern interpretation of *War of the Worlds*, a hyper-realistic alien invasion movie promo that would create mass hysteria and great promotional value. What measures would be taken to protect users from an intrusive invasion of their reality, and who would define the legal and moral boundaries of reality 'ownership'? These big questions need to be asked sooner rather than later.

Real-Time augmented filters will provide beautification layers that could have projected makeup, or other facial and body feature enhancement. These could be developed to a far more creative and expressive layer than we currently have, creating endless possibilities and representations of one's presence and identity through the use of augmentation. Will our identity be defined by the digital content that we apply to our physical body, and will it cause further fragmentation or enrich our social relationships, interactions and rituals? It may sound hypocritical to debate this, since procedures that are much more intrusive – such as plastic surgery, tattooing and makeup – are perfectly legal and socially acceptable. But Identity ownership and manipulation can take a completely different twist with the use of augmented facial mapping. Identity hacking would be a much easier task once one's appearance and physical features can be duplicated and applied.

"ALICE: WHY, SOMETIMES I'VE BE-LIEVED AS MANY AS SIX IMPOSSI-BLE THINGS BEFORE BREAKFAST."

— Lewis Carroll, Alice's Adventures in Wonderland

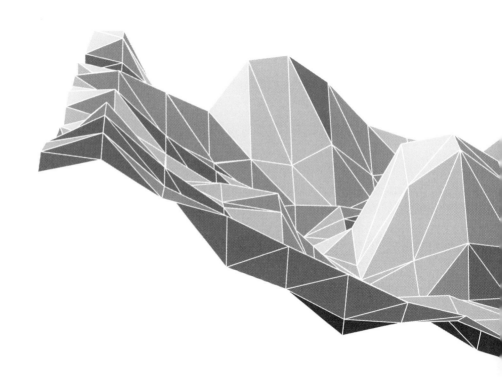

6.0 CATERPILLARS & BUTTERFLIES

Caterpillar & Butterflies

'Reality' Redefined

Once we accept the evident advantages and benefits Augmented Reality offers at the experiential level, we need to consider how it will influence our perception of reality itself.

6.1 Grasping Reality

Plato's cave is an allegory for the human concept of reality. Although this was originally used to explain the value of knowledge acquisition, it's also a great description of how limited our perception of reality is. In the allegory, there is a cave in which a group of people live, chained to the cave's wall and unable to turn their heads. Their faces are turned away from the entrance of the cave, and their only input is the shadows cast upon the wall. One of these prisoners is a philosopher who is freed from his shackles, and manages to see the true nature of their reality – the actual figures, objects, and source of the shadows – which are not visible to the group in the cave. The philosopher attempts to convince the group about what he has seen, so they too can be free and experience the true nature of reality. Yet he encounters resistance, as the others refuse to replace what they consider as the only possible reality.

This allegory reflects on our lives on many levels. We construct our perception of reality based on a limited input system. In an open-source information age, with unlimited input channels and sources, the need to be 'freed' does not seem to be relevant anymore. As consumers and creators of content, we become active participants in forming our own reality.

We may have influence, but we still need to filter and evaluate the endless stream of content coming our way. Monitoring this data influx is a time and energy consuming task. The amount and immediacy of available content inevitably compromises how we process data quality, nuance and reliability. This forces us to rely on embedded filtering systems, with preference-built algorithms [which may be custom-tailored in the future] that make these choices for us. Artificial Intelligence technology and behaviour-based data analysis are more likely to gain our trust. With analysis systems that could simulate human thought and react on a human cognitive level, Augmented Reality would be the best platform where it could be implemented. Augmented Reality has the potential to achieve a true state of mixed reality – where the synergy between data analysis systems and digital simulation blend into our everyday action and interaction.

This is indeed an extremely exciting prospect. Yet, with Plato's cave in mind, we need to remember how impressionable we are. Especially as these processes reach unprecedented levels of physical proximity and trust. Even when we seek objective foundations and safeguards, our choices derive from personal, social and spatial proximity. In short, we tend to more quickly trust people, cultures and environments that we can relate to.

> **In the age of the data spectacle we merge social systems and content input into one data channel. With multiple new channels lighting everything in our overcrowded cave, we are mesmerised by the dancing shadows projected onto the walls.**

We find it harder to distinguish between the remote and the near, fabricated and authentic, and in our desperate need to make sense of it all, we fall into the traps of confirmation biases, more easily accepting online feeds as facts and our online friends as soulmates. Perhaps this is a necessary reaction, yet it results in the shifting boundaries of our perception of reality, content and social hierarchies, ultimately shaping personal and social moralities and values. But with a constant augmented content, the differentiating between the real-world content and the augmented layer might be altogether impossible.

6.0 Caterpillar to Butterflies

Plato's Cave
Reality is interpreted via
our [physical and cognitive]
limitations, as well as the medium
and context by which our
content [input] is delivered.
Author's Image, 2017.

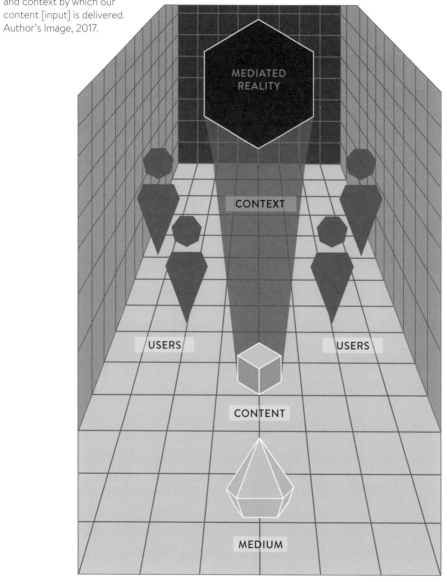

MEDIATED
REALITY

CONTEXT

USERS   USERS

CONTENT

MEDIUM

UNMEDIATED
REALITY

6.2 The Real Fake

Let's begin by exploring our perception of 'realness'. 'Real' and 'fake' are
co-dependent terms – each validates and defines the quality of the other.
When we come to define the 'realness' of 'things', the criteria are quite simple.
The term 'real' is normally related to two core qualities: the need for objects to
actually exist within the physical reality, and *authenticity* – the objective source
of the subject's existence. The first is normally measured by whether or not the
subject can be sensed or processed via a tangible input or sensation [including
having 'real feelings' for someone]. For the second, let's use the example of
faux leather. Although it might look, feel and smell like real leather, and even
mimic all the qualities of leather for its designated purpose, it is artificially
manufactured or synthesised in order to obtain these characteristics. This is
where realness becomes an important cultural term – since we use authenticity
and the tangibility of experiences to determine quality, value, and personal
status. The entire value systems of products, entities, institutes, and brands
rely heavily on establishing a claim of authenticity, and often include systems
of unique features that can be evaluated to maintain the claim.

Integrating a digital layer positions 'realness' in a different context. Since a
digital layer is inherently synthetic, constantly shifting on the spectrum
between 'window' and 'mirror' attributes, we move to a different value system
that is much more ambiguous. Innovation and technology are largely based on
creating an open process for diffusion and creation, removed from traditional
systems of centralisation and control. This might create a more dynamic value
system, yet leaves the user with a central role in establishing the 'realness' and
value of the subject.

> We might still consider the qualities of the virtual realm as artificial
> since "...online worlds are simply another arena, alongside offline
> worlds, for expressive practice, and there is no reason to privilege
> one over the other."[1] But the cognitive value we give it is in many
> cases as influential as [if not more than] a physical realm.

6.0 Caterpillar to Butterflies

Our individual cognitive comprehension of 'realness' is based on:

#01 Cultural/societal acquired knowledge
[what we are told/taught to be real]

#02 Experiential acquired knowledge
[what we have experienced as real in the past,
and thus assume to be real in the present]

#03 Sensory input and processing
[the actual experience]

#04 External factors and situational disposition
[environmental, contextual, circumstantial etc.]

This is hardly the manner to negotiate a universal or communal sense of 'real' or 'fake' value. We cannot avoid 'unpacking' our reality on an individual sensory level, however technology plays an important role in contextualising the experience. With technology targeting a more personalised content flow, it's no wonder that we construct a culture [or cult] of individualism, where we are utterly convinced that our specific reflective fragment represents an accurate depiction of reality.

The real flaw within our perception of reality is rooted in the most wonderful and imperfect processing machine used to comprehend it – our brain. Cognitive psychology has proven that the repression, alteration and implantation of memories enables us to modify, create and erase real events and experiences. This implies that our perception of reality is fluid, with the potential to be manipulated. Even if we consider a hypothetical neutral space – which offers a cohesive, complete and objective context [and please, let me know when you find this space] – we are still limited and conditioned by our individual experience of realness. Our perception of the ultimate definition of 'real' is heavily based on our individual perception, which by definition is subjective. Only the collective accumulation of all individuals composes a 'universal' reality, but individuals can rarely [if at all] map or experience a universal reality.

Augmented Reality, in contrast with Virtual Reality, has the advantage of offering a certain level of hypermediacy. When looking at issues of immediacy, hypermediacy and remediation Bolter and Grusin state that "Hypermediacy can also manifest itself in the creation of multimedia spaces such as theme parks or video arcades. In every manifestation, hypermediacy makes us aware of the medium or media reminding us of our desire for immediacy."[2] Let's recall, however, that 'knowing' that something is not real does not prevent us from experiencing it as real. Our minds allow us to emotionally and mentally immerse in a fabricated world, shedding a tear whilst reading a sad story, shrieking with fear as a killer creeps behind the victim in a thriller movie, and admiring television characters for their fabricated actions. As Augmented Reality technology improves – delivering Real-Time, user-targeted content – the line between real and augmented experiences will blur. A new perception of reality will emerge, as well as those who would truly experience a 'digital reality' – who view the 'virtual continuum' as simply the 'reality continuum'.

In order to achieve this perception of reality, we need to create experiences that align well with physical reality, feedback and cognitive perception. Masahiro Mori, a robotics professor from the Tokyo Institute of Technology, defined *"The Uncanny Valley"*[3] model in 1970. Mori was exploring human reaction to human-like robots, AKA androids. What he discovered is that our positive feelings about robots grow in alignment with the robot's resemblance to human physical appearance. For example, an industrial machine might not evoke any emotion, while there is more affinity for a toy robot. As the robot's features more closely resemble those of a human, there is a certain spectrum where positive emotions drop and turn into a negative sensation of eeriness and rejection. Mori named this section the *"Uncanny Valley"*. This spectrum occurs once the robot's appearance starts to get very close to human appearance, yet still gives a 'fake' human impression. For example, a prosthetic limb that resembles a real limb, but is evidently not, evokes this same sensation. Once the humanoid resemblance increases and reaches a 'fully human' appearance, our affinity towards it once again soars.

The HBO television series *Westworld* [based on the 1973 movie] explores the concept of reality simulation through android role-playing experiences inside a massive entertainment park. An interesting feature in the series is how the

6.0 Caterpillar to Butterflies

park developers purposefully incorporate Artificial Intelligence algorithms to enhance the visitor's experience of the android by having the android portray 'unnecessary' human gestures, such as tucking a loose lock of hair behind an ear or 'unconsciously' touching their own lips. These little imperfections, or behavioural 'hiccups', are mundane behaviours that create a sense of intimacy, as the visitors recognise themselves and other humans in these gestures. Between Siri's lame knock-knock jokes and the Rumba autonomous vacuuming robot getting stuck in the corner of the room, inserting quirky 'human-like' behaviours [whether intentionally or unintentionally] can unveil nuances of imperfection that trigger a sense of trust and affiliation.

What we can conclude is that, in order to create convincing augmented experiences, we need to create engagement tools that produce high-fidelity perceptual elements, on both the physical and mental level. To be perceived as 'real', the experience needs to synchronise with our multisensory processing systems. This could be challenging and time consuming to perfectly simulate, but – great news! – it would be layered on a high-definition, multisensory experience that we already know how to interact with, and that has an embedded social platform. We simply call it 'reality'.

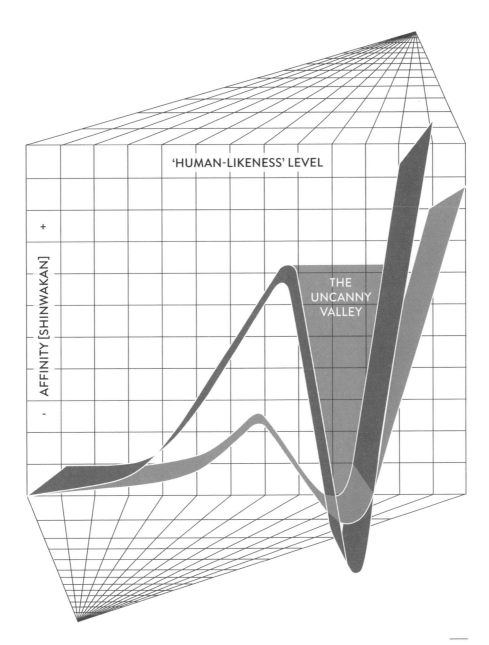

'HUMAN-LIKENESS' LEVEL

+

AFFINITY [SHINWAKAN]

-

THE
UNCANNY
VALLEY

'The Uncanny Valley'
Author's image, 2017.
[Adaptation from Masahiro Mori, 1970].

6.0

Caterpillar to Butterflies

6.3 I See, Therefore It Is

Many factors influence our perception of reality, including physiological and biological characteristics, evolutionary and survival-driven behaviours, influenced behavioural patterns, acquired acknowledge, and even social consensus. We cannot separate, for example, the value and influence of our emotional input in processing our reality [or vice versa]. Certain psychological patterns, such as anxiety, have been found to be both socially conditioned and also hereditary. In a famous Dutch research study on babies conceived during World War II, researchers found that elevated traumatic incidents can influence the mental and physiological conditioning for generations to come.

Today we know that all neurological processes occur in the human brain, including the generation of emotional reactions and sensations. Our brains are sophisticated input machines. On a physiological level, we simultaneously collect data via multiple sensory devices [eyes, ears, mouth, skin], and receptors [taste buds, nervous system]. Various neurological processes organise the input sensation channelled through our sensory receptors, and process them into vision [the sense of seeing], auditory [the sense of hearing], tactile [the sense of touch], olfactory [the sense of smell], vestibular [the sense of balance], gustation [the sense of taste], interoception [the sense of internal organ function] and proprioception [the sense of one's body position in space]. Sensory processing and multisensory integration are combined with cultural and individual contextualisation, and then translated into our sense of reality.

Even though various forms of sensory augmentation could be applied to reach different aspects of immersion, Augmented Reality development is primarily focused on the visual aspect. This is understandable, since 70% of our sensory receptors relate to visual processing.[4] For the digital layer to be convincingly perceived as part of the environment, it will need to mimic our vision system. What makes our vision unique [and gives computer vision developers the biggest challenge] is our ability to have a Semantic Depth of Field.[5] This means the ability to form a visual focal point while blurring the background, which helps us focus our attention – cinematic and photographic depth of field aid in simulating this focused intention. Another unique human feature is our ability to identify geometric shapes, understand objects' spatial arrangement,

translate and form visual patterns and hierarchies, and – most importantly – understand their semantic meaning in relation to each other and to the environment they are in, even if we only obtain partial or distorted information. This is where image capturing and processing devices start encountering new difficulties – from a simple perspective and vicinity problem, such as a bug approaching the lens and covering 20% of the field of view, or balancing the exposure when a camera is taking a snapshot of an interracial couple, to deciphering variables within the context of the object. For example, when Google invited employees' kids to march in front a parked self-driving car on Halloween to help its algorithm identify costumed children.[6]

Yet the key for a truly convincing Augmented Reality implementation is the application of a seamless multisensory experience. Although we have a wide understanding of individual sensory effects, the impact of combined multisensory stimulation has not been fully explored due to the difficulty with measuring the wide range of non-linear interactions and impact. A recent study conducted by Schreuder, van Erp, Toet, & Kallen,[7] attempted to create a more coherent outline of a multisensory response framework. Some considerations can be drawn from their research for Augmented Reality as an added layer of stimuli:

» As emotional responses to an environment are context dependent, there will need to be a responsive way to 'tune' the level of augmentation on both mono and multisensory levels.

» Seamless application of multisensory stimuli within the augmented system and in combination with the environment may positively enhance experiential aspects. Inconsistency and overlap of multisensory stimuli could result in a negative response to the augmented input, resulting in a negative emotional context of the experience, and the technology.

The recommendation is to limit and phase in the multisensory aspects of augmentation until we can perfect the core individual elements.

Niccolo Machiavelli, Renaissance man and founder of modern political science, saw mass communication as a tool that could be used to shape public opinions and political marketing. Though many have attempted to colour

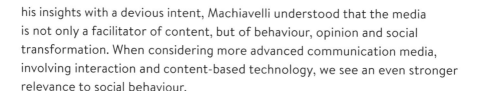

his insights with a devious intent, Machiavelli understood that the media is not only a facilitator of content, but of behaviour, opinion and social transformation. When considering more advanced communication media, involving interaction and content-based technology, we see an even stronger relevance to social behaviour.

'The medium is the message' implies precisely that – technology shapes social interaction and knowledge systems via the content delivery method itself. We have seen this from scrolls [ancient knowledge], to printed publishing [common knowledge], to screens [user led], mobile devices [user made] and integrated surfaces [fluid access]. Augmented Reality could transcend reality itself to become a digital communication medium; a transcending – borderline spiritual – concept that communicates and exists on a unified physical-digital frequency.

6.4 Post- and Hyper-Realism

Remember our discussion about science fiction anticipating scientific and technological advances? Consider *Flatland: A Romance of Many Dimensions*, Edwin Abbott Abbott's novella that was first published in 1884. The satirical story describes a two-dimensional world [AKA Flatland], where males and females are represented by geometric shapes. After a visit to the three-dimensional dimension [AKA Spaceland] a male polygon, called "A Square", reveals the true nature of his existence and the possibility of lower and higher order dimensions. This story presents the idea that spatial perception is a relative, and – hold on to your seats – there is a scientific theory that supports it. Based on String Theory's holographic principle, a group of physicists concluded that it is quite possible that we are two-dimensional beings that merely have a perceptual notion that we exist in a three-dimensional space. It is possible that the universe itself is an information network, and we decipher its information as a notion of volume and space. This implies that a physical and a digitally-generated three-dimensional experience are equally as 'real', differing from one another only by whether they are man-made or part of the existing information network in our realm.

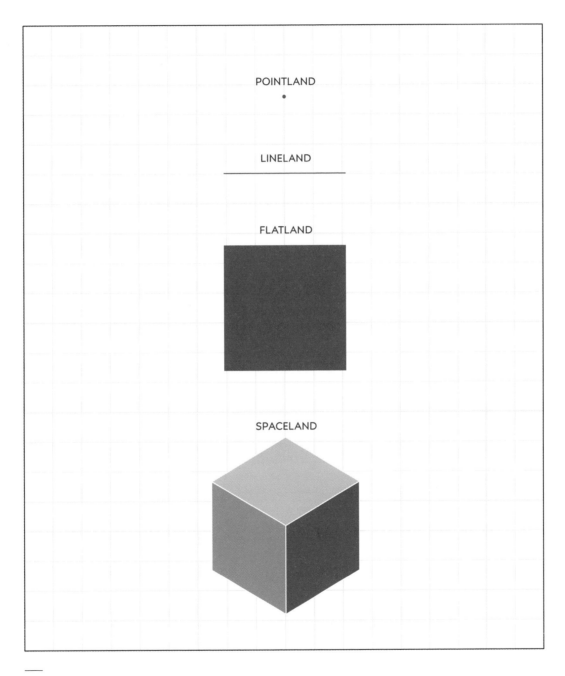

POINTLAND

LINELAND

FLATLAND

SPACELAND

—

From Pointland to Spaceland

Author's Image, 2017.

6.0 Caterpillar to Butterflies

Augmented Reality has the potential to eventually cease to represent a technological definition, transforming into an inseparable expression of reality. As soon as our brains become accustomed to being duped into experiencing a digital layer as an integral part of the physical environment, it would become [in all regards] the only reality. We are already living in a technological post-realism world, which allows us to create high-fidelity digital representations of reality. We constantly document, record, store, rehash, and replay reality via multimedia and data storage devices. Yet authentic experiences are instantaneous – Augmented Reality would allow us to form a Real-Time stream of interactive augmented content, achieving a continuous flow and alternate reality state within the virtual continuum.

Our sophisticated brain-machines constantly collect and decipher input, converting it into patterns and feedback. We have several mechanisms that place our sensory processing on a higher level than intelligent machines. Namely, we can contextualise multiple abstract signals and connotations to create a cohesive perception of reality. This is due to our ability to have associated learning [filling the necessary gaps to understand a situation and its context], conditional learning [connecting certain behavioural phenomena and feedback patterns with each other [classical or 'Pavlovian' conditioning], and the ability to establish certain social and behavioural hierarchies. These paradigms are very much dependent on cultural and environmental context and circumstances. For example, if we see a person wearing a police uniform arresting another person, we assume the uniformed individual is indeed an employee of the police, we associate that person with the values the police represent, and we tend to evaluate the arrested person as a criminal. In a corrupt society, we might be more likely to assume that the policeman might be harassing the person for no reason. Adding another layer, if there was a film crew and camera in the background, we would be likely to believe that we have witnessed a scene from a movie.

Contextual and cultural nuances are things that computers and some people on the autism spectrum find difficult to decipher. They might be taught to associate them, but may still lack the ability to form new associations and pattern recognition outside their 'pattern library'. Other decision-making factors relate to the possibility that our belief processes are built on false

positives [believing something is real when it's not], or false negatives [not believing something is real when it is]. From an evolutionary standpoint, instinctively complying with the hints provided by reality tended to aid humans in escaping predators.

Our perception of reality is also reliant on what is called 'truth proximity', a process that creates hierarchy in our belief systems – both inside-out and outside-in. Meaning that we construct our perception of reality based on our own experiences, and then cross reference with those who are close to us

Input/Output/Reality Perception
Sensory input, our celebral processing and our
perception of reality are intertwined.
Author's Image, 2017.

HOUR BRAINS ARE BELIEF
ENGINES...THAT IS [WHY]
WE CONNECT THE DOTS
BETWEEN Λ AND B.

— Dr. Michael Shermer, 2011[9]

[our family or 'tribe', and a familiar cultural context and so on. This aids in both bonding on a social level, and obtaining a shared knowledge pool that prevents us from: 1] individually, empirically processing and analysing each variant within our environment, and 2] experiencing it anew to prove and rationalise its context and meaning. However, this reliance has also accelerated the evolution of mass media and new media platforms, allowing for the widespread creation, representation and alteration of alternative truths. It has also led to our having a complex and ambivalent relationship with the representation of reality.

Manipulation in image capturing started almost as soon as photography appeared, with incidents such as the 1917 'Cottingley Fairies', a series of photos that 'captured' Elsie Wright's and Frances Griffiths' encounters with fairies. The two young British cousins ultimately admitted to fabricating the images, but in the meantime swayed an entire generation into debating the existence of magical creatures. As soon as digital photography emerged, retouching and digital editing software appeared, enabling professionals and amateurs to manipulate both photography and video content. The incorporation of high-quality image and video capture in mobile devices quickly led to image enhancing applications such as Instagram and the inevitable Augmented Reality filters and applications, which led to the popularity of applications such as Snapchat and MSQRD. The next generation of reality manipulation could quite conceivably be the ability to edit in or out environmental and experiential assets.

Our exposure to manipulated content and imagery has made society more gullible, and more susceptible to being triggered by digital content, whether it is generated by mainstream media sources or an anonymous source with a mobile device. The immediacy of this content creates new levels of exhilaration and anxiety. Even after endless disaster movies, the impact of the 9/11 attacks was far-reaching because of the 'realness' factor of its live-stream broadcasting. The broadcasting of this attack, in Real-Time and via multiple sources, created visual trauma on a global scale. A study published in the *Journal of Traumatic Stress*[10] reveals "how the attacks impacted the psychological processes of those not directly exposed to the event. The study, which focused on college students in Massachusetts, found that even those who were not directly connected to New York or Washington showed increased stress responses to run of the mill visual images."[11]

6.0 Caterpillar to Butterflies

When we realise the impact of visual triggering, it is a not an unhinged possibility that augmented visual tools could be used to influence and terrorise entire populations. Perhaps triggering a reverse effect of avoidance mechanism. Mechanisms where augmented alternative realities are formed in which individuals, objects and situations are perfected, bypassing trauma, complexity and distress. In the new augmented realms we could upgrade the way we look, update our home interiors weekly and simply erase collective and personal traumas. A reality in which loved ones would live forever and the Twin Towers would still stand tall. We should be concerned about such a transformation, where our reality becomes a Real-Time amusement park.

6.5 The Ultimate Immersion

Going back to Plato's cave, we are, indeed, prisoners stuck in our subjective experience of reality. In the search for a definitive sense of reality, spirituality defines the link we draw between everyday reality and the "ultimate reality."[12]

Andrew Newberg, MD, an American neuroscientist who investigated the notion of *The Spiritual Brain* also explored experiences of "everyday" versus "ultimate" reality. His research benchmarks our perception of reality against religious practices and near-death experiences, applying scientific measurements to theological experiences [or Neurotheology] by scanning the brains of people who engage in deep spiritual practices.

The everyday reality is more connected to the material world. Alternatively, the ultimate reality seeks the context of reality beyond our everyday experiences. The two can be benchmarked – at least somewhat – using specific criteria:

#01 We experience objects and environments through our sensory input [sound, vision, etc.]

#02 We experience reality with consistency and persistence over time

#03 We can cross-reference and compare elements within the reality, meaning we can describe and share similar perceptions and elements

Newberg found that people who have had religious or mystical experiences tend to have a consistent and deep mental reference to such an experience, which represents a more fundamental form of reality a conscious reality. In short, spiritual experiences are longer-lasting and have more impact on one's approach to reality. One could argue that the objective value of consciousness overrides the experiential/material reality, providing an ultimate sense of reality that is detached from the immediate impression of a subjective experience. While Newberg's findings may not prove the existence of the divine, they do assert the impact of spiritual experiences on the human brain's functions and belief systems.

Since our understanding of reality is still heavily based on sensory perception, so too is our 'spiritual brain' and the triggering of our belief systems. Most belief systems [whether a science or an established religion] base their expectancy and diffusion on both a theological/ideological layer, and by incorporating a layer of sensory signals and proofs that confirm their existence as a higher order – at least in their conception.

Polytheism and natural religions see the divine as part of the continuum of the physical world, where each natural element has a specific myth that speaks to its purpose or source. Thunder and lightning bolts, for example, are both natural phenomena that can be found in Greek mythology as a weapon used by Zeus, or Norse mythology as an outcome of Thor's hammer wielding. Monotheistic religions such as Judaism, Christianity, and Islam still credit nature to a [single] divine creator, but also provide a detached metaphysical layer of divinity. As human society and monotheistic religions evolve, so grows the divine distance between God and human. Even within these religions, major theophany [appearances of a God] or prophetic messages involved a physical expression that could be perceived via sensory input, namely vision and/or sound – for example, the pillars of cloud and fire, or the burning bush.

God speaks directly to Adam and Eve in the Garden of Eden, as well as to Abraham. Later, one can see a more selective and indirect communication of divine messages, such as through angels, saints and prophets. In more primitive cultures, hearing, seeing and experiencing spiritual or other metaphysical and abnormal visions is considered acceptable, and even part of social rituals and conventions. In modern societies, we tend to be more sceptical and judgemental of individual testimonies of visions and experiences.

6.0 Caterpillar to Butterflies

Without casting judgement on the validity of spiritual experiences, we need to acknowledge the role myths play in the construction of cultural elements, social structures and hierarchies. These experiences are utilised not only during the conception of religions, but repeated and remediated through rituals and storytelling during their institutionalisation and delivery. Institutionalised religions, in turn, have developed centralised belief, monetary, social, legal and political structures. They also play an influential role in mediating and developing innovation systems. If we look at the development of communication – documentation and archiving, writing skills, specific language dominance, and printed media – these elements are clearly communicated in the media channels controlled by religions.

Whereas controlled media is one story, multichannel media presents a conflict for institutionalised religion. Since the Pope holds a Twitter account, the incorporation of religious dogma within the augmented space would be inevitable. Yet the paradox of a religious augmented layer would be baffling, since it will form an individual and unmediated spiritual presence and ritual, diminishing the role of the designated religious spaces and mediating figures, and with that the hierarchy system that is in place. Certain religious streams such as Amish and Hasidic Judaism already ban access to modern technologies, with official concerns that it will lead to moral and sexual corruption. This is an effective way to avoid conflict between its religious belief system and an ever-changing world. In the case of Hasidic Rabbis, despite imposing bans on television, the Internet and smartphones, the diffusion of integrated computing has seeped into all layers of everyday existence. Smartphones and computers have become essential for conducting basic personal and business functions. Their solution was to introduce 'Kosher' devices that incorporate restricted features, limiting exposure to information.[14]

While screens can still be somewhat controlled and viewed by others, once individual HMDs and retina displays are common devices, control over the content will surely become a consideration. Will Augmented Reality herald the end of institutionalised religion, or will it enhance religious dogmas and content streaming? After all, the printing press significantly aided in spreading Christian ideals across Europe, and shifted the religious content delivery system away from priests and monks hand-copying religious scripts to printed pamphlets that could be distributed to a wider audience. Religion has always treated new

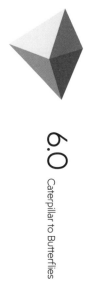

media forms with suspicion, eventually adapting them to influence existing and potential followers.

Religion and spirituality will catch up with, and most likely cash in on, augmentation at the interactive and/or monetary level. Eventually, we will consider the divine existence within augmented churches, and embed augmented spiritual rituals in our everyday environment. Since prayer and confession-texting already exists, augmentation would be able to offer an integrated spiritual layer within our everyday lives. Allowing any Catholic to be granted forgiveness by the augmented Pope, facilitating Telepresence pilgrimages or even the ability to 'witness' augmented spiritual revelations on a whim.

6.6 Digital Dreamtime

As Augmented Reality eliminates the boundaries between reality and fiction, it will only be limited by our imaginations and resources. After all, all this content does not come free of charge. Reality could become the sandbox to our imagination – blending concepts of past, present, future, real and holistic. Much like the Australian Aboriginal concept of 'Dreamtime'.

Virtual Reality is considered to have a higher potential for immersive experience and dependency. Yet, as Augmented Reality progresses and overcomes its technical limitations, the combination of quality delivery, multisensory stimulation, and the introduction of sophisticated deep-learning algorithms will deliver a multi-layered experience that we would perceive as a natural continuum to our reality. Augmented Reality could become so engaging and immersive that it creates an elevated experiential standard to our everyday activities, perhaps even conditioning us to achieve a dependency on augmentation. The couch potatoes of yesterday will be the immersive potatoes of tomorrow. Augmented Reality has the true potential to form experiences that are perceived as being so deep, that bare reality just won't be enough.

The question remains, what dose of augmentation will the user like and be able to consume? There is always the chance that a pendulum effect occurs, making unmediated experiences more exclusive. We have already seen this happen. Overly accessible work practices have become so diffuse,

6.0

Caterpillar to Butterflies

that certain executives choose to reinstate their status paradigms by restricting their digital connectivity and accessibility.

I remember being struck by a drug prevention lecture I attended when I was 20. It was given by a former addict, who explained the problems with using heroin. He told us that the high the drug provides is a transcending experience that cannot be naturally achieved. The user becomes addicted because they are always chasing the same sensation, while each time they use it there is a diminishing effect. This causes the user to increase their dosage, often leading to overdose. Mar Gonzalez Franco, a Microsoft researcher, predicts that future Virtual Reality experiences will be so impactful that they will have hallucinatory qualities:

> "By 2027 we will have ubiquitous virtual reality systems that will provide such rich multisensorial experiences that will be capable of producing hallucinations which blend or alter perceived reality. Using this technology, humans will retrain, recalibrate and improve their perceptual systems."[15]

This renders the comparison of Augmented and Virtual Reality with addictive substances, and – like the drug addict's experience – the human attempt to maintain and become addicted to superior sensations, so much so that they might not be able to cope without the use of the technology.

We can expect a highly immersive quality for Augmented Reality via narrative-based and multisensory applications that will layer engagement triggers used in game mechanics.[16] The successful incorporation of perceptual, cognitive and physical experience elements will create deep immersion. Reflecting on the narrative world, if we are already expecting singularity that will eventually define the rights of machines, we should also expect to discuss the rights of augmented beings and storylines.

Even without achieving a 'perfect' augmented experience, the moment when Augmented Reality users shift towards a continuous experience of Augmented Reality through behaviours, rituals and belief systems will position the technology as part of a 'natural' immersive state. From that moment on,

the 'Augmediated Reality' will be the only acceptable experience of reality, and might lead many users to consider the non-augmented 'vanilla' reality as unacceptable [vanilla is a term taken from gaming, which describes the original version of a platform].

Alain de Botton states "The desire for high status is never stronger than in situations where 'ordinary' life fails to answer a median need for dignity and comfort."[17] The Hyper-Augmented Reality would take over on an absolute and everyday level. It remains to be seen whether the Augmented Reality will become our primary or secondary perception of reality. Some key considerations include how that would shift our link between the physical and metaphysical, whether we would be able to trust our internal sensory input and processing mechanisms, and how willing the user would be to control such an [augmented] reality versus experiencing a passive experience stream. Who will construct this new reality for the user, and how will it shift social and political structures and hierarchies?

Fundamental societal and cultural outcomes will include shifting the needle on the ambiguous standards our society gives to individuals that experience a different sense of reality – those currently labelled 'insane', 'genius' or 'enlightened', depending on the intensity of the experience, context and outcome. Once 'experiencing' is a practice, how will our common understanding of reality shift? How will we be able to define, individually, if what we are seeing is real, augmented, a hallucination, or a vision? The more Augmented Reality becomes merged with our physical reality, the less separation we would experience between our everyday and absolute reality. Reality will become a fluid state that can be altered, edited and tailored by users, and – more alarmingly – by covert stakeholders.

And here's the final catch: Augmented Reality contains the ultimate key to embedding technology within a physical environment. Once we do this, it will be an almost irreversible passage – all due to one little brain candy molecule called dopamine. Dopamine is an organic chemical synthesised in the brain and kidneys, vital to various functions both motoric – such as moving and sleeping, and cognitive – such as reasoning, arousal and reinforcement.

6.0
Caterpillar to Butterflies

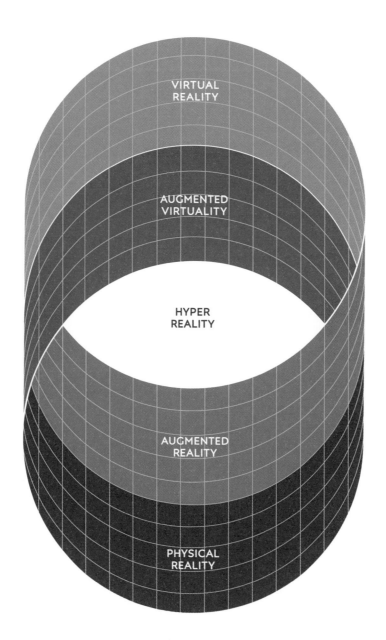

The Virtual Continuum – Revisted.
Author's Image 2017.

Dopamine plays a big role in our mood and motivation, most importantly in our reward system.[18] It plays the role of 'Charlie' to our 'inner Angels' – causing us to develop an appetitive [predatory] behaviour that stimulates our seeking mechanism. So, when we 'feel like' doing something, we are most likely looking to elicit a dopamine release. Dopamine seeking is what drives our 'gimme more' approach that results in basic survival and development behaviours, such as procreation, eating and curiosity. This means that innovation and progress in human society are basically the result of satisfying our dopamine itch.

The reason that this survival mechanism is successful is because it is nearly impossible to override. It's a simple catch-22 – the dopamine sends us out to seek gratification, and we will keep searching until we find it. Yet once it is 'mission accomplished', and we receive rewards and pleasure [from the brain's opioid release system], our gratification does not last. Instead, we are wired to keep seeking more, creating an endless behavioural loop. This gratification-seeking-loop is also the harbinger of addiction.

Let's jump back to technology. Systems are currently built on consistent feedback to entice quick gratification, platform experiences and interfaces designed around micro-tasking and triggering interaction, gamification, push notifications, constant content streaming and Real-Time interactions. These have been designed to feed and trigger the dopamine loop. Now let's consider Augmented Reality – a platform that will be based on sensory stimulation, Real-Time feedback and immersive user-tailored content layered on top of our everyday activities. It's the perfect platform for triggering – dare I say it – 'Pavlovian' behaviour.

The roles and applications of Augmented Reality may vary from simple game platforms to content and information delivery, and from training and education to integrated control and interface systems. The 'what' is less concerning than the 'how'. As reward-driven practices are further integrated into platform architectures, brand content, and marketing strategies, the user will experience continuous dopamine triggers, stimulating and perhaps overstimulating the user to remain in the augmented loop. For adults, the result may be dependency, leading to Augmented content addiction.

6.0 Caterpillar to Butterflies

For minors, dependency may trigger a deep, long-term emotional reliance on digital feedback and rewards, causing tectonic behavioural and social shifts.

Another addiction-related theory highlights the need to balance high-tech and high-touch interactions and applications. Bruce Alexander is a Canadian psychologist whose work considered the influence of external stimuli on addiction in rats. Alexander built a stimulus-deprived environment, and a separate high-stimulation 'Rat Park' to establish the core influence factors in opiate drug addiction. The study mainly identified influences from the environment over physical-based dependency. Alexander's extensive work in the field concludes, "Addiction cannot be understood simply as an affliction of certain individuals with genetic or acquired predispositions to addiction in otherwise well-functioning societies. The most powerful risk factors for addiction are social and cultural rather than genetic or individual."[19]

What this implies is that, even where technology has addiction-triggering features, there needs to be a social or emotional void that enables the actual addiction. Thus, the role of developers should be to use technology as a tool to enhance – or augment – human connections. This further highlights Augmented Reality's potential to be a potent social intensifier and enabler. We are nearing the phase where an emerging technology could truly transcend our experience and perception of reality – transforming our reality into a new state of digital dreamtime.

▼

"IMAGINATION IS THE ONLY WEAPON IN THE WAR AGAINST REALITY," SAID THE CHESHIRE CAT.

— Lewis Carroll, Alice's Adventures in Wonderland

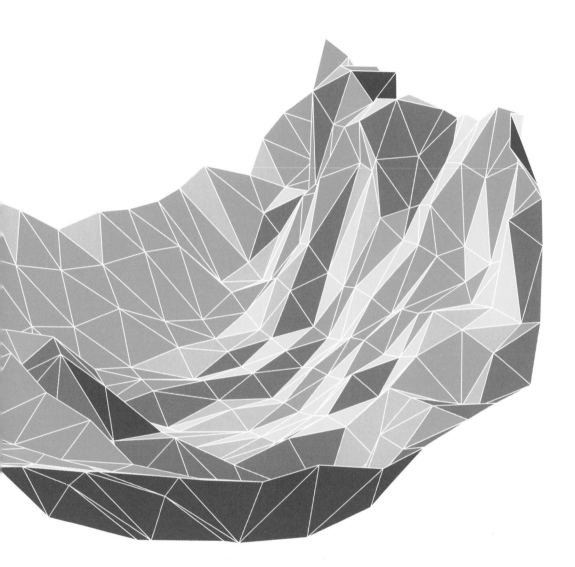

7.0 THE HUMAN / CYBER CONTINUUM

The Human/Cyber Continuum

Conclusions and Tools

7.1 This is the Age of Humans

Back in 1995, MIT's founding director, Nicholas Negroponte, predicted that "Computing is not about computers anymore. It is about living."[1] Yet we have spent the last few decades as guests in our own reality, relying on technology developments to determine our interaction, stream our content input, and organise our lives. It is time to break free and reclaim our independence. I am not calling for the rejection of technology, but I believe that technology advances mean that we no longer need to apply technology to compensate for our human imperfections – but rather to complement them.

We tell ourselves we create technology to help us gain control and access, but the truth is that we are becoming increasingly reliant on smart systems and stream data, to the extent where technology platforms have just as much to gain from our interaction. Our core gain through the application of technology is to elevate capabilities based on efficiency and accuracy, though these sometimes remain as external rather than acquired skills. For example, technology enhanced our ability to navigate the globe. We can chart, time, view and get live navigation routes to almost any point on Earth. The price we pay for this elevated navigation system is a diminished ability to independently decipher and connect with our surroundings. Having smart mobile devices enables us to store multiple layers of communication and information on our smartphones, yet using them may diminish our cognitive skills.[2] If you insist on disputing that, please test yourself by: whether you have memorised the phone numbers of your closest friends or family, or can you recite your meeting schedule for the coming week, do some simple math calculations, and...what did you say the time was again?

We have let go of core human skills since we lean toward performance over long-term skill acquisition or the acceptance of our human imperfections. One example is the autocorrect function. It may make our emails and text appear more professional, but it also relieves us from the need to learn correct punctuation and grammar. Perhaps we shouldn't be too concerned, since this is where emojis and multimedia instant messaging come into place – bringing us full circle from a visual and oral storytelling society to a data society, and back again into a [digitally] audio/visual society.

Applying technology in our everyday lives takes away our sense of technological wonder, making technology an integral part of our lives. This leads to a changing sense of its value and even of what 'qualifies' as technology. For example – we don't seem to consider a wristwatch as 'technology' anymore, unless it has digital or advances multimedia features embedded in it. We have reached the point where we can control almost 'everything' with the edge of our fingertips, able to control and influence all aspects of our lives. This internal sense combined with interaction game engagement mechanics, keep us hooked on technology. Technology streams our behaviours and experiences like never before. We use it to monitor everyday functional actions such as navigation and scheduling, to lifestyle choices such as improving our nutrition and sleep patterns – we are even seeing examples of wearable devices alerting us that we need to get 'drenched'. However, there is a difference between applying technology to elevate our everyday behaviours and applying it with sole purpose of quantifying them. And modified behaviours don't necessarily qualify as improved ones. We can see how Real-Time, constant online access overtakes knowledge acquisition – forming behavioural patterns designed to avoid boredom at all costs, to compulsively engage with digital content streams, and thrive on external affirmation.

> "Instead of demanding that our technologies conform to ourselves and our own innate rhythms, we strive to become more compatible with our technologies and the new cultural norms their timelessness implies." Rushkoff rightfully stated "We misapply the clockwork era's goals of efficiency and productivity over time to a digital culture's asynchronous landscape. Instead of working inside the machine, as we did before, we must become the machine."[3]

7.0

The Human/Cyber continuum

We are on the verge of many great technological strides, approaching an amazing era where technology will finally catch up with our imagination. Soon, we will be able to form new experiences that are complementary to our behavioural and biological needs. The more we progress, the more organic systems will become human-centric. As artificial neural networks are applied to machine learning, and interaction experiences base their feedback systems on cognitive processes, they form a new virtual/physical continuum. Augmented Reality application would conclude this quest and supply the seamless interaction platform that bridges the virtual and physical realms. Our augmented experiences will intensify and alter our perception of reality, sense of identity and our relationships with people, places and 'things'.

As we step over the new threshold to a new crescendo of visual/sensory interaction, we must learn from our past mistakes, and create human-centric experience applications. Trusting that it is the funny, quirky, human way that will truly elevate the way we experience, communicate and learn from our physical reality, but at the same time building safeguards that would prevent the exploitation of the influence inherent to immersive technology.

Emerging technologies, like any other human phenomena – from religion to work ethics – has the potential to be taken to the extreme, abused and used in ways that were never intended. This is inevitable, yet we must recall that a digital Dreamtime would have implications for core cultural and social values, and we need to have an open and honest debate about what this entails.

Even though the breadth and depth of the impact of implementing emerging technologies has the potential to be unpredictable, we do know that we have been too lenient and slow in comprehending or reacting to applications that have recently reconstructed social, economic and political systems. We are not a college grad sitting in his dorm, wondering about the impact of creating a social media platform called 'Thefacebook'. In this Information Age, stakeholders cannot hide behind 'not knowing' what may come next. The industry has the moral and professional responsibility to ensure that Augmented Reality is applied in an ethical way.

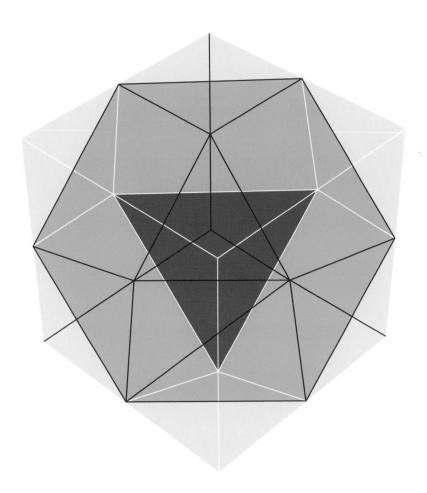

The Human/Cyber Nexus
Technology and humanity are intertwined,
their interaction results in mutual evolution.
Author's Image, 2017.

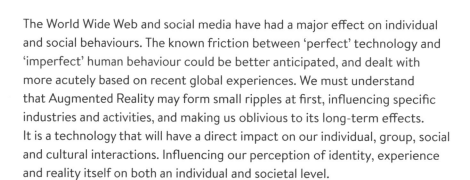

7.0

The Human/Cyber continuum

The World Wide Web and social media have had a major effect on individual and social behaviours. The known friction between 'perfect' technology and 'imperfect' human behaviour could be better anticipated, and dealt with more acutely based on recent global experiences. We must understand that Augmented Reality may form small ripples at first, influencing specific industries and activities, and making us oblivious to its long-term effects. It is a technology that will have a direct impact on our individual, group, social and cultural interactions. Influencing our perception of identity, experience and reality itself on both an individual and societal level.

> Augmented interaction and content will bring back human-centric interaction, and reinstate heritage mental and physical skills. No more adapting to machine thinking, but building on human intelligence and emotional value. We will be talking more and more about Affective Computing that "relates to, arises from, or deliberately influences emotions or other affective phenomena."[4]

7.2 The Final Frontier

At this point we can and should construct scenarios and hypotheses regarding the endeavour of implementing Augmentation. It is more likely to take the obvious route of being applied via traditional accelerating industries – the military, gaming, entertainment and porn [highly underestimated for its power to diffuse, test and make emerging technologies accessible]. Despite our educated guessing, guidance and strategising, it is ultimately the user who will define how quickly and through which game mechanics and interaction realms it will best be implemented.

Augmentation would stretch beyond our digital interactions as it crosses the screen boundary and layered on top of physical elements within our environment. We would find new ways to explore and bond with technology, and the role of social/behavioural psychology embedded within its development will aid in applying it in a wider and more sustainable context. What is certain is that there will eventually be an absolute synergy between the information economy and the experience culture. While behavioural marketing was based on identifying and enticing usage patterns, the new value

of augmented experience would be based on finding new ways to facilitate, create and curate digital content that is reactive and complementary to physical behaviours and social nodes, and that explores and enhances obstacles and opportunities that are rooted in the way we interact and experience our physical world. This would be a new age of exploration, reinterpretation and remixing of the digital and physical realm. With mixed reality, Tangible User Interface and multisensory experiences becoming a norm within communication and content delivery.

The shift would be towards a societal and experiential brand, product and value creation – a truly heterogeneous system that would immerse the user, not only on a sensory level, but with a deeper alignment between values and emotional bonding. The alignment between product, brand, content and marketing will need to become seamless. You can see that tech service agencies such as Cognizant and Accenture are already moving towards branching and clustering through having acquisition, creative, digital, innovation, service and design disciplines all under one roof. Yet, the biggest question is how do the systems builders approach, develop and create applications and platforms – learning from past mistakes and building a new experiential platform that would benefit users, creators and curators alike – guaranteeing a new level and value of digital experience.

Technology is as restrictive as the tools it supplies to the user – open platforms of content creation can unlock new levels of creativity. Minecraft is a 'digital Lego' game – and as digital architecture leaks into our physical space, we will be able to create a new open world within the confinements of our existing one.

> New experiential applications may include Augmented Synesthesia – where we link new experiential layers within specific spaces or interaction levels. A multisensory ability to mediate new layers of experience on top of our physical reality may allow us to re-experience segments of our life – your honeymoon or first date, whenever your spouse is in the room.

Or imagine the interior of an Art Deco movie theatre with the scent and sound of popcorn cracking as you settle into a binge-watching weekend of your favourite TV series. The ability to weave experiential layers into our private and public realms would mean that we can construct multiple versions and

COMPUTING IS NOT ABOUT COMPUTERS ANYMORE. IT IS ABOUT LIVING.

— Nicholas Negroponte, 1995

experiential layers – bending our 'limited' perception of physical Spacetime as we upload and tap into the past, present, or remote locations.

Certain terms such as Augmented, Augmediated and Mixed Reality will become more dominant as we attempt to describe the experience quality rather than its functional aspect. For example, the term 'Mixed Reality' may have a cultural significance beyond the spatial mapping layer it currently offers, instead manifesting our ability to reconstruct our reality with the aid of augmented technologies.

> If our reality is to be augmented, we should not reduce augmentation and experience building into a mere commodity. Instead, we need to harness the potential of Augmented Reality into newly formed intimacies with the world around us and the worlds within us, so we can apply technology in a meaningful way that truly integrates the best of both the digital and physical worlds.

7.3 Experiences That Matter

The unprecedented impact that Augmented Reality has the potential to bring, also means that the technology's application is likely to form extreme usage patterns – either becoming the new experience standard, or being left in the dusty drawer of 'great technologies that just did not make it'.

Augmented Reality is a platform that could bring the human/machine interaction to an unprecedented level. However, the combination of predictive analytics, and emerging technologies' heterogeneity – especially in terms of integrating advanced Artificial Intelligence algorithms – means that it will also have unprecedented influence and 'nudge power' over consumer behaviour. So far, the relative separation between physical and digital has created a defined boundary between the user and technology, yet a fully immersive and gamified experience could create an 'undetectable' decision-making process.
The current digital noise is already unbearable. We are bombarded with nudges and information overload until we become digitally numb, expressed

7.0

The Human/Cyber continuum

by declining and shifting values from 'quality' and 'authenticity' to data 'quantity'. A gamified environment and decision-making system would be characterised in a highly content and trigger-saturated reality – beautifully visualised by Keiichi Matsuda's Hyper-Reality video, which envisions user's future existence within a constant stream of digital stimuli, exposed to shifting status fluxes, and based on digital currency and streamed identity.

Experience building should not merely be a marketing stunt – it needs to provide real value to the user before, during and after the moment of use. Building on authentic value and a meaningful user experience is not only the path for building great brands, products, platforms and technologies, but a necessity for those who would like to create sustainable ecosystems around them. Over the long-term, it is the best way to establish a sustainable business model. The users are more than consuming machines. They are an integral part of the value ecosystem. Especially since technology platforms are moving away from a role of content creation, and towards one of curation and facilitation.

To have a user-driven process requires the creation of a truly user-minded culture and design process. It starts with intimate insights into user needs, building reactive processes and platform architecture, and having a multidisciplinary team mix [including users] that allows for out-of-silo development. Perhaps finally moving beyond the 'disruptive innovation' concept and considering a more 'constructive innovation' work model. Brand and platform builders will play an important role in setting the process framework [within the boundaries of ethics and purpose], while the user will use the product or service to shape and explore content and experience.

> At some point, the digital experience will become an extension of the physical one, and we need to understand how to prepare for it. Augmented Reality is a technology that has the potential to unlock opportunities for interaction and content creation, beyond 'pushing' content and opportunities to form interactive storytelling, to elevating [positive impact] and disrupting [negative impact] our physical reality. Over-access may not be an issue once we transform the digital noise into quality experiences. Balancing meaningful and casual exploration of our reality, relationships and identity through Augmented Reality could transcend the technology and its socio-cultural nuances.

7.4 Digital Ethics

We are only now 'catching up' with the impact of the World Wide Web and social media. Already in 1993, Wellner identified one of the core issues of the information age:

> "Computer-augmented environments raise many issues, both technical and social. They may require a complex, distributed infrastructure, precise alignment between the real and electronic worlds, novel input and output devices, and great care for people's privacy."[5]

Even though we are developing social and legislative norms regarding online presence and behaviours, law-making is a slow process that is still trailing behind technology's advancements. The reality is that the digital layer has already gravitated into our public, private and intimate environments, altering our perception of identity, society, and culture. This is quite alarming, considering that we increasingly use digital content as a core source of information and experience, and will continue to do so in more and more areas of interaction and consumption.

The evolution of User Interface [UI] and User Experience [UX] is also leading to the oversimplification of data representation and some cognitive risks. It plays into our tendency to 'flatten' and ignore complexities – accepting online behaviours, feedback and facts as a reliable representation of reality; and substantially shaping our own beliefs, behaviours and ethics. *Glass* and *Pokémon Go* both raised issues of privacy invasion and ownership in physical and virtual spaces. As augmentation becomes a diffused interface, we will witness more of these conflicts.

The cyber dimension surpasses legislative boundaries, and in many cases platforms and systems are mainly regulated via the initiating entities rather than governments. This gives platform builders further social and political influence that can at times, exceed those of governing bodies. The 2016 dispute between the FBI and Apple went viral when the US federal government demanded that Apple unlock cryptographically protected content from iPhones, as part of a terror activity investigation. Apple declined the request, the case went to court, and was ultimately resolved via third-party hacking. The merging of the physical and digital domain will continue to challenge users, entities and legislative bodies on issues such as accountability, ownership, and conduct regarding digital presence, privacy and content.

While the importance of Corporate Social Responsibility [CSR] codes increases for companies, many still only focus on the physical aspects, such as sustainability issues. Digital responsibility should be considered as an integral part of social responsibility regulation. Since social responsibility relates to our quality of life as a society, we cannot pretend that our society exists solely within the physical realm. Some tech companies have already arrived at this conclusion. As Google dives into machine learning, it has also set up an Ethics Board. As admirable as that is [and I would hope that all technology moguls and start-ups will start to embrace ethical accountability], we need to remember that these boards are still following their subjective corporate ethics and needs. What is needed is an independent framework that can oversee and regulate the implications of technology.

Virtual, Augmented and Mixed Reality researchers in the US have initiated a discussion with members of the government regulatory agency,[6] hoping to promote further research and considerations related to long-term influences and ethics. Many developers think that technology needs to be free from any regulation, and are concerned about how it may become a slippery slope to institutionalised censorship, based on political gains and 'out of date'/regressive thinking. My answer to them is twofold. Firstly, 'with great power comes great responsibility' – right now the regulatory power lies within the tech conglomerates that are running the platforms. Let us not pretend that they are not driven by commercial motives that are beneficial for their entity's growth first with user, and any social benefit will come later – if at all. Secondly, I truly wonder why we ignore the fact that Silicon Valley is rooted in social idealism, with many founders of the biggest tech conglomerates being former hippies. The Augmented Reality versions we may construct could either enrich our private and social experience, or form divisive 'reality bubbles' that may be harmful on many levels. The responsibility lies in the hands of policymakers, Augmented Reality developers, and users alike.

"Digital technologies are used to imagine specific futures and cultural styles. Increasingly the digital itself is a prominent building block in shaping people's futures."[7]

The shift in power over defining social agendas is occurring. We are moving from geopolitical frameworks to corporations, media, and ultimately technology corporations – which for-profit entities are not fully obliged to have a moral code and transparency model. This is problematic. The user, accustomed to free and open platforms, may condemn institutionalised restrictions, but also demand to be able to report and control content. Facebook's reporting system is aimed at removing offensive content, yet it is often used as a political or ideological tool to target and suspend an individual user's digital presence.

The lawsuit against the creators of *Pokémon Go* by a New Jersey property owner is only the first in a wave of cases addressing the legal and moral responsibilities of the builders and developers of augmentation platforms. In this case, Niantic placed *Pokéstops* and *Pokémon gyms* on private property, disturbing the owner and encouraging trespassing in pursuit of the augmented assets and activities. Other inappropriate placements included memorials and cemeteries. Niantic claimed that users are encouraged not to intrude on private property, and to 'adhere to the rules of the human world', which should be enough for it to claim no responsibility. This strange argument implied that, on one hand, they realise that the augmented content and engagement effect the real world, yet should not be considered an integral part of it. This is quite contradictory for Augmented Reality developers' who aspire to create persuasive, immersive technology, while maintaining trust value.

As Augmented Reality moves the virtual continuum closer and closer to the physical world, the idea that technology is an abstract 'thing' that exists in a 'separate' realm is no longer true or relevant. As virtual and augmentation technologies mature, so will their influence on our morals and behaviour – both socially and privately. Can we control all consequences and outcomes? I think not! Should we be responsive to and conscious about the advancements we make, and anticipate what will inevitably happen? This is our role as individuals and as a society. If we don't do that, someone else surely will.

7.0

The Human/Cyber continuum

7.5 Design With Intent

What can we do to improve the application Augmented Reality? Let's start by designing these platforms and experiences with the intention to create value rather than filling a market gap. 'Goddamn digital hippie,' you roll your eyes. 'You forgot about ROI, investors, costs and of course [drum roll] our double-digit growth forecast!' Well, no I did not.

> Even whilst cosidering finanacial factors such as Return On Investment [ROI] there is room, and in fact there is a need to develop and apply technologies in an intelligent and prosocial way instead of the for-profit and pro-speed. And the beauty of it all is that it does not contradict a financial model. In this era of transparency and immediacy, design with intent is what makes a sustainable impact. It is also intelligent business.

Most of us believe that the petrochemical, tobacco, mining, and consumer goods industries have a responsibility for ensuring safe processes and products at the user, social and environment level. Considering the role emerging technologies take in shaping the present and future global economy, society and quality of life, they should be held to the same standard. Especially when we consider technologies such as Augmented Reality, which are focused on directly laying content on, and manipulating our interaction with, reality. There are a few key principles we can use – instead of helplessly witnessing the 'inevitable' implementation pains and errors – to ensure a more productive and positive effect from the diffusion of Augmented Reality.

The optimisation of Augmentation involves many stakeholders, from platform builders, content creators, and policymakers to users. We need to lay down clear rules of engagement and an ethical code regarding the manipulation of reality from the get-go. Ensuring high standards for the development and implementation of Augmented Reality would protect the safety, privacy, physical and cognitive state of the user. This is not just common sense, but it is also good business sense – ensuring a sustainable framework for the technology to operate in, as it is heavily reliant on smooth integration with existing physical and behavioural frameworks.

The rise in popularity of 'disruptive innovation' as a holistic mindset sometimes makes me feel quite weary. A disruptive element is a 'given' in relation to any dynamic advancement or process, yet this popular combination of tech and disruption as a core value for innovation generation, implies an accelerated process that is enforced upon the market and the user, ignoring existing cycles and relationships. Part of my motivation to wave the flag for Augmented Reality is as the name indicates – an elevation on an existing system. Hopefully this blend of positive elements of technology, together with social innovation will form a more socially responsible process that will ensure a positive-minded implementation of Augmented Reality.

7.6 Here's to Augmented Kittens

We have witnessed how social media and diffused access to online content has led to radical transparency of brands, governments, and social systems. We need to consider whether Augmented Reality can further this trend, or induce radical escapism.

Augmentation, like any technology, will reflect the Zeitgeist during its implementation, and it is highly likely that we will witness applications that amplify human behaviours and interactions – for better, and for worse. Augmented Reality has the potential to enrich our interaction within our physical environments; and create a new cyber/human ecosystem that intersect traditional and digital environments, tools, and interactions to form new experiential layers. This ecosystem has the capacity to bring back heritage knowledge, visual, behaviour and gesture-based interaction [in your face digital natives...], and construct a comprehensive and widespread interaction platform within developed and developing countries. Augmented Reality may also be used to create 'less serious' content – from environment-hacking filters to rainbow-pooping kittens. Fun is not a problem if it is a meaningful tool to reach engagement and improve our lives.

The concern is whether Augmented Reality would be reduced to a divisive, avoidant, anxious, flat and commercially driven digital hell – where augmented flaming kittens influence us to drink soft drinks as we walk off a cliff,

"**WE ARE JUST AN ADVANCED BREED OF MONKEYS ON A MINOR PLANET OF A VERY AVERAGE STAR...BUT WE CAN UNDERSTAND THE UNIVERSE. THAT MAKES US SOMETHING VERY SPECIAL.**"

- *Stephen Hawking, 1988*

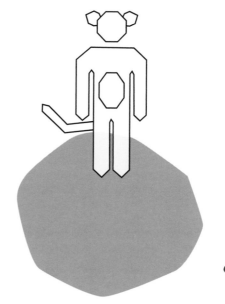

oblivious of our own physical surroundings. It is our choice to either ignore or acknowledge the negative potential inherent in the technology. As Alvin Toffler surmises; change and progress are inevitable, and the process of human/technology evolution is intertwined: "If our images of reality are changing more rapidly, and the machinery of image-transmission is being speeded up, a parallel change is altering the very codes we use."[8] Researchers compared Western/modern and non-Western/remote people, and found that technology use results in developing different biases within our visual processing, suggesting that we are already going through a rapid perceptual evolution due to the application of technology.

Earlier I mentioned that technology is perfect. On its own, it can do us no harm. It is the human factor in the development and application of technology that concerns me. I do have faith in humans, and agree with Stephen Hawking who declares that

"We are just an advanced breed of monkeys on a minor planet of a very average star. But we can understand the Universe. That makes us something very special."[9]

I hope this book provides a better understanding about the potential and challenges of augmentation. I invite you to explore, and responsibly develop and use the technology to augment everything around you... Heralding a bold new era, where no [wo]man has gone before.

7.0

The Human/Cyber continuum

7.7   Establishing Augmented Reality Design Principles

The impact of Augmented Reality implementation is beyond a business/tech case – it represents a new way of creating content and communication as an experience platform [the tangible WWW]. Developers need to consider what Augmented Reality implementation means on a societal and behavioural level. Considering these consequences in advance is necessary for its successful adoption and implementation, and does not contradict innovation/moving forward. Here are some key principles that will aid developers in measuring the development of augmented experiences.

> We are Not AR-Wired. Yet.

We are still in the early days of experimenting and exploring Augmented Reality, and we need to consider this within development and launch processes. Many developers are tempted to launch prototypes as products, which makes a lot of sense in terms of being able to test the product. Yet, since Augmented Reality has an additional layer that developers should 'not forget' about – the physicality related to its implementation might cause a harmful backlash for the specific application and the entire industry. There are many variables in play [on a functional and behavioural level], making the diffusion of AR more susceptible to rejection. We need to consider and balance the development and diffusion pace of AR with the behavioural and mental readiness of individuals and societies.

Developers should aspire to build better development processes that enable them to act and implement a highly reactive strategy, attuned to the needs of core users. Agile and lean development formulas exist, but more often than not are replicated rather than adapted to specific product or industry needs and context. It is the developers' role to hack, check and test methodologies, boundaries and never underestimate usage testing, and users' behavioural nuances.

To achieve deep impact and sustainable adoption of Augmented Reality, we need to create clear benefits for the user. Although it is only natural that, at first, intoxication with the new technology may lure many users to engage with Augmented Reality applications and features. Developers and the AR industry will therefore, eventually need to be clear about the value proposition that they are offering to the user, hopefully building on existing needs and gaps rather than forging false desires.

Augmented Reality can build on existing Virtual Reality expertise and learnings, as well as those from storytelling, and multimedia and interactive design. However, it is a unique discipline of its own that will require further exploration and insights based on wider diffusion and behavioural feedback. We are entering a phase of development concession that relies [more than ever] on the user's feedback or reactive development based on Real-Time behaviours. Augmented Reality should [and will] become a stand-alone discipline that will create and develop existing disciplines from:

- » Augmented environments design

- » Creating and curating augmented content design

- » Multisensory and haptic design

- » Augmented digital and Tangible User Interface

- » Material and surface innovation

- » Behavioural, ergonomic and gesture research

- » Augmented experience and narrative creation and curation [concept and production]

- » Augmentation game mechanics exploration [on a physical and psychological level]

- » Augmented marketing and branding

- » Augmentation platform developments and education

These are just top-line areas that may diversify and intensify the knowledge and job market in the next few years. Although some augmentation engines and platforms offer free and open-source learning, we will require a much wider knowledge base, and professionals that can enable and sustain the growth and maintenance of the Augmented Reality industry.

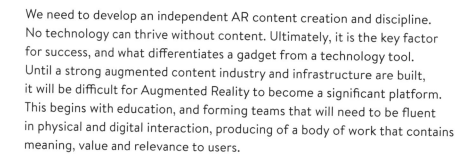

We need to develop an independent AR content creation and discipline. No technology can thrive without content. Ultimately, it is the key factor for success, and what differentiates a gadget from a technology tool. Until a strong augmented content industry and infrastructure are built, it will be difficult for Augmented Reality to become a significant platform. This begins with education, and forming teams that will need to be fluent in physical and digital interaction, producing of a body of work that contains meaning, value and relevance to users.

The path to creating sustainable value for augmented content requires having systems in place that ensure the continuous creation of quality content. Content makers need to carefully consider how the narrative and context become a 'gravitational point' that would form a meaningful experience. Applying one or choosing a more sophisticated combination of the steps below can pave the road to a sustainable application of Augmented Reality:

» Define the added [personal] value of the application.

» Determine the functional value
   [enhanced performance, data prioritisation and filtering, time-saving or efficiency].

» Consider the unsolicited entertainment value
   [surprise and delight].

» Entice curiosity
   [newness, non-purpose learning, independent experiences].

» *Create an open system, based on inclusive interaction*
   [that can sustain communication between users and non-users].

» *Share the love – make sure this is a value-sharing platform.*

» *Ensure interaction newness that triggers and sustains engagement*
   [for-profit and non-profit activities].

» *Integrate self-affirmation and self-development systems.*

» *Ensure access and development for knowledge and skill growth.*

Actually, it seems like we should consider the future based on an Augmented-Virtuality perspective. Augmented Reality is also limited by the need to build on the existing versus forming a fantastic and free-form alternative experience. Each one has its value and role, and eventually Augmented and Virtual technology will merge, offering a hybrid experience that combines the physical, augmented and virtual experience. A deep cyber-physical hybrid system would integrate and interchange the experience modes, allowing us to augment the existing or jump into a completely virtual experience forming an alternative presence realm. This might mean that we lose our day job, though.

The 12 steps to creating meaningful augmentation:

#01 ADMIT

Admit that we have become powerless over technology.
That our lives have become unmanageable through its over-use.

#02 BELIEVE

Believe that our tech sanity can be restored.

#03 CONFESS

Confess to Cyber-God, ourselves & other human beings
the exact nature of our wrong [tech] doings.

#04 COMMIT

Commit to turning Augmented Reality into a sustainable
technology platform.

#05 REPLACE

Replace our Return On Investment obsession
with a long-term value system.

#06 STEP AWAY

Step away from the tech silos. Talk to users [a lot of them]
so you can design for their needs – not just for market gaps
or technological possibilities.

#07 OLD SCHOOL

Start with 'old school' by building on intuitive interaction, combining future and heritage knowledge.

#08 DESIGN WITH INTENT

Augmentation as a tool needs to have a function.
Augmentation as a platform needs to have a cause.

#09 DESIGN FOR HUMANS

By harnessing Augmented Reality's attributes to deepen knowledge and empathy, and enhance personal and social exploration.

#10 ACCOUNTABILITY

Build for best-worst-case-scenarios. Assuming that Augmented Reality applications will be misused, aspire to eliminate or at least diminish negative implementation.

#11 STAY CONSCIOUS

In continuing to take a personal inventory as we develop the Augmented Reality application, and when we are wrong – promptly admit it.

#12 MAKE REALITY GREAT AGAIN

Build on the most immersive experience there is – the world around us. Augmentation should not be perceived as the ultimate system to filter or redesign reality, but as a new way to experience it.

7.0

The Human/Cyber continuum

#01 ### Admit that we have become powerless over technology – that our lives have become unmanageable through its over-use

There is value in technology and there are, indeed functions that improve our life's quality. However – choosing machine knowledge and mediated content to a level that overrides human qualities is a way to disengage from meaningful experiences, rather than elevate our lives.

#02 ### Believe that our tech sanity can be restored.

Technology is wonderful in the sense that we can adapt its usage and purpose in a relatively short time. This is more about refocusing the goal of its application and development, to ensure its human-positive implementation.

#03 ### Confess to Cyber-God, ourselves & other human beings the exact nature of our wrong [tech] doings

Remember 'Don't be evil'? This is where the industry needs to have some genuine soul-searching. Users live under the illusion that they can protect their privacy, yet big data and over-connectivity ensure the monitoring and monetisation of every online activity. Once we merge the digital layer into our physical experience layer, we are creating an inseparable node that disables users from ever being disconnected. Unless Augmented Reality developers form a transparent business model and ethical platform that puts the user at the centre [not as a monetary value generator, but as a human being with the right to be unquantified], Augmented Reality should not, and perhaps will not, be diffused. The threshold of privacy may be breached initially, but eventually, invasive applications of the technology will be harmful and lead to irreversible consequences – compromising the nature of the technology application.

As new social and user paradigms emerge, the user expectation to obtain meaningful applications will move AR away from a commercially driven application as a kick-off point for the technology's relevance. Creating high-stimuli, gimmicky applications may work, but they take away our ability to

explore Augmented Reality's potential as a multi-experiential, added value and truly innovative-by-nature technology.

#04 Commit to turning Augmented Reality into a sustainable technology platform

A sustainability mindset is not just about fixing broken systems; it is also about constructing lasting alternatives. Use Augmented Reality wisely, and consider the best and worst paths that the user may take so you can future-proof the platform.

#05 Replace our Return On Investment obsession with a long-term value system

Augmented Reality developers and stakeholders need to decide if they want the technology to be an inclusive experience that benefits and reinforces social structures, or one that only provides an experiential and content value to those who have access and resources.

Experience is an entirely internal process, even when it occurs externally to our bodies; it requires sensory input, stimulation and comprehension processes. Users' intrinsic drives seek meaning through experience. It is the basis for customer decision-making. Considering, linking to and anticipating users' intrinsic needs is a vital part of the innovation process/value, and is also good business.

#06 Step away from the tech silo

Talk to users – a lot of them. Design for their needs, not just to fill market gaps or explore technological possibilities. By solving users' [real, and preferably significant] needs you would create a more [personally, socially and culturally] valuable application of the technology. To ensure its success you need to take care that Augmented Reality technology is not developed, tested, and applied by developers for developers. You also need to consider how to build Augmented Reality applications that do not form socio-technological silos where subgroups,

7.0

The Human/Cyber continuum

predispositions, developed preferences, and content access become the core determining factor of one's identity and status. The idea of having a tech-related citizenship is more plausible than you might think, considering the capital, reach and data power behind some of the current technology conglomerates.

#07 Start with Old School

By building on existing behavioural patterns and social platforms, you are creating an added value based on intrinsic motivation and an invisible implementation of highly sophisticated technology. You can maintain relevance through the application of accessible innovation that built on basic social engagement and emotional needs. The user should not experience augmentation filters or tools as a 'technology' feature – rather just as a great interaction feature.

#08 Design with Intent

Augmentation as a tool needs to have a function.
Augmentation as a platform needs to have a cause.

Assuming that the [perceived or actual] 'wow factor' can overcome issues such as aesthetics or UI design, and convince the user to adopt a technology despite basic flaws, is naïve at best. I am a believer that 'still water runs deep' – using more subtle cues to form sophisticated and meaningful nodes, building on a more intimate and effective impact, looking at the imperfection and various layers of the human existence to build experiences that dare to explore awkwardness, nostalgia, unsolicited fun and meaning. I am a fan of creating an augmented realm over an augmediated one, at least to begin with.
Remember that helping the user get use to augmentation is already a big step.

#09 **Design for humans**

Design for humans. They are imperfect, complex, and generally speaking worth our respect and consideration. Forming genuine long-term emotional hooks would be a more effective tool to ensure deeper engagement and heightened value for the technology. Augmented Reality technology should be designed with individual and social needs in balance, ensuring its inclusive nature and positive integration. Social interaction is critical in obtaining the value and further developing Augmented Reality applications and features. This does not mean that every platform should contain a social platform, but it should contain both unique and personalised features, that demonstrate inclusive behaviour.

#10 **Build for best-worst-case-scenarios**

Assuming that Augmented Reality applications will be misused, aspire to eliminate or at least diminish negative implementation.
You can't win them all but you should try.

#11 **Stay Conscious**

By continuing to take a personal inventory as we develop the Augmented Reality application, and when we are wrong – promptly admit it.
Basic emotional triggers work on humans. After all, we are biological creatures with embedded emotional triggers, hooks and drives – all there to sustain our survival and evolution as a species. But these should not be abused to impose dependency. There will be no escape from augmentation's influence once it is applied. So be gentle. By offering meaning and value, you will help to maintain a healthy human/cyber balance.

Respect and consider social needs when introducing Augmented Reality. Look into the social context via moral and legal lenses within the environment. Embrace the philosophy of 'Function follows behaviour.' Public space, private space and intimate space – the integration of Augmented Reality crosses all these thresholds, and causes new challenges and layers of complexity. Augmented Reality will not be confined to one, and thus its development

7.0

The Human/Cyber continuum

7.0

The Human/Cyber continuum

and implementation cannot be inconsiderate of the other layers. You cannot develop AR for the public space without understanding the implications for one's private and intimate space, and vice-versa.

Humans are easily blinded by the functional and emotional triggers of technology application, with little regard for the price they may be paying. Since we are in a data economy, the price is our privacy. We are happy with 'good enough' privacy and data protection, leaving us wide open for data gathering, hacking and manipulation. The more integrated/invisible UI and interaction become, the less we are aware of and alerted to data collection. As the breadth and depth of tech access spreads, the more sophisticated and accurate the application of big data becomes. Those who hold the keys to that data, and have the potential to combine it with Augmented Reality, will be the ones to rule our interaction and perception of reality.

#12   Make reality great again

We shouldn't constantly attempt to override life, by creating technologies that compensating for its complexities. Rather, we should embrace reality's harsh truths and complexity as the beautiful building blocks that form our reality.

> Augmentation should not be perceived as the ultimate system to filter or redesign reality, but as a new way to experience it. Augmented Reality should add to the physical experience rather than attempting to replace it.
>
> We can utilise Augmented Reality to make our physical reality experiences better by building on the most immersive experience there is – the world around us.

"YES, THAT'S IT!"
   SAID THE HATTER WITH A SIGH,
"IT'S ALWAYS TEA TIME"

— Lewis Carroll, Alice's Adventures in Wonderland

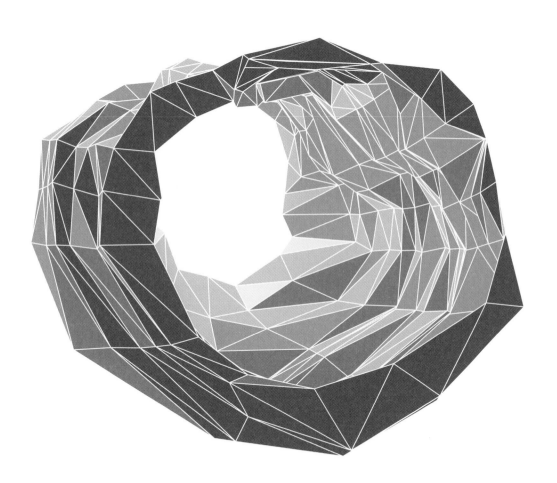

8.0 APPENDICES

8.0 Appendices

All That Virtual Jazz

Definitions

The key to success for every discussion is to ensure a common understanding of core concepts. This is my attempt to create clear and concise definitions, contextualising my use of specific terms.

Narrative

Narrative is an essential part of storytelling and experience building. It relates to the manner in which the story elements create a cohesive story flow and context. There are three key characteristics that define and distinguish a narrative:[1]

1. Situation – time, location, conflict and developments,

2. Character – main and sub characters, and how they contribute and react to story events,

3. Form – the artistic structure and flow of the story.

Embedded Narrative

Embedded narrative is directly related to the pre-existing knowledge and hierarchies within a story world. The embedded narrative contextualises the plot, characters, hierarchies and interaction within the story. It can be delivered indirectly, be assumed or unravel as the story evolves.

Interactive Narrative

Interactive narrative allows the recipient to actively participate in and influence the story flow, story world or experience. It is non-linear, and requires feedback systems that can incorporate the user's input into the experience or story progression.

8.0 Appendices

Flow

'The state of flow' is a term coined by Hungarian psychologist Mihály Csíkszentmihályi, and describes the state where a person is positively engaged in an activity, entering an immersive psychological state within the action or process.

Immersion

Immersion describes a mental state where the user is absorbed and engaged on a cognitive level with an experience or flow state.

Hertzian Space

Coined by critical designers and technology researchers Anthony Dunne and Fiona Raby, 'Hertzian space' describes the micro-environment that encapsulates an electronic device and all of its cultural interactions. It looks at the interface between the device's electromagnetic waves [whether visual, aural or digital] and the human experience. Virtual spaces and augmented spaces are Hertzian spaces, where the digital layer impacts the human experience.

Interface

Interface is the place or the system by which interaction between the user and an artifact [physical or digital] occurs.

Tangible User Interface [TUI]

The tangible user interface may include the physical input and interaction point [handle, buttons] or the visual attributes of an object or system that aids in communicating and mapping the interaction and usage.

Graphic User Interface [GUI]

Graphic User Interface refers to the display of information via graphic elements. The Xerox *Star 8010* workstation interface is considered to be the first commercial GUI, which was later followed by Apple's Lisa interface. The value of GUI is that by using visual cues and interaction, it eliminates the user's need to have 'backdoor' know how, such as programming and coding, to interact with the digital system or framework. Computer scientist Ivan Sutherland's 1963 Sketchpad is the first GUI system ever created.

Interactivity

Interactivity relates to the state where feedback and outcome can be altered, based on the user's input. The level of interaction is defined by the quality and quantity of decision-making the user can engage in, as well as variations and nuances within the feedback and outcome.[2] Interactivity requires several conditions to be effective, including a clear mental model, input and output systems, and feedback. Interlacing between input, output and feedback systems helps to elevate the quality and immersive attributes of the interactive experience.

Katie Salen and Eric Zimmerman talk about four game-specific modes of interactivity in their book Rules of Play, which many consider as the 'Bible' of the game design. Their modes are adapted here to fit general interactive modes:

1. Functional interactivity refers to the interaction with the real or virtual interface and feedback components

2. Explicit Interactivity is the action/reaction and choice making chain and dynamics, delivered through the narrative framework/ gameplay that constructs the experience

3. Cognitive interactivity refers to the psychological, emotional and intellectual bond the user develops through the interaction and the experience

4. Beyond-the-object-interactivity is when the magic happens, and the user creates a new cultural layer that exceeds the intended interaction cycle

The Rocky Horror Picture Show is a great example of a [passive] viewing media form, which, as a result of its cult following, turned into an interactive experience via ritualistic actions made by the avid fans during public screenings.

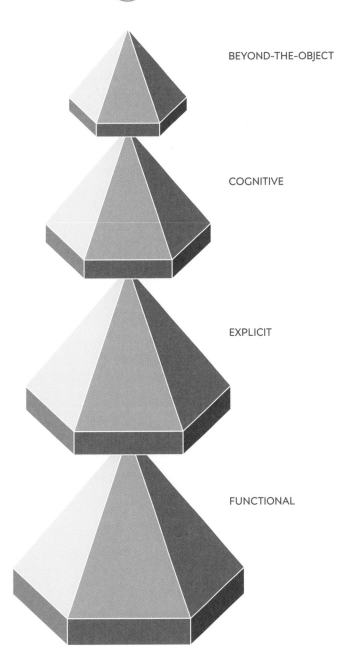

BEYOND-THE-OBJECT

COGNITIVE

EXPLICIT

FUNCTIONAL

The Four Layers of Interactivity
Author's Image, 2017.
[Representation based on Salen and Zimmerman. 2004].

Clear Mental Model

A clear mental model describes a state where the purpose and use of an interaction are clear to the user throughout the design flow, forming a clear 'usability map'.

Remediation

Remediation relates to the translation of older media forms to create new interactions and interface design models that can easily be understood by the user. Often, interface designers use shapes and visual cues that relate to physical objects that the user is already familiar with.[1] This invites the user to apply heritage knowledge in a new context – for example, using a trash bin on the computer to dispose of digital files, or page scrolling and digital volume dials.

Input Systems

Input systems transmit physical or sensory action via interaction devices. These include voice receptors, haptic devices and sensors [such as video game controllers and digital gloves], motion trackers, keyboards, touch input devices [including touch screens], etc.

Feedback

Feedback is the indicator that an action has been identified within the system.

Output Systems

Output systems are used to communicate the feedback to the given input. These include visual display systems, audio output systems, haptic feedback devices, etc.

Somatosensory

A sensation that can be sensed anywhere in the body, in contrast to a localised sensation that relates to a specific organ. An example of somatosensory sensations are temperature, pain, tactility, pressure and relief.

Haptic Interaction

Haptic interaction relies on our somatosensory nervous system, and the physical sensation processed via our tactile sensing subsystem. Good examples of haptic interaction include heat, vibration, and force resistance feedback.

Gesture Recognition

Gesture recognition transmits human gestures into signal processing, and is a key development area in Artificial Intelligence. Gesture recognition and feedback work together to create an interactive input system, and will be essential to creating an Augmented Reality experience that is immersive and intuitive. We group eye tracking and facial expression recognition together with gesture processing – utilising facial micro-expressions, eye movement and focal changes for interacting, and predicting the user's conscious and unconscious intentions.

Big Data

Big data is a literal description of the collation and analysis of large amounts of data to create Real-Time responsive and predictive algorithm systems.

Deep Learning

Deep learning is a data analysis method that is used when the amount of data is so great that it cannot be processed using conventional methods. Deep learning typically simulates the brain's neural networks, replicating neurons of the neocortex, and using non-linear content association methods rather than linear calculation and data processing. Deep learning is commonly used in Artificial Intelligence interactions and analysis, primarily within the context of human-to-machine interactions, such as voice recognition and behavioural targeting.

Blue Brain Project

Blue Brain is based on neuromorphic engineering, which describes computing systems that use a process that simulates the human brain. The term 'Blue Brain' is derived from IBM's *Blue Gene* Computer.

8.0 Appendices

Full human brain simulation is expected by 2023,[3] and will result in the ability to mimic and expand on biological problem-solving and processing capabilities, marking a major contribution to research and development into an artificial neural network.

Singularity

'Technology singularity' is a term coined by Ray Kurzweil, and describes the state when computer-based intelligence [Artificial Intelligence] reaches the level of consciousness. Kurzweil predicts this will be achieved by 2045.

Ubicomp

'Ubiquitous Computing' or 'Ubicomp' is a term that was coined in a 1988 lecture and 1991 article by Mark Weiser, a chief scientist at Xerox PARC. It describes the embedding of technology within everyday objects and environments. Ubicomp systems are applied in mobile devices, smart devices, and the Internet of Things. The concept was the basis for design and technology theories and insights later developed by user-centric design leader Don Norman, in his 1999 book *The Invisible Computer*, and futurist Ray Kurzweil, in his 1999 book *The Age of Spiritual Machines*. Norman looked at how to achieve a user-centric approach to technology development and render an invisible level of technology, AKA completely integrated in the design of information appliances. Ray Kurzweil, on the other hand, looked at different applications of invisible computing, incorporating technology in everyday objects and surfaces, leading to eventual singularity.

Real-Time

Real-Time computing [RTC] relates to content streaming immediacy [formerly referred to as 'live broadcasting'] and processing. Together with his team, engineer/inventor Douglas Engelbart made the first Real-Time presentation in December 1968. In the presentation [later referred to as "The Mother of All Demos"], he showed various features of modern computing and interaction systems, including teleconferencing, interactive editing and the use of the computer mouse.[4]

Simulation Localisation and Mapping [SLAM]

Within the context of technology, simulation localisation enables a device to map its surroundings, and successfully navigate it and update it in Real-Time. This technique is used by autonomous vehicles.

Head Mounted Displays [HMDs]

Head Mounted Displays are wearable devices, mostly used for the display of Augmented Reality and Virtual Reality imagery, data or content. HMDs are sometimes also referred to as 'headsets'.

Virtual Reality [VR]

The digital representation or recreation of a three-dimensional reality/ environment [existing or imaginary] through a display, sensory headset or device. The first Virtual Reality device was Morton Heilig's *Sensorama* machine, which was conceptualised in 1955 as a multisensory theatre, and prototyped in 1962.

Augmented Reality [AR]

The act or process of augmentation means to intensify, enhance or elevate. Augmented Reality relates to a variety of techniques used to add a digital layer within a physical environment. Even though Augmented Reality is commonly used to describe the application of a graphic layer, it could relate to any sensory augmentation.

Spatial Augmented Reality [SAR]

Spatial Augmented Reality refers to Augmented Reality that is based on projection mapping, where a series of sensors and optical devices map and layer digital information directly onto an environment or object.
The *Digital Desk* is the first example of Spatial Augmented Reality. William Newman and Pierre Wellner, then researchers at University of Cambridge and Xerox EuroPARC, presented a paper at the 1991 Symposium on User

Interface Software and Technology conference proceedings titled *The Digital Desk Calculator: Tangible Manipulation on a Desktop Display*. The *Digital Desk* incorporated elements of Tangible Augmented Reality [TAR], emulating and integrating physical surfaces, objects and gestures as interaction layers within the Augmented Reality projection.

Recent SAR applications include:

» Microsoft *RoomAlive* – maps a physical space and transforms the environment and players located there into an interactive game experience[5]

» The Volkswagen Group – uses SAR in their design and development process, projecting 2D user interfaces onto a white 3D automotive model

See-through Augmented Reality

See-through Augmented Reality refers to the mediation of the digital layer via a screen or display. This includes screens, mobile devices [phone, tablet] or near-eye HMDs and eyewear. The University of Washington's Human Interface Technology Laboratory has made new progress in research and development with virtual retinal display [Virtual Reality].

Recent see-through Augmented Reality applications include:

» IKEA's 2013 launch of an augmented catalogue and application that allows users to place virtual products within their physical environment,

» HoloLens – a Microsoft HMD system that comprises eye tracking goggles that enable the user to interact with high-definition hologram projections

» Layer – an application that enables the user to embed and view an Augmented Reality layer within printed media

» Mercedes' 2012 CES presentation of an Augmented Reality concept for the dashboard touchscreens and voice-control interfaces

8.0 Appendices

Tangible Augmented Reality [TAR]

Tangible Augmented Reality [TAR] interfaces incorporate Augmented Reality interaction via the [intuitive] manipulation of physical objects.
Notable applications include:

» *Digital Desk* – **Pierre Wellner's work aimed at emulating and integrating physical surfaces, objects and gestures with Augmented Reality projections** [6]

» *AR Sandbox* – **Using a Kinect 3D camera and projection system, the augmented sandbox generates Real-Time digital topographic contour lines, according to the physical altitude of the surface** [7]

Mixed Reality [MR]

Mixed Reality relates to a spatial Augmented Reality, but differs in the manner in which objects are integrated into – and are responsive to – the physical space. In the case of Mixed Reality, the digital layer considers environmental restrictions. For example, when an augmented image uses spatial mapping, it will react to its position in physical space, and the objects around it. The augmented object is displayed within the space as if it had physical properties, visualised as if it were positioned behind, under or within environmental elements. Magic Leap is a key player in the development of Mixed Reality.

Telepresence

A digital representation of a user's bodily form in a remote environment via Virtual Reality or Augmented Reality technology.

References

————————————

& Notes

Chapter 0.0

[1] Record $2.3 billion VR/AR investment in 2016. [2017]. [Blog] Digi-capital.
Available at: http://www.digi-capital.com/news/2017/02/record-2-3-billion-vrar-investment-in-2016/#.WSqfQFLL2jR [Accessed 1 Mar. 2017].

[2] Crunchbase.com. [2017]. Magic Leap | crunchbase. [online] Available at:
https://www.crunchbase.com/organization/magic-leap#/entity [Accessed 10 Apr. 2017].

[3] Bellini, H., Chen, W., Sugiyama, M., Shin, M., Alam, S. and Takayama, D. [2016]. Profiles in
Innovation – Virtual & Augmented Reality. 1st ed. [PDF] Goldman Sachs Group Inc.
Available at: http://www.goldmansachs.com/our-thinking/pages/technology-driving-innovation-folder/virtual-and-augmented-reality/report.pdf [Accessed 2 Feb. 2017].

[4] Glasner, J. [2017]. Despite Hype, VR Investment Fades In Q1 2017 - Crunchbase. [online]
Crunchbase. Available at: http://about.crunchbase.com/news/despite-hype-vr-investment-fades-q1-2017/ [Accessed 22 Apr. 2017].

[5] Godin, B. [2010]. 'Meddle Not With Them That Are Given to Change': Innovation as Evil. 1st ed.
[ebook] Montreal: Project on the Intellectual History of Innovation Working Paper No. 6. Available
at: http://www.csiic.ca/PDF/IntellectualNo6.pdf [Accessed 4 Jan. 2016].

[6] Live at the Beacon Theater. [2011]. [DVD] Directed by L. C.K. New York, NY, USA: Pig Newton.

[7] Vankin, D. [2016]. The arts buzzword of 2016: 'immersive'. [online] latimes.com.
Available at: http://www.latimes.com/entertainment/arts/la-ca-cm-immersive-arts-20161225-story.html [Accessed 2 Feb. 2017].

[8] Cole, J., Suman, M., Schramm, P. and Zhou, L. [2015]. Surveying The Digital Future. 1st ed.
[ebook] Center for the Digital Future. Available at: http://www.digitalcenter.org/wp-content/uploads/2013/06/2015-Digital-Future-Report.pdf [Accessed 25 Jul. 2016].

Chapter 1.0

[1] McGonigal, J. [2012]. Reality is broken. 1st ed. London: Vintage, p.12. eBook edition.
[2] Milgram, P. and Kishino, F. [1994]. A Taxonomy of Mixed Reality Visual Displays. IEICE
Transactions on Information and Systems, E77-D[12], pp.1321-1329.
[3] Mann, S. [2013]. Steve Mann: My "Augmediated" Life. [online] IEEE Spectrum: Technology,
Engineering, and Science News. Available at: http://spectrum.ieee.org/geek-life/profiles/steve-mann-my-augmediated-life [Accessed 11 Apr. 2016].
[4] Bimber, O. & Raskar, R. [2005]. Spatial Augmented Reality. Wellesley, Mass.: A K Peters.
[5] E, Thorp. [1998]. The Invention of the First Wearable Computer. IEEE Int'l Symp. Wearable
Computers, pp. 4-8.

[6] Kushner, D. [2013]. Oculus Rift Takes Virtual Reality Mainstream. [online] IEEE Spectrum. Available at: http://spectrum.ieee.org/consumer-electronics/gaming/oculus-rift-takes-virtual-reality-mainstream [Accessed 2 Apr. 2015].

[7] Von Hippel, E. Open User Innovation. The Encyclopedia of Human-Computer Interaction, 2nd Ed. Aarhus, Denmark: The Interaction Design Foundation. [PDF, pp 1107- 1136]. Retrieved from: https://www.interaction-design.org/encyclopedia [Hippel, 1123]

[8] Oculus.com. [n.d.]. Gear VR powered by Oculus | Oculus. [online] Available at: https://www.oculus.com/gear-vr/ [Accessed 10 Aug. 2016].

[9] [10] Prasuethsut, L. [2016]. Palmer Luckey: Oculus Rift's success depends on a 'virtual cycle'. [online] Wareable. Available at: https://www.wareable.com/vr/palmer-luckey-oculus-rift [Accessed 3 Apr. 2016].

[11] Essential Facts About the Computer and Video Game Industry. [2014]. [PDF] Entertainment Software Association. Available at: http://www.theesa.com/wp-content/uploads/2014/10/ESA_EF_2014.pdf [Accessed 4 Feb. 2016].

[12] Kushner, D. [2013]. Oculus Rift Takes Virtual Reality Mainstream. [online] IEEE Spectrum. Available at: http://spectrum.ieee.org/consumer-electronics/gaming/oculus-rift-takes-virtual-reality-mainstream [Accessed 2 Apr. 2015].

[13] Ma, B., Nahal, S. and Tran, F. [2016]. Future Reality: Virtual, Augmented & Mixed Reality [VR, AR & MR] Primer. 1st ed. [PDF] Bank of America Merrill Lynch. Available at: https://www.bofaml.com/content/dam/boamlimages/documents/articles/ID16_1099/virtual_reality_primer_short.pdf [Accessed 4 Dec. 2016].

[14] Digital Desk by Pierre Wellner, 1991. [2008]. [image] Available at: https://www.youtube.com/watch?v=S8ICetZ_57g [Accessed 8 Jun. 2017].

[15] Raskar, R., Welch, G. and Fuchs, H. [1998]. Spatially Augmented Reality. [PDF] San Francisco: First International Workshop on Augmented Reality, pp.63-72. Available at: http://citeseerx.ist.psu.edu/viewdoc/download?doi=10.1.1.439.7783&rep=rep1&type=pdf [Accessed 5 Mar. 2016].

[16] Kato, H., Billinghurst, M., Poupyrev, I., Tetsutani, N. and Tachibana, K. [2002]. Tangible Augmented Reality for Human Computer Interaction. The Journal of the Society for Art and Science, 1[2], pp.97-104.

[17] Raskar, R., Welch, G., Cutts, M., Lake, A., Stesin, L. and Fuchs, H. [1998]. The Office of the Future: A Unified Approach to Image-Based Modeling and Spatially Immersive Displays. [PDF] Orlando: SIGGRAPH 98. Available at: https://pdfs.semanticscholar.org/05de/05f242f62bd597666c7821d99dc568d47b6c.pdf [Accessed 24 Apr. 2016].

[18] Bolter, J. and Gromala, D. [2005]. Windows and mirrors. 1st ed. Cambridge, Mass.: MIT.

[19] Sparkes, M. [2014]. James Dyson invented Google Glass over a decade ago. [online] Telegraph.co.uk. Available at: http://www.telegraph.co.uk/technology/news/10865808/James-Dyson-invented-Google-Glass-over-a-decade-ago.html [Accessed 3 Mar. 2016].

[20] [21] Mann, S. [2013]. Steve Mann: My "Augmediated" Life. [online] IEEE Spectrum: Technology, Engineering, and Science News. Available at: http://spectrum.ieee.org/geek-life/profiles/steve-mann-my-augmediated-life [Accessed 11 Apr. 2016].

[22] Strauss, K. [2013]. Google Glass: A Fashion Failure. [online] Forbes.com. Available at: https://www.forbes.com/sites/karstenstrauss/2013/06/04/google-glass-a-fashion-failure/#58aa22482df4 [Accessed 16 Jun. 2016].

[23] Purdy, K. [2013]. What's new with Glass since it launched?. [online] ITworld. Available at: http://www.itworld.com/article/2833269/mobile/what-s-new-with-glass-since-it-launched-.html [Accessed 3 Feb. 2016].

[24] Sharma, M. [2014]. Google Glass will not succeed: FitBit designer Gadi Amit. [online] The Advocate. Available at: http://www.theadvocate.com.au/story/2314908/google-glass-will-not-succeed-fitbit-designer-gadi-amit/?cs=32 [Accessed 21 Mar. 2016].

8.0

Appendices

[25] Lynley, M. [2016]. With 500M downloads, Pokémon Go is coming to the Apple Watch. [online] TechCrunch. Available at: https://techcrunch.com/2016/09/07/pokemon-go-the-hottest-game-on-the-planet-is-coming-to-the-apple-watch/ [Accessed 9 Sep. 2016].

[26] Annino, E. [2016]. Forbes BrandVoice: Understanding The Pokémon Go Craze. [online] Forbes. Available at: https://www.forbes.com/sites/sap/2016/07/22/understanding-the-pokemon-go-craze/#497b17bb5824 [Accessed 8 Aug. 2016].

[27] Kawa, L., Verhage, J. and Treene, A. [2016]. Investors Are Already Bidding Up Secondary Plays on Pokemon GO. [online] Bloomberg.com. Available at: https://www.bloomberg.com/news/articles/2016-07-14/investors-are-already-bidding-up-secondary-plays-on-pokemon-go [Accessed 17 Jul. 2016].

[28] Crecente, B. [2016]. Spurned Pokemon Go players file complaints with federal government. [online] Polygon. Available at: https://www.polygon.com/2016/9/28/13082056/pokemon-go-ftc-complaints [Accessed 1 Oct. 2016].

[29] Annino, E. [2016]. Forbes BrandVoice: Understanding The Pokémon Go Craze. [online] Forbes. Available at: https://www.forbes.com/sites/sap/2016/07/22/understanding-the-pokemon-go-craze/#497b17bb5824 [Accessed 8 Aug. 2016].

[31] Harlow's Study on Monkeys' Attachment. [2012]. [video] Available at: https://www.youtube.com/watch?v=C5PlcmVao64 [Accessed 18 Jan. 2016].

Chapter 2.0

[1] Economist.com. [2015]. Paris climate talks: Local policies can combat emissions where international ones fall short. [online] Available at: http://www.economist.com/news/international/21679695-mayors-turn-local-policies-can-combat-emissions-where-international-ones-fall-short [Accessed 25 Mar. 2017].

[2] World City Report 2016: Urbanisation and Development Emerging Futures. [2016]. 1st ed. [ebook] UN Habitat. Available at: http://wcr.unhabitat.org/wp-content/uploads/sites/16/2016/05/WCR-%20Full-Report-2016.pdf [Accessed 7 Feb. 2017].

[3] Economist.com. [2015]. Paris climate talks: Local policies can combat emissions where international ones fall short. [online] Available at: http://www.economist.com/news/international/21679695-mayors-turn-local-policies-can-combat-emissions-where-international-ones-fall-short [Accessed 25 Mar. 2017].

[4] Common.com. [n.d.]. Available at: https://www.common.com [Accessed 9 Sep. 2016].

Cutler, K. [2017]. Common, The Co-Living Startup From A General Assembly Founder, Opens Its First Building in Brooklyn. [online] TechCrunch. Available at: https://techcrunch.com/2015/10/19/common-building-opening/ [Accessed 9 Sep. 2016].

[5]Urbanus.com.cn. [2017]. DenCity · a Reachable Utopia in Shenzhen | URBANUS 都市实践. [online] Available at: http://www.urbanus.com.cn/projects/dencity/?lang=en [Accessed 5 Jan. 2017].

[6] Toffler, A. [1970]. Future Shock. 1st ed. New york: Bantam Books, p.59.

[7] Toffler, A. [1970]. Future Shock. 1st ed. New york: Bantam Books, p.55.

[8] Vashti, H. [2015]. Consumer lifestyle: Digital Nomads. [online] Stylus Innovation Research & Advisory. Available at: http://www.stylus.com/qpjnhl [Accessed 16 Sep. 2016].

[9] Naisbitt, J. [1983]. High tech/high touch. 1st ed. [Zeeland, Mich.]: [Herman Miller], p.12.

[10] De Botton, A. [2005]. Status Anxiety. 1st ed. London: Penguin Books Ltd.

[11] Johnson, E. [2015]. The Real Cost of Your Shopping Habits. [online] Forbes.com. Available at: http://www.forbes.com/sites/emmajohnson/2015/01/15

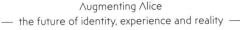

the-real-cost-of-your-shopping-habits/#696d57e921ae [Accessed 12 Jul. 2016].

[12] solis, B. and MacLeod, H. [2015]. Attention is a Currency. 1st ed. [ebook] Linkedin, p.7. Available at: https://business.linkedin.com/content/dam/me/business/en-us/marketing-solutions/cx/2016/pdfs/gapingvoid-attention-is-a-currency.pdf [Accessed 13 Nov. 2016].

[13] TED 2017 [2017]. His Holiness Pope Francis: Why the only future worth building includes everyone. [video] Available at: https://www.ted.com/talks/pope_francis_why_the_only_future_worth_building_includes_everyone?language=en#t-272162 [Accessed 26 Apr. 2017].

[14] Prensky, M. [2001]. Digital Natives, Digital Immigrants Part 1. On the Horizon, 9[5], pp.1.

[15] Boroujerdi, R. and Wolf, C. [2017]. Themes, Dreams and Flying Machines. 1st ed. [PDF] Goldman, Sachs & Co. Available at: http://www.goldmansachs.com/our-thinking/pages/macroeconomic-insights-folder/what-if-i-told-you/report.pdf [Accessed 19 Sep. 2016].

[16] Prensky, M. [2001]. Digital Natives, Digital Immigrants Part 1. On the Horizon, 9[5], pp.1-2

[17] Sparks & Honey trend report via Slideshare. [2014]. Meet Generation Z: Forget Everything You Learned About Millennials. [online] Available at: https://www.slideshare.net/sparksandhoney/generation-z-final-june-17 [Accessed 14 Mar. 2016].

[18] Cole, J., Suman, M., Schramm, P. and Zhou, L. [2015]. Surveying The Digital Future. 1st ed. [ebook] Center for the Digital Future. Available at: http://www.digitalcenter.org/wp-content/uploads/2013/06/2015-Digital-Future-Report.pdf [Accessed 25 Jul. 2016].

[19] An extensive research examining various aspects of new media interaction from gaming to social media we can see how U.S. youth is using new media interaction to socially engage, as well as to explore their personal identities.

[20] Ito, M. and Horst, H. [2009]. Living and learning with new media: Summary of findings from the digital youth project. 1st ed. Cambridge, Mass.: MIT Press. [Kindle Locations 689-694]. Kindle Edition.

[21] Ito, M. and Horst, H. [2009]. Living and learning with new media: Summary of findings from the digital youth project. 1st ed. Cambridge, Mass.: MIT Press. [Kindle Locations 71-73]. Kindle Edition.

[22] Ito, M. and Horst, H. [2009]. Living and learning with new media: Summary of findings from the digital youth project. 1st ed. Cambridge, Mass.: MIT Press. [Kindle Locations 710-712]. Kindle Edition.

[23] Ito, M. and Horst, H. [2009]. Living and learning with new media: Summary of findings from the digital youth project. 1st ed. Cambridge, Mass.: MIT Press. [Kindle Locations 109-113]. Kindle Edition.

Chapter 3.0

[1] Ishii, H. and Ullmer, B. [1997]. Tangible Bits: Towards Seamless Interfaces between People, Bits and Atoms. CHI 97. P 234

[2] Cooper, A. [2004]. The inmates are running the asylum. 1st ed. Indianapolis, Indiana: Sams. [Kindle Locations 655]. Kindle Edition.

[3] MiniBrew is a great example for a personalised, small batch beer production system https://www.minibrew.io

Another interesting in relation to this is Reflow Filament. Aiming at Making 3D printing 'sustainable, global and community driven' by building an international network of small-scale 3D printing production. http://reflowfilament.com/

[4] Dengel, A. [2016]. Digital Co-Creation and Augmented Learning. KMO '16 Proceedings of the 11th International Knowledge Management in Organizations Conference on The changing face of Knowledge Management Impacting Society Article No. 3; ACM New York, NY, US. P 2

8.0 Appendices

[5] [6] Ross, A. [2016]. The industries of the future. 1st ed. New York: Simon & Schuster. [Kindle Locations 2266-2267]. Kindle Edition.

[7] Metz, C. [2017]. Bitcoin Will Never Be a Currency—It's Something Way Weirder. [online] Wired.com. Available at: https://www.wired.com/2017/01/bitcoin-will-never-currency-something-way-weirder/ [Accessed 7 Jan. 2017].

[8] Soon, C., Brass, M., Heinze, H. and Haynes, J. [2008]. Unconscious determinants of free decisions in the human brain. 1st ed. [PDF] Nature Publishing Group. Available at: http://www.rifters.com/real/articles/NatureNeuroScience_Soon_et_al.pdf [Accessed 17 Feb. 2017]..

Max Planck Society for the Advancement of Science [2008]. Unconscious decisions in the brain. [online] Mpg.de. Available at: https://www.mpg.de/research/unconscious-decisions-in-the-brain [Accessed 5 Feb. 2017].

[9] Wood, H. [2014]. Sales-Boosting Beacons: Targeted Mobile Marketing. [online] Stylus Innovation Research & Advisory. Available at: http://www.stylus.com/spsdcw [Accessed 18 Sep. 2016].

[10] Boroujerdi, R. and Wolf, C. [2017]. Themes, Dreams and Flying Machines. 1st ed. [PDF] Goldman, Sachs & Co. Available at: http://www.goldmansachs.com/our-thinking/pages/macroeconomic-insights-folder/what-if-i-told-you/report.pdf [Accessed 19 Sep. 2016].
– also see –
4th Installment of the Innovation Imperative Polling Series: Portrait of Generation Z. [2012]. 1st ed. [PDF] Boston, Massachusetts: Northeastern University. Available at: http://www.northeastern.edu/innovationsurvey/pdfs/Innovation_Summit_GenZ_Topline_Report.pdf [Accessed 13 Oct. 2016].

[11] Bry, D. [2015]. Mast Brothers: taste-testing $10 chocolate bars as controversy boils over. [online] the Guardian. Available at: https://www.theguardian.com/lifeandstyle/2015/dec/20/mast-brothers-chocolate-bars-scandal [Accessed 8 Jan. 2017].

[12] Mike Stoner [2012]. Elmer Wheeler - Don't Sell The Steak, Sell the Sizzle. [video] Available at: https://www.youtube.com/watch?v=eUmxGqsuKmY [Accessed 9 Apr. 2016]. Also – for a free copy of "Tested Sentences That Sell" go to http://www.elmerwheeler.net

[13] FITC [2015]. You are not a storyteller - Stefan Sagmeister. [video] Available at: https://vimeo.com/98368484 [Accessed 17 Dec. 2016].

[14] Kenzo [2016]. Kenzo World. [video] Available at: https://vimeo.com/180668935 [Accessed 29 Aug. 2016].

[15] Millman, D. [2011]. Brand Thinking. 1st ed. New York, NY, USA: Allworth Press.

[16] Dengel, A. [2016] Digital Co-Creation and Augmented Learning. KMO '16 Proceedings of the 11th International Knowledge Management in Organizations Conference on The changing face of Knowledge Management Impacting Society Article No. 3. New York, NY, USA: ACM

[17] Crawford, C. [2013]. Chris Crawford on interactive storytelling. 1st ed. [Berkeley, Calif.]: New Riders, p.80.

[18] Ma, B., Nahal, S. and Tran, F. [2016]. Future Reality: Virtual, Augmented & Mixed Reality [VR, AR & MR] Primer. 1st ed. [PDF] Bank of America Merrill Lynch. Available at: https://www.bofaml.com/content/dam/boamlimages/documents/articles/ID16_1099/virtual_reality_primer_short.pdf [Accessed 4 Dec. 2016].

[19} Masunaga, S. and Khouri, A. [2015]. Tesla's Elon Musk and his big ideas: A brief history. [online] latimes.com. Available at: http://www.latimes.com/la-fi-hy-elon-musk-big-ideas-story-so-far-20150501-htmlstory.html [Accessed 27 Jun. 2015].

[20] Ross, A. [2016]. The industries of the future. 1st ed. New York: Simon & Schuster. [Kindle Locations 2406]. Kindle Edition.

[21] Csikszentmihalyi, M. and Csikszentmihalyi, I. [2000]. Beyond boredom and anxiety. 1st ed. San Francisco: Jossey-Bass, P4

[22] Stewart, J. [2016]. Facebook Has 50 Minutes of Your Time Each Day. It Wants More... [online] Nytimes.com. Available at: https://www.nytimes.com/2016/05/06/business/facebook-bends-the-rules-of-audience-engagement-to-its-advantage.html?_r=2 [Accessed 2 Feb. 2017].

[23] Vanian, J. [2017]. Facebook CEO Mark Zuckerberg To Spend Billions More On Virtual Reality. [online] Fortune.com. Available at: http://fortune.com/2017/01/18/facebook-mark-zuckerberg-virtual-reality-billions/ [23] http://www.forbes.com/companies/apple/ [Accessed 2 Feb. 2017].

[24] Forbes [2017] Forbes World's Biggest Public Companies. [online] Available at: http://www.forbes.com/companies/apple/ [Accessed 14 Mar. 2017].

[25] Badenhausen, K. [2016]. Apple, Google Top The World's Most Valuable Brands Of 2016. [online] Forbes.com. Available at: https://www.forbes.com/sites/kurtbadenhausen/2016/05/11/the-worlds-most-valuable-brands/#3b9fc9b536ec [Accessed 31 Oct. 2016].

[26] Murphy, A., Clinton, D. and Munster, G. [2017]. This Is Going to Be Apple's Next Hit. [online] Fortune.com. Available at: http://fortune.com/2017/03/30/apple-augmented-reality-iphone-pokemon-go-glasses-tim-cook/ [Accessed 1 Apr. 2017].

[27] Beattie, A. [2015]. The Story Behind Google's Success. [online] Investopedia. Available at: http://www.investopedia.com/articles/personal-finance/042415/story-behind-googles-success.asp [Accessed 6 Jan. 2017].

[28] Cadwalladr, C. [2014]. Are the robots about to rise? Google's new director of engineering thinks so.... [online] the Guardian. Available at: https://www.theguardian.com/technology/2014/feb/22/robots-google-ray-kurzweil-terminator-singularity-artificial-intelligence [Accessed 3 Jun. 2014].

[29] Kurzweil is considered a lead futurist in areas of AI, He is the author of key ground breaking literature such as 'The Age of Intelligent Machines', 'The Age of Spiritual Machines' and 'The Law of Accelerating Returns'

[30] Cadwalladr, C. [2014]. Are the robots about to rise? Google's new director of engineering thinks so.... [online] the Guardian. Available at: https://www.theguardian.com/technology/2014/feb/22/robots-google-ray-kurzweil-terminator-singularity-artificial-intelligence [Accessed 14 Jun. 2016].

[31] Economist.com. [2017]. The world's most valuable resource is no longer oil, but data. [online] Available at: http://www.economist.com/news/leaders/21721656-data-economy-demands-new-approach-antitrust-rules-worlds-most-valuable-resource [Accessed 9 May 2017].

The article appeared in the Leaders section of the print edition under the headline "The world's most valuable resource"

[32] Bleed, J. [2016]. Alexa a Witness to Murder? Prosecutors Seek Amazon Echo Data. [online] Bloomberg.com. Available at: https://www.bloomberg.com/news/articles/2016-12-28/alexa-a-witness-to-murder-prosecutors-seek-amazon-echo-data [Accessed 29 Dec. 2016].

[33] Attributed to Socrates by Plato, according to Patty, W. and Johnson, L. [1953]. Personality and adjustment. 1st ed. New York: McGraw-Hill, p.277.

Chapter 4.0

[1] Illouz, E. [2007]. Cold intimacies. 1st ed. Cambridge: Polity, p.21.

[2] Stevenson, S. [2016]. Snapchat Releases First Hardware Product, Spectacles. [online] WSJ. Available at: https://www.wsj.com/articles/snapchat-releases-first-hardware-product-spectacles-1474682719 [Accessed 24 Sep. 2016].

8.0 Appendices

[3] Nietzsche, F. [1887]. The Gay Science. 1st ed. Leipzig: Verlag von E. W. Fritzsch, p.371.

[4] LSteinberg, L. [2014]. The Case for Delayed Adulthood. [online] Nytimes.com. Available at: https://www.nytimes.com/2014/09/21/opinion/sunday/the-case-for-delayed-adulthood.html?_r=0 [Accessed 6 Nov. 2017].

[5] Barry Schwartz, Professor of Psychology at Swarthmore College author of The paradox of choice. [2009]. New York, N.Y.: HarperCollins.

[6] First mentioned by Rene Descartes' [1637]. Discourse on the Method of Rightly Conducting the Reason, and Seeking Truth in the Sciences. [in Latin 'Cogito ergo sum']

[7] Rushkoff, D. [2013]. Present Shock. 1st ed. New York: Current, p.73.

[8] For more information read one of the most cohesive books [in my mind] about String Theory, by theoretical physical Brian Greene

Greene, B. [2010]. The fabric of the cosmos. 1st ed. New York: Vintage eBooks.
Semi-nerds can his 2005 TED talk 'Brian Greene: Making sense of String Theory'

[9] Qoute from The Book of Genesis, Vatican version, available online on http://www.vatican.va/archive/bible/genesis/documents/bible_genesis_en.html

[10] Hassan, R. [2008]. The information society. 1st ed. Cambridge: Polity, p.105.

[11] billions] [2016]. Mobile phone users worldwide 2013-2019 | Statistic. [online] Statista. Available at: https://www.statista.com/statistics/274774/forecast-of-mobile-phone-users-worldwide/ [Accessed 20 Sep. 2016].

[12] Aley, J. [2016]. How Snapchat Built a Business By Confusing Olds. [online] Bloomberg.com. Available at: http://www.bloomberg.com/features/2016-how-snapchat-built-a-business/ [Accessed 21 Sep. 2016].[13] Frier, M. [2016]. Snapchat Passes Twitter in Daily Usage. [online] Bloomberg.com. Available at: http://www.bloomberg.com/news/articles/2016-06-02/snapchat-passes-twitter-in-daily-usage [Accessed 21 Sep. 2016].

[14] Eadicicco, L. [2016]. How Snapchat Spectacles Could Become a Huge Hit. [online] Time.com. Available at: http://time.com/4507081/snapchat-spectacles-release-date-price/ [Accessed 28 Sep. 2016].

[15] Mathematical Tables and Other Aids to Computation Mathematical Tables and Other Aids to Computation Coverage: 1943-1959. [1953]. 1st ed. Providence, RI: American Mathematical Society, p.Vii. 73.

[16] Gleick, J. [1999]. Faster. 1st ed. New York, NY: Hachette, p.68.

[17] Gleick, J. [1999]. Faster. 1st ed. New York, NY: Hachette, p.41.

[18] Rushkoff, D. [2013]. Present Shock. 1st ed. New York: Current, p.2.

[19] Legorburu, G. and McColl, D. [2014]. Storyscaping : Stop Creating Ads, Start Creating Worlds. 1st ed. Wiley. Kindle Edition.

[20] Rosenfeld, M. and Thomas, R. [2012]. Searching for a Mate. American Sociological Review, 77[4], pp.523-547.

[21] Watt Smith, T. [2015]. Book of Human Emotions: An Encyclopaedia of Feeling from Anger to Wanderlust. 1st ed. London: Profile books LTD.

[22] Mobile phones and tablets had a similar effect on the visual engagement, grabbing the visual attention and eventually become a reality lens or filer even when capturing an image or motion. Social behaviour and appropriation shift as individual immersive states and narratives gain more and more importance.

8.0

Appendices

Chapter 5.0

[1] Harvey, D. [1989]. The Condition of Postmodernity: An Enquiry into the Origins of Cultural Change. 1st ed. Oxford: Blackwell Publishers, p.135.

[2] Harvey, D. [1983]. The Limits to Capital. 1st ed. Oxford: Blackwell Publishers, p.35.

[3] Hassan, R. [2008]. The information society. 1st ed. Cambridge: Polity, p.120.

[4] Zach, D. [2016]. Facebook against the world. [online] Mako. Available at: http://www.mako.co.il/nexter-internet/social-networks-facebook-lost-it/Article-d8ce56f9aac1951006.htm?sCh=9cde8f126c9d8510&pId=173113802 [Accessed 29 Dec. 2016].

[5] Fan, Y. [2017]. China Bans Augmented Reality Games, Citing Security Concerns. [online] Radio Free Asia. Available at: http://www.rfa.org/english/news/china/china-bans-aungmented-reality-games-citing-security-concerns-01112017120933.html [Accessed 12 Jan. 2017].

Translated and written in English by Luisetta Mudie.

Kain, E. [2017]. 'Pokémon GO' Banned In China. [online] Forbes.com. Available at: https://www.forbes.com/sites/erikkain/2017/01/10%20/pokemon-go-isnt-coming-to-china-any-time-soon/#72a884e854bd [Accessed 12 Jan. 2017].

[6] Horst, H. and Miller, D. [2014]. Digital anthropology. 1st ed. London [etc.]: Bloomsbury Academic, an imprint of Bloomsbury. Kindle Edition.

[7] Shavit, V. [n.d.]. [Blog] Digital Dust. Available at: http://digital-era-death-eng.blogspot.nl [Accessed 27 Mar. 2017].

[8] Life Insurance Finder [n.d.]. What Happens Online When You Die? [Infographic] Available at: https://www.finder.com.au/infographics/life-insurance/what-happens-online-when-you-die/ [Accessed 27 Mar. 2017].

[9] Rubin, C. [2010]. A Virtual World Spawns a Very Real Lawsuit. [online] Inc.com. Available at: https://www.inc.com/news/articles/2010/05/second-life-virtual-land-dispute.html [Accessed 13 Feb. 2017].

En.wikipedia.org. [n.d.]. Bragg v. Linden Lab. [online] Available at: https://en.wikipedia.org/wiki/Bragg_v._Linden_Lab [Accessed 16 Dec. 2016].

New World Notes. [2013]. Class Action Lawsuit Against Linden Lab for Suspended Accounts Settled for $172,000 Paid in Linden Dollars UPDATE: Legal Expert Says "Looks like Linden Lab lost". [online] Available at: http://nwn.blogs.com/nwn/2013/06/linden-lab-class-action-settlement.html [Accessed 16 Dec. 2016].

[10] Hippel, E. [2007]. The sources of innovation. 1st ed. New York, NY: Oxford Univ. Pr., p.292.

[11] Tufte E.R. [2003]. The Cognitive Style of PowerPoint. Cheshire, CT: Graphics press

[12] Lo, R., Chen, A., Rampersad, V., Huang, J., Wu, H. and Mann, S. [2013]. Augmediated reality system based on 3D camera selfgesture sensing. 1st ed. [PDF] Toronto: IEEE International Symposium on Technology and Society. Available at: http://www.eyetap.org/papers/docs/IEEE_ISTAS13_Selfgesture_Lo_etal.pdf [Accessed 15 Aug. 2016]. P20

[13] Heath, A. [2017]. Families of Americans killed by ISIS are suing Twitter for allegedly providing 'tremendous utility and value' to the terrorist organization. [online] Business Insider. Available at: https://www.businessinsider.nl/twitter-sued-isis-victims-families-france-belgium-attacks-2017-1/?international=true&r=US [Accessed 21 Jan. 2017].

[14] Asai, N. [2014]. Omote / Real-Time Face Tracking & Projection Mapping. [video] Available at: https://vimeo.com/103425574 [Accessed 12 Mar. 2016].

8.0

Appendices

[15] Asai, N. [2016]. 花鳥風月 [kacho-fugetsu] / real-time face tracking and projection mapping. [video] Available at: https://vimeo.com/186075386 [Accessed 23 Dec. 2016].

[16] Cuthbertson, A. [2016]. Could Amazon Echo help solve a murder case?. [online] Newsweek. Available at: http://europe.newsweek.com/amazon-echo-may-have-overheard-murder-536585?rm=eu [Accessed 29 Dec. 2016].

[17] My Friend Cayla. [n.d.]. My Friend Cayla. [online] Available at: http://www.myfriendcayla.com [Accessed 21 Jan. 2017].

[18] Oakley, N. [2015]. Watch children's doll quote 50 Shades and Silence of the Lambs - it's creepy. [online] mirror. Available at: http://www.mirror.co.uk/news/technology-science/technology/friend-cayla-doll-can-hacked-5110112 [Accessed 22 Nov. 2016].

Lion, P. [2017]. Parents ordered to destroy talking My Friend Cayla Doll over hacking fears. [online] mirror. Available at: http://www.mirror.co.uk/news/uk-news/parents-ordered-destroy-talking-friend-9838125 [Accessed 21 Feb. 2017].

[19] Kain, E. [2017]. 'Pokémon GO' Banned In China. [online] Forbes.com. Available at: https://www.forbes.com/sites/erikkain/2017/01/10%20/pokemon-go-isnt-coming-to-china-any-time-soon/#72a884e854bd [Accessed 12 Jan. 2017].

[20] Gilmore, L. [2017]. How to balance security and usability with data analytics. [online] The Next Web. Available at: http://thenextweb.com/worldofbanking/2017/01/03/how-to-balance-security-and-usability-with-data-analytics/ [Accessed 10 Jan. 2017].

[21] Ahprojects.com. [2017]. HyperFace Camouflage – Adam Harvey. [online] Available at: https://ahprojects.com/projects/hyperface/ [Accessed 19 Feb. 2017].

[22] Mitnick was described as FBI's 'most illusive hacker'.

Mitnick, K. and Simon, W. [2011]. Ghost in the wires. 1st ed. London: Little, Brown.

Chapter 6.0

[1] Horst, H. and Miller, D. [2014]. Digital anthropology. 1st ed. London [etc.]: Bloomsbury Academic, an imprint of Bloomsbury, p.386.

[2] Bolter, J. D., & Grusin, R. Hypermerid [1999], p.34.

[3] Uncanny Valley = "Bukimi No Tani"[不気味の谷] find more information on http://spectrum.ieee.org/automaton/robotics/humanoids/the-uncanny-valley

[4] Merieb, E. N. & Hoehn, K. [2007]. Human Anatomy & Physiology 7th Edition, Pearson International Edition.

[5] Kosara, R., Miksch, S. and Hauser, H. [2001]. Semantic Depth of Field. 1st ed. [ebook] Kosara. Available at: http://kosara.net/papers/2001/Kosara_InfoVis_2001.pdf [Accessed 20 Aug. 2016].

[6] Coldewey, D. [2017]. Google's Self-Driving Cars Use Halloween to Learn to Recognize Costumed Kids. [online] NBC News. Available at: http://www.nbcnews.com/tech/innovation/googles-self-driving-cars-use-halloween-learn-recognize-costumed-kids-n455901 [Accessed 12 Mar. 2016].

[7] Schreuder, E., van Erp, J., Toet, A. and Kallen, V. [2016]. Emotional Responses to Multisensory Environmental Stimuli. SAGE Open, 6[1], p.215824401663059.

[8] Bagchi, A., Basu, R., Grumiller, D. and Riegler, M. [2014]. Entanglement entropy in Galilean conformal field theories and flat holography. 1st ed. [ebook] Arxiv org. Available at: https://arxiv.org/pdf/1410.4089.pdf [Accessed 30 Oct. 2017].

[9] Science at Melbourne. Recorded at the Copland Theatre, University of Melbourne [2017].

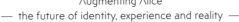

8.0

Appendices

The Believing Brain - Presented by Dr Michael Sherme. [image] Available at: https://www.youtube.com/watch?v=R6ijdDtOLLo [Accessed 28 May 2017].

[10] Tso, I., Chiu, P., King-Casas, B. and Deldin, P. [2011]. Alterations in affective processing of attack images following September 11, 2001. Journal of Traumatic Stress, 24[5], pp.538-545.

[11] ScienceDaily. [2011]. Emotional impact of 9/11 attacks seen in brain's response to negative visual images. [online] Available at: https://www.sciencedaily.com/releases/2011/09/110909074915.htm [Accessed 28 Jan. 2016].

[12] do5e [2007]. Andrew Newberg, M.D – on God, Reality and Everything. [image] Available at: https://www.youtube.com/watch?v=OZEVOenOwYU [Accessed 18 Nov. 2016].

[13] Newberg, A. [2017]. The Spiritual Brain: Science and Religious Experience. [online] English. Available at: http://www.thegreatcourses.com/courses/the-spiritual-brain-science-and-religious-experience.html [Accessed 23 Feb. 2017].

[14] Toor, A. [2015]. Ultra-orthodox Jews are using WhatsApp to defy their rabbis' internet ban. [online] The Verge. Available at: http://www.theverge.com/2015/10/27/9620752/whatsapp-hasidic-jewish-internet-ban [Accessed 9 Oct. 2016].

[15] Microsoft Corporate Blogs [2017]. 17 for '17: Microsoft researchers on what to expect in 2017 and 2027 Read more at https://blogs.microsoft.com/next/2016/12/05/17-17-microsoft-researchers-expect-2017-2027/#sm.00001bmddzi8fvepwpm7dyiil5im8 [Accessed 27 Jan. 2017].

[16] Sutton-Smith, B. [1986]. Toys as culture. 1st ed. New York, N.Y.: Gardner Press, p. 69–72.

[17] De Botton, A. [2005]. Status Anxiety. 1st ed. London: Penguin Books Ltd.

[18] Weinschenk Ph.D., S. [2012]. Why We're All Addicted to Texts, Twitter and Google. [Blog] psychologytoday.com. Available at: https://www.psychologytoday.com/blog/brain-wise/201209/why-were-all-addicted-texts-twitter-and-google [Accessed 23 Oct. 2016].

[19] Alexander, B. [2014]. Rise and Fall of the Official View of Addiction. [online] Brucekalexander.com. Available at: http://www.brucekalexander.com/articles-speeches/277-rise-and-fall-of-the-official-view-of-addiction-6 [Accessed 20 Jun. 2016].

Chapter 7.0

[01] Nicholas Negroponte, Being Digital, 1995.

[02] https://www.psychologytoday.com/blog/glue/201501/is-your-smartphone-making-you-dumb

[03] Rushkoff, D. [2013]. Present Shock. 1st ed. New York: Current, p.95.

[04] Picard, R. [1997]. Affective computing. 1st ed. Cambridge: The MIT Press.

[05] Wellner, P., Mackay, W. and Gold, R. [1993]. Computer-augmented environments. 1st ed. New York, NY: Association for Computing Machinery.

[06] Crecente, B. [2017]. Experts set to meet with fed government about need for VR ethics, more research. [online] Polygon.com. Available at: https://www.polygon.com/2017/3/24/15055542/vr-government-regulation [Accessed 28 Mar. 2017].

[07] Horst, H. and Miller, D. [2014]. Digital anthropology. 1st ed. London [etc.]: Bloomsbury Academic, an imprint of Bloomsbury. Kindle Edition, Kindle Locations 5428-5429.

[08] Toffler, A. [1970]. Future Shock. 1st ed. New york: Bantam Books, p. 169

[09] Original interview was made in German, on Der Spiegel. [1988]. Wir alle wollen wissen, woher wir kommen - Der Spiegel 42/1988. Availble online via Spiegel.de. Available at: http://www.spiegel.de/spiegel/print/d-13542088.html [Accessed 11 Mar. 2016].

8.0 Appendices

Chapter 8.0

[1] Miller, J. H [n.d.]. Narrative. 1st ed. [ebook] N/A. Available at: http://engl273-3-stair.wikispaces. umb.edu/file/view/j.+hillis+miller+-+narrative.pdf [Accessed 8 Nov. 2016].

[2] Based on 'Interactivity' from Zimmerman, E. [2004]. Rules of play. 1st ed. Cambridge, Mass.: MIT Press, pp 56–69]

[3] Avula, S., Pakale, V. and Kashid, S. [2013]. Blue Brain - The Future Generation. 1st ed. [ebook] International Journal of Application or Innovation in Engineering & Management. Available at: http://www.ijaiem.org/Volume2Issue3/IJAIEM-2013-03-28-091.pdf [Accessed 10 Jan. 2017].

[4] Watch MarcelVEVO [2012]. The Mother of All Demos, presented by Douglas Engelbart [1968]. [video] Available at: https://www.youtube.com/watch?v=yJDv-zdhzMY [Accessed 15 Feb. 2016].

[5] Watch Microsoft Research [2014]. RoomAlive: Magical Experiences Enabled by Scalable, Adaptive Projector-Camera Units. [image] Available at: https://www.youtube.com/watch?v=ILb5ExBzHqw [Accessed 8 May 2016]. https://www.youtube.com/watch?v=S8ICetZ_57g

[6] Watch AR Sandbox [n.d.]. See the AR Sandbox in action. [image] Available at: https://arsandbox.ucdavis.edu [Accessed 12 Sep. 2016].

Graph List

Chapter 0.0

Augmented & Virtual Reality Market worth. Author's Image, 2017.
Multiple sources. See chapter 0.0

Moore's Law in Practice, 120 years overview. Author's Image, 2017.
Based on TED.com. [2005]. Ray Kurzweil: The accelerating power of technology. [online] Available at: http://Ray Kurzweil: The accelerating power of technology [Accessed 21 Aug. 2016].

The One Ring to Rule Them All. Author's Image, 2017.

Chapter 1.0

The Virtual Continuum. Author's Image, 2017.
Adapted from: Milgram, Paul & Kishino, Fumio, [1994] A taxonomy of Mixed Reality Visual Displays; IEICE Transactions on Information Systems, Vol E77-D, No.12 December 1994

An effective solution for wearable technology success Author's Image, 2017.

The Augmented Reality landscape. Author's Image, 2017.

Core challenges in Virtual Reality diffusion. Author's Image, 2017.

CH 2.0

Global Patterns of Urbanisation. Author's Image, 2017.
Based on: World City Report 2016: Urbanisation and Development Emerging Futures. [2016]. 1st ed. [ebook] UN Habitat. Available at: http://wcr.unhabitat.org/wp-content/uploads/sites/16/2016/05/WCR-%20Full-Report-2016.pdf [Accessed 7 Feb. 2017].

Maslow's Hierarchy of Needs. Author's Image, 2017.

Rogers' Innovation Adoption Curve. Author's Image, 2017.
Based on Rogers, E. [2005]. Diffusion of innovations. New York: Free Press. [1st ed. 1983].

8.0

Appendices

US Online Connectivity. Author's Image, 2017. Based on Cole, J., Suman, M., Schramm, P. and Zhou, L. [2015]. Surveying The Digital Future. 1st ed. [ebook] Center for the Digital Future. Available at: http://www.digitalcenter.org/wp-content/uploads/2013/06/2015-Digital-Future-Report.pdf [Accessed 25 Jul. 2016].

Chapter 3.0

Shifting Economies. Author's Image, 2017.

Augmented Reality Big Players. Author's Image, 2017.

Chapter 4.0

Digital Interaction Evolution. Author's Image, 2017.

The Spacetime Continuum. Author's Image, 2017.

Adapted from on Example of a light cone. Created in Lightwave by stib

The Rise of Online Intimacy. Author's Image, 2017. Based on Rosenfeld, M. and Thomas, R. 2012. Searching for a Mate. American Sociological Review, 77[4], pp.523-547

Gestures can be tricky. Author's Image, 2017.
Inspired by Munari, B. [2005]. Speak Italian. San Francisco: Chronicle Books. [1st ed. 1963]

Chapter 5.0

The 8 Veillances. Author's Image, 2017.
Adapted from Mann, S. [2017]. Veillance and Reciprocal Transparency: Surveillance versus Sousveillance, AR Glass, Lifelogging, and Wearable Computin. 1st ed. [ebook] Toronto, Canada: SurvVeillanCeNTRE. Available at: http://wearcam.org/veillance/veillance.pdf [Accessed 6 Jan. 2017].

Chapter 6.0

Plato's Cave. Author's Image, 2017.

'The Uncanny Valley'. Author's Image, 2017.

Adapted from Mori, M. [2012]. The Uncanny Valley: The Original Essay by Masahiro Mori. [online] IEEE Spectrum: Technology, Engineering, and Science News. Available at: http://spectrum.ieee.org/automaton/robotics/humanoids/the-uncanny-valley [Accessed 9 Dec. 2016].

From Pointland to Spaceland. Author's Image, 2017.

Input/Output/Reality Perception. Author's Image, 2017.
Adapted from Oscar Reutersvärd' Penrose triangle.

The Virtual Continuum [Revisted]. Author's Image, 2017.
Based on En.wikipedia.org. [n.d.]. Spacetime. [online] Available at: https://en.wikipedia.org/wiki/Spacetime [Accessed 12 Feb. 2017].

Chapter 7.0

The Human/Cyber Nexus. Author's Image, 2017.

Chapter 8.0

The Four Layers of Interactivity. Based on 'Interactivity' from Zimmerman, E. [2004]. Rules of play. 1st ed. Cambridge, Mass.: MIT Press, pp 56–69]

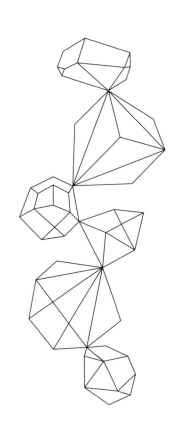